S0-ANW-447

School Violence

ARNOLD P. GOLDSTEIN
Psychology Department and Center for Research on Aggression,
Syracuse University

STEVEN J. APTER
Division of Special Education and Rehabilitation and Center
for Research on Aggression, Syracuse University

BERJ HAROOTUNIAN
Division for the Study of Teaching and Center for Research on Aggression,
Syracuse University

PRENTICE-HALL, INC., Englewood Cliffs, New Jersey 07632

Library of Congress Cataloging in Publication Data
Goldstein, Arnold P.
    School violence.

    Includes bibliographies and index.
    1.   School violence–United States.   2.   Moral education
–United States.   3.   Behavior modification.   4.   Socializa-
tion.   I.   Apter, Steven J. (Steven Jeffrey), 1945–
II.   Harootunian, Berj.   III.   Title.
LB3013.3.G64   1983   371.5'8'0973   83-8670
ISBN 0-13-794545-0

Editorial/production supervision and
   interior design: Kate Kelly
Cover design: Diane Saxe
Manufacturing buyer: Ron Chapman
Front cover photo: Ted Jursek

To the American teacher

Printed in the United States of America

10   9   8   7   6   5   4   3   2   1

ISBN 0-13-794545-0

Prentice-Hall International, Inc., *London*
Prentice-Hall of Australia Pty. Limited, *Sydney*
Editora Prentice-Hall do Brasil, Ltda., *Rio de Janeiro*
Prentice-Hall Canada Inc., *Toronto*
Prentice-Hall of India Private Limited, *New Delhi*
Prentice-Hall of Japan, Inc., *Tokyo*
Prentice-Hall of Southeast Asia Pte. Ltd., *Singapore*
Whitehall Books Limited, *Wellington, New Zealand*

Contents

Preface

Violence in America's 84,000 schools has for several years posed a largely unresolved national problem of the first magnitude—to teachers and student victims, to school property, to the community, and to the educational process in general. Approximately 270,000 physical assaults occur annually in primary and secondary schools in the United States, and approximately 500 million dollars in damage from vandalism, arson, and theft are visited upon school property each year. Even though the collective rates of such incidents have leveled off in recent years, they are—in an absolute sense—very high and, thus far, generally resistant to significant reduction.

It is the basic position of this book that our national failure to reduce aggression in America's schools is in large part a failure of perspective. Viable controls, alternative models, and prevention techniques *do* exist, but they have been utilized in a piecemeal, often unsystematic, and, especially, unidimensional manner. When a teacher or student is beaten in school, corrective steps must focus not only upon the student involved, not only upon the teacher and his or her colleagues, not only upon the school and its curricula and organization, and not only upon the community or state in which the school is located, but simultaneously upon *all* of these levels of potential relevance and potential intervention. To reduce the likelihood that another beating will occur, or another window will be broken, or another fire started, and to increase the likelihood that prosocial, rather than antisocial, values and behaviors will be demonstrated and reinforced, our optimal interventions should occur concurrently at the student, teacher, school, and community levels. This sytems approach to aggression controls, alternatives, and prevention lies at the heart of this book.

Following a presentation and consideration, in Chapter 1, of the scope, trends, and economic and social costs of school violence in the United States, as well as an overview of existing control and remedial efforts, we turn in Chapter 2 to a discussion of the classroom teacher as manager, organizer, and executive. Our focus here is on teacher selection and decision-making behavior as he or she chooses, adapts, and implements specific classroom procedures selected from a broad array of those available. This view of teacher as decision maker is provided largely to aid the reader in making decisions about the choice, adaptation, and use of the various aggression-control and prevention procedures presented in the chapters which then follow.

Specific aggression-relevant techniques must, first of all, be directed toward youngsters themselves. Several such behavior-modification (Chapter 3) and humanistic and psychodynamic (Chapter 4) techniques of demonstrated value for the control and reduction of aggressive, antisocial, and disruptive behaviors exist, and are described in rather complete detail in these two chapters. Teachers faced with such behaviors and armed with these techniques will be able to make significant inroads in reducing aggression in their classrooms.

Teacher efforts aimed directly at youngsters themselves will more fully succeed if in addition to the control of aggression they also reflect attention to aggression alternatives. That is, school violence will diminish most when student-oriented efforts to control and reduce it are combined with explicit teaching of what to do instead. The systems approach at the heart of this book urges use of concurrent efforts to both reduce the antisocial and to directly teach the prosocial. Chapter 5 describes the major contemporary approaches to teaching prosocial values; Chapter 6 places analogous focus on teaching explicit prosocial behaviors. Both foci are included as evidence of our belief that results are optimized when teaching efforts are targeted on both underlying values and overt behaviors.

Techniques designed to enhance the control of aggression or to foster aggression alternatives are exceedingly important contributors toward our overall goal of violence-free American schools. But preventive efforts are at least as significant. It is in this realm in particular that our systems orientation becomes explicit. Both the school itself and the larger community of which the school is a part can and should be mobilized in this endeavor. The school's curriculum, preferred instructional methods, formal organization, and prevailing climate all may serve aggression-prevention goals, as Chapter 7 seeks to describe. Similarly, Chapter 8 portrays community-level efforts directed toward the same ends. In this chapter, *Beyond the School*, parents, families, community resources, government interventions, and other potential, extraschool resources are considered for their aggression-prevention potential.

Thus, youngsters in school, their teachers, the school itself, and the larger community are each in turn the focus of our attention. How techniques implemented with each may serve the companion goals of aggression control, alternatives, and prevention is this book's concern. In the last chapter, we seek to pull these separate efforts at different levels of intervention into a coherent whole. We fully believe that the overall goals of reducing school violence, preventing its occurrence, and enhancing prosocial behavior will be most adequately achieved when these interventions are implemented simultaneously at all levels. This multilevel stance— youngster, teacher, school, community—is further described in Chapter 9.

American public education has contributed immeasurably to this nation's strength and global impact. It now suffers from the malaise of violence characteristic of so many aspects of American life. It is our hope that this book will serve as a small but useful contribution to reducing and preventing such violence, thereby permitting America's schools to get on with the educational tasks and accomplishments they can do, and have in the past done, so very well.

A. P. G.
S. J. A.
B. H.

1
The Problem

I do not agree with the apostles of gloom and despair who tell us that we are poised on the brink of a declining era in American education, marked only by the burnt out hopes of an institution that tried to do too much. The spirit, sense of purpose, willingness to strive, and the desire to accomplish that were the hallmarks of the American educational effort over our first 200 years, are alive and flourishing in schools across our country today. As we enter our third century, we are obviously facing grave problems in American education, but we have in the past confronted such challenges and have succeeded in producing a public educational system with a breadth and depth unmatched in the history of the world. Indeed, it seems that the very strengths of the system are forged through the experience of overcoming numerous obstacles throughout our history. Today we face yet another challenge, but while there may be reason for concern there is no need for discouragement. Anyone who has worked closely with the educational community cannot fail to be impressed with the vitality and confidence of the students, teachers, administrators, and parents confronting and successfully overcoming the problems of violence and vandalism. With the cooperation and commitment of all elements of the educational community, I am confident that we can succeed in exchanging the adversity and strife, so harmful to education in our schools, for the diversity and debate so necessary for learning . . . (Senator Birch Bayh, 1978)

Aggression and America are long and intimate companions. Both historically and today, collective and individual aggression are prominent features of the American scene. Collective aggression, born in a frontier spirit and irregularly enhanced by both the sanctioned collective aggression of warfare and the ready availability of guns in the United States, has historically found diverse expression in vigilante movements, feuding, agrarian and labor strife, racial lynchings, and, in the 1960s, in student and antiwar riots. Individual aggression in America is more difficult to capture in objective historical perspective for two reasons. First, the major means utilized in the United States for systematically recording and enumerating individual criminal acts, the Federal Bureau of Investigation's Uniform Crime Reports, was not begun until 1933. Thus, less systematic and comprehensive historical accounts must be relied upon for information regarding pre-1933 levels of criminal aggression in America. Second, certain other forms of individual aggression, notably child and spouse abuse and a few classes of juvenile "misbehavior," were not a matter of

1

TABLE 1.1 Index of Crime in the United States, 1960–1978

POPULATION	TOTAL CRIME INDEX	VIOLENT CRIME	PROPERTY CRIME	MURDER AND NON-NEGLIGENT MAN-SLAUGHTER	FORCIBLE RAPE	ROBBERY	AGGRAVATED ASSAULT	BURGLARY	LARCENY/THEFT	MOTOR-VEHICLE THEFT
Number of offenses:										
1960: 179,323,175	3,363,700	286,890	3,076,800	9,060	17,130	107,570	153,140	906,600	1,543,100	327,100
1961: 182,002,000	3,466,800	287,800	3,179,000	8,690	17,160	106,400	155,560	943,800	1,500,300	334,000
1962: 185,771,000	3,729,500	209,860	3,420,600	8,480	17,490	110,580	163,310	988,300	2,075,800	365,600
1963: 188,483,000	4,084,400	315,230	3,769,200	8,590	17,590	116,180	172,880	1,079,800	2,282,000	401,900
1964: 191,111,000	4,537,100	362,210	4,174,800	9,310	21,350	130,500	201,500	1,205,800	2,497,800	471,200
1965: 193,526,000	4,710,800	385,260	4,325,500	9,010	23,330	138,340	213,680	1,274,700	2,555,600	495,200
1966: 195,576,000	5,102,000	427,840	4,761,100	10,980	25,730	157,590	283,530	1,401,500	2,803,300	559,300
1967: 197,457,000	5,888,100	497,290	5,370,800	12,170	27,580	202,400	255,190	1,622,200	3,001,000	637,600
1968: 199,399,000	6,680,300	501,980	6,088,300	13,730	31,580	262,180	284,510	1,847,600	3,450,700	781,000
1969: 201,385,000	7,410,900	661,870	6,749,000	14,760	37,170	298,850	311,090	1,981,900	3,888,600	878,500
1970: 203,235,298	8,098,000	738,820	7,359,200	16,000	37,990	349,860	334,970	2,205,000	4,225,800	928,400
1971: 206,212,000	8,588,200	816,500	7,771,700	17,780	42,260	387,700	368,700	2,399,300	4,424,200	948,200
1972: 208,230,000	8,248,800	834,900	7,413,900	18,670	46,850	376,290	393,090	2,375,500	4,151,200	882,200
1973: 209,851,000	8,718,100	875,910	7,842,200	19,640	51,400	384,220	420,650	2,565,500	4,347,900	928,800
1974: 211,392,000	10,253,400	974,720	9,278,700	20,710	55,400	442,400	456,210	3,039,200	5,262,500	977,100
1975: 213,124,000	11,256,600	1,026,280	10,230,300	20,510	56,090	464,970	484,710	3,252,100	5,977,700	1,000,500
1976: 214,659,000	11,304,800	986,580	10,318,200	18,780	56,730	420,210	490,850	3,089,800	6,270,800	957,600
1977: 216,332,000	10,935,800	1,009,500	9,926,300	19,120	63,020	404,850	522,510	3,052,200	5,905,700	968,400
1978: 218,059,000	11,141,300	1,061,830	10,079,500	19,560	67,130	417,040	558,100	3,104.500	5,983,400	991,600

Rate per 100,000 inhabitants:

Year										
1960	1,875.8	160.0	1,715.8	5.1	0.5	60.0	85.4	505.6	1,027.8	182.4
1961	1,804.5	157.3	1,737.2	4.7	0.4	58.1	85.0	515.7	1,038.5	183.0
1962	2,007.6	161.4	1,846.2	4.6	9.4	59.5	87.9	532.0	1,117.4	196.8
1963	2,167.0	167.2	1,999.8	4.6	9.3	61.6	91.7	572.9	1,211.0	213.9
1964	2,373.7	189.5	2,184.2	4.9	11.2	68.0	105.4	630.9	1,306.8	246.5
1965	2,434.2	199.1	2,235.1	5.1	12.1	71.5	110.4	658.7	1,320.5	255.9
1966	2,654.7	218.8	2,435.9	5.6	13.2	80.6	119.4	716.6	1,433.4	286.0
1967	2,971.8	251.8	2,720.0	6.2	13.9	102.5	129.2	821.5	1,565.4	333.0
1968	3,350.2	296.9	3,053.3	6.9	15.8	131.5	142.7	926.6	1,735.1	391.7
1969	3,658.1	327.0	3,331.1	7.3	18.4	148.0	153.3	978.2	1,918.2	434.8
1970	3,960.9	361.7	3,599.1	7.8	18.6	171.7	163.6	1,078.4	2,065.5	455.3
1971	4,140.0	394.0	3,716.0	8.6	20.4	187.5	177.5	1,156.4	2,131.3	458.3
1972	3,937.8	398.9	3,538.9	8.9	22.4	180.3	187.3	1,133.9	1,980.4	421.6
1973	4,129.7	415.3	3,714.4	9.3	24.4	182.6	198.9	1,245.1	2,058.2	441.1
1974	4,821.4	458.8	4,362.6	9.7	26.1	208.8	214.2	1,429.0	2,473.0	160.6
1975	5,281.7	481.5	4,800.2	9.6	26.3	218.2	227.4	1,525.9	2,804.8	469.4
1976	5,266.4	459.6	4,806.8	8.8	26.4	195.8	228.7	1,439.4	2,921.3	446.1
1977	5,055.1	466.6	4,588.4	8.8	29.1	187.1	241.5	1,410.9	2,729.9	447.6
1978	5,109.3	486.9	4,622.4	9.0	30.8	191.3	255.9	1,423.7	2,743.9	454.7

Source: F.B.I. Uniform Crime Report, 1979.

general public concern and attention until the late 1960s. Such societal relative indifference to these behaviors has changed quite dramatically in recent years.

Much of what can be reported more or less factually about recent trends in individual aggression, especially of a criminal nature, is depicted in Table 1.1. This table, drawn from the F.B.I. Uniform Crime Reports, 1960 through 1978, is derived from crime statistics voluntarily submitted to the F.B.I. by police departments across America. It enumerates both the absolute number and relative rate (per 100,000 inhabitants) of major violent and property crimes in the United States. Violent crimes are defined to include murder, forcible rape, robbery, and aggravated assault. Property crimes include burglary, larceny/theft, and motor-vehicle theft. We are presenting these data here in order to provide a broad context for our later, more specific examination of similarly aggressive behaviors directed towards persons or property in a school setting.

The statistical levels and trends depicted in Table 1.1 are the focus of very considerable attention and often diverse interpretation in the United States. Our overall understanding of these data, in agreement with Kushler and Davidson (1981), Feldman (1977), and Nietzel (1979), views crime in America as increasing in a consistent but moderate manner during the fifteen-year period from 1960 to 1975, and then essentially stabilizing in rate since that time. In support of the oft-heard contention that individual aggression and vandalism in schools tends to directly reflect the levels of such behaviors in the community at large, we illustrate later in this chapter that much the same conclusion may appropriately be drawn for the rates of aggression toward people and property in the school context—namely, substantial increases until the mid-1970s, then stabilization of (high) rates since then.

Table 1.1 also shows exceptions to this recent rate-stabilization trend, and unfortunately two such exceptions are particularly aggressive criminal acts—forcible rape and aggravated assault—both of whose rates have continued to increase. Further, even in the case of certain crimes whose rates of occurrence have largely stabilized, the level or intensity of associated violence has increased. In 1967, for example, one in five robbery victims was physically injured during the commission of the robbery. In 1977, the comparable injury statistic was one in three. Similarly, Neill (1977) and Rubel (1977) have each observed that in America's schools, the intensity of violence associated with diverse acts of aggression or vandalism has discernibly escalated in the last few years. To further set the stage for our consideration of aggression in schools, and intervention therein, we now examine more fully issues of types, rates, and trends in school violence and vandalism.

AGGRESSION TOWARD PERSONS

We are concerned in this book with aggression in schools, toward either people or property. In American public education for the many decades preceding the twentieth century, such aggression apparently was infrequent in occurrence, low in intensity, and—at least in retrospect—almost quaint in character. "Misbehavior," "poor comportment," "bad conduct" and the like in the form of getting out of one's seat, insubordination, throwing a spitball, sticking a pigtail in an inkwell, or even the rare breaking of a window seem like, and truly are, the events of another era, events so mild in comparison to the aggression of today that it becomes difficult to conceptualize them as the extremes of a shared continuum. Commenting on Westin's study of urban school violence for the years 1870 through 1950, Bayh (1975), observes: "If, however, the system has never been totally immune from incidents of student misbehavior, such problems have historically been viewed as a relatively minor concern seldom involving more than a few sporadic and isolated incidents" (p. 3). Rubel (1977) has correspondingly noted that fights between students have changed from words and fists to aggravated assault with lethal weapons. In a manner consistent with our interpretation of nonschool violence in Table 1.1, the years prior to the 1960s may appropriately be called the "preescalation period" in American school violence. Consistent with Bayh's observations, a 1956 National Education Association survey reported that two-thirds of the 4,270 teachers sampled from across the United States reported that fewer than 1 percent of their students caused instances of disruption or disturbance, and "... 95 percent [of the responding teachers] described the boys and girls they taught as either exceptionally well behaved, or reasonably well behaved" (National Education Association, 1956, p. 17).

We noted earlier that crime in general in America rose rapidly in the 1960 to 1975 period. Table 1.2, drawn from the 1975 F.B.I. Uniform Crime Report, indicates that a similar trend is also descriptive for one of the age groups of particular interest to this book, 15 to 17 year olds. Note that across types of offenses, the percent increment in arrest rate for the two periods compared is consistently substantial. Can analogous conclusions be drawn for acts of aggression toward persons and property in a school context? As is seen later, the answer is an unequivocal yes.

In 1975, the Bayh Senatorial Subcommittee issued its Safe School Report. This survey of 750 school districts indicated that in America's schools between 1970 and 1973, homicides increased by 18.5 percent, rapes and attempted rapes increased by 40.1 percent, robberies increased by 36.7 percent, assaults on students increased by 85.3 percent, assaults on teachers increased by 77.4 percent, burglaries in school increased by 11.8 percent, drug and alcohol offenses increased by 37.5 percent, and the number of weapons confiscated by school personnel (pistols, knives, chunka sticks, and even sawed-off shot guns) increased by 54.4 percent. The National Association of School Security Directors reported that, in 1974, there were 204,000 assaults and 9,000 rapes in American schools. Matters had gone a very long way from spitballs and pigtails. There were 18,000 assaults on teachers in 1955, 41,000 in 1971, 63,000 in 1975; by 1979, the number of such attacks had risen to 110,000. The level of assaults on teachers in America's public schools is sufficiently high that the vocabulary of aggression has been expanded to include what Block (1977) has called the "battered teacher syndrome": a combination of stress reactions including anxiety, depression, disturbed sleep, headaches, elevated blood pressure, and eating disorders.

TABLE 1.2. Actual Percent Increases in Arrest Rates of 15 to 17 Year Olds (1953-1974)[a]

OFFENSE	POPULATION, 1953[b]	ARREST RATE, 1953[c]	POPULATION, 1974[b]	ARREST RATE, 1974[c]	PERCENT INCREASE OF ARREST RATE; 1974 OVER 1953[a]
Assault	6.490	2.5365	12.651	13.6909	440
Burglary	6.490	32.7037	12.651	80.3479	150
Larceny/Theft	6.490	43.1557	12.651	142.8089	230
Total Part I	6.490	87.2347	12.651	291.2210	230
Total Part II	6.490	160.3079	12.651	511.6645	220

[a]The actual percent increase controls for: (1) changes in the UCR arrest population over time by using rates per 100,000 population and (2) changes in the number of juvenile arrests as a function of changes in the youth population of the same age group.
[b]Population expressed in thousands.
[c]Rate expressed in terms of 100,000 population.

Source: F.B.I. Uniform Crime Report, 1975.

The seriousness of these attacks on teachers notwithstanding, it must be remembered that most aggression in America's schools is directed toward other *students*. Victimization data from twenty-six major American cities surveyed in 1974 and 1975 indicated that 78 percent of personal victimizations in schools (rapes, robberies, assaults, and larcenies) were students (McDermott, 1979). Ban and Ciminillo (1977) report that in a national survey the percent of principals who report "unorganized fighting" between students had increased from 2.8 percent in 1961 to 18 percent in 1974. Examining much of the data on correlates of aggression toward students, Ianni (1978) reports that seventh graders are most likely to be attacked, twelfth graders the least likely; at about age 13 the risks of physical attack tend to be greatest. Fifty-eight percent of such attacks involve victims and offenders of the same race; 42 percent are interracial. It has also been demonstrated that the smaller the size of a minority group in a school, the more likely its members will be victimized by members of other racial groups.

As we elaborate upon later in this book, the nature of leadership and governance in a school can be a major correlate of violence within its walls. A firm, fair, consistent principal-leadership style, for example, has been shown to be associated with low levels of student aggression. High levels of arbitrary leadership and severe disciplinary actions tend to characterize schools experiencing high levels of aggression. School size is a further correlate of school violence: The larger the school, the more likely its occurrence. Such a relationship, it has been proposed, may grow from the easier identification of students and by students in smaller schools, and such consequences of larger schools as nonparticipation in governance, impersonalness, and crowding. Crowding is a particularly salient school-violence correlate, as aggressive behavior in fact occurs more frequently in more crowded school locations—stairways, hallways, and cafeterias—and less frequently in classrooms themselves. Other often-chronic "casuality zones" include lavoratories, entrance and exit areas, and locker rooms. Student violence is most likely during the time between classes, and, for reasons that may have to do with "spring-fever effects," during the month of March. With a number of exceptions, school violence also correlates with the size of the community in which the school is located. The proportion of American schools reporting serious levels of aggressive behavior is 15 percent in large cities, 6 percent in suburban areas, and 4 percent in rural areas.

AGGRESSION TOWARD PROPERTY

School vandalism, defined as acts that result in significant damage to schools (Greenberg, 1969), has been characterized, in terms of perpetrator motivation, as predatory, vindictive, or wanton (Martin, 1961) and, in terms of perpetrator perception, as acquisitive, tactical, ideological, revengeful, playful, and malicious (Cohen, 1971). Across motivational or perceptual subtypes, vandalism viewed collectively is an expensive fact of American educational life. Though estimates for some years show not inconsiderable variability, several reports lead to a consensus view that, in more or less direct parallel to incidence statistics for aggression toward people in schools, aggression toward property increased substantially in the several years ending in the mid-1970s, and then generally leveled off at what is best described as an absolutely high level (Casserly, Bass, & Garrett, 1980; Inciardi & Pottieger, 1978; Rubel, 1977). One hundred million dollars of such school vandalism is reported to have occurred in 1969, 200 million dollars in 1970, 260 million dollars in 1973, 550 million dollars in 1975, and 600 million dollars in 1977.* In 1977, 24,000 of America's 84,000 public schools reported the occurrence of some major vandalism each month. Concretely, in the 84,000 schools, each month there were substantial reports of trespassing (10.9 percent), breaking and entering (10 percent), theft of school property (12.3 percent), property destruction (28.5 percent), fires or false alarms (4.5 percent), and bomb threats (1.1 percent). In 1979, America's schools reported 20 million thefts and 400,000 acts of property destruction. Arson, a particularly dangerous form of vandalism, perhaps deserves special comment. From 1950 to 1975, while the number of students in average daily attendance in American public schools was increasing by 86 percent, school arson increased 859 percent (Rubel, 1977). The annual cost of school fires increased from 17 million dollars in 1950 to 106 million dollars in 1975. Even discounting inflationary influences, the cost of school arson increased by 179 percent in constant dollars during this period. Though window breaking is the most frequent single act of aggression toward property in schools, arson is clearly the most costly, typically accounting for approximately 40 percent of total vandalism costs annually.

Although early research suggested that most vandalism was committed by lower-class minority males (Bates, 1962; Clinard & Wade, 1958), vandalism has since apparently become distributed in a more egalitarian manner. The school vandal of today is just as likely to be white as nonwhite (Goldmeir, 1974), middle class as lower class (Howard, 1978), and (at least for graffiti and similar acts) female as male (Richards, 1976). Most vandals are 11 to 16 years old (Ellison, 1973); are no more disturbed on formal psychological evaluations than youngsters who do not vandalize (Richards, 1976); are frequently students who have been left back (Nowakowski, 1966); are often truant (Greenberg, 1974), and have frequently been suspended from school altogether (Yankelovich, 1975).

In connection with school correlates of student vandalism, Greenberg (1969) reports that rates tend to be highest in schools with obsolete facilities and equipment and low staff morale. Leftwich (1977) found a similarly strong relationship between high teacher turnover rates and level of vandalism. In contrast, vandalism has been found to be unrelated to teacher-student ratios, to the proportion of mi-

---

*As the National Education Association's (1977) Report indicates, as these years passed and vandalism costs grew, approximately half of such costs were directly due to property damage incurred, and the remaining half represented indirect vandalism costs associated with hiring and supporting a security force, use of security devices, and so forth. These total vandalism cost figures typically have not included one additional and major hidden cost of such property destruction: insurance.

nority students in the school, or to the percent of students whose parents were on welfare or unemployed (Casserly et al., 1980). As we stress in later chapters, community characteristics are also often important influences upon in-school events. In this connection, school vandalism tends to be correlated with community crime level, geographic concentration of students, degree of nonstudent (intruder) presence in school, and nature of family discipline.

We have focused thus far in this section on costs and correlates of school vandalism. It is also instructive to note factors associated with *low* levels of aggression toward property in schools. These include informal teacher-teacher and teacher-principal interactions, high levels of teacher identification with the school, and low student-dropout rates (Goldman, 1961). The Safe School Study (Bayh, 1975) also reported vandalism to be lower when school rules were strictly but evenhandedly enforced, parents supported strong disciplinary policies, students valued teachers' opinions of them, teachers avoided use of grades as disciplinary tools, and teachers avoided use of hostile or authoritarian behavior toward students.

In addition to those violence and vandalism correlates described thus far in this chapter that may prove in subsequent research to be causatively related to aggression in schools, a large number of factors have already been proposed as just such antecedents. Aggression toward persons or property in schools has been held to result, in part, from low student self-esteem, student frustration associated with learning disabilities or emotional problems, insufficient student participation in school rule making, student exclusion, truants, intruders, gang influences, and student alcohol and drug abuse. Also implicated has been an array of purported teacher inadequacies: disrespectfulness, callousness, disinterest, incompetence, and middle-class bias. Schools themselves have been considered as wellsprings of violence and vandalism when they are too large, impersonal, unresponsive, nonparticipatory, over-regulated, oppressive, arbitrary, or inconsistent. American society at large, in less direct but perhaps more basic senses, has been implicated as a multiple source of aggression in schools, as a function of widespread aggression out of school, the breakdown of the American family, television influences, ethnic conflict, unemployment, poverty, inadequate health services, and an array of related social ills.

We have stated that the human and economic costs of aggression toward people and property in America's schools is very substantial. After decades of what, at least in retrospect and probably in reality, seem like negligible incidence rates, both classes of aggression increased precipitously during the late 1960s and early 1970s. Their plateauing at very high levels since that time can give us little cause for comfort. In fact, there are several reasons to suspect that even these apparent current levels may be serious underestimates. Inconsistent and imprecise definitions of violence and vandalism, inaccurate or nonexistent record keeping, unwillingness to report acts of aggression, fear of reprisal, wide variance in reporting procedures, and school administrator concern with appearing inadequate each may lead to markedly underestimated and underreported incidence statistics. In fact, it has been estimated that actual levels of school violence and vandalism may be as much as 50 percent higher than that generally reported (Ban & Ciminillo, 1977).

POTENTIAL SOLUTIONS

As expressed by Senator Bayh in the quotation which opened this chapter, the response of the educational community to this immense and unremitting problem has been energetic, creative, and sustained. A very large number of potential solutions has emerged, some aimed at students themselves, others at teachers, administrators, or the wider community in which the school functions. Hoped-for solutions have been almost as varied as they are numerous: humanistic, behavioral, electronic, architectural, organizational, curricular, administrative, legal, and more. Table 1.3 is a comprehensive presentation of these intended solutions to aggression in school, a presentation we include here to provide both a sense of the sheer scope and number of such efforts, as well as further introduction to the chapters which follow, in which several of the more promising of these solutions are examined in depth. All of these interventions have in fact been implemented in one, and often many, American schools. Some have been systematically evaluated for their impact on violence and vandalism, others have been examined more cursorily, and still others not at all.

As earlier sections of this chapter made quite clear, the magnitude and social and economic costs of school violence in the United States are substantial. Table 1.3

TABLE 1.3. Attempted Solutions to School Violence and Vandalism

---

I. STUDENT ORIENTED

Diagnostic learning centers
Regional occupational centers
Part-time programs
Academic-support services
Group counseling
Student advisory committee
Student patrols (interracial)
Behavior modification: contingency management
Behavior modification: time out
Behavior modification: response cost
Behavior modification: contracting
Financial accountability
School transfer
Interpersonal skill training
Problem-solving training
Moral education
Value clarification
Individual counseling
More achievable reward criteria
Identification cards
Peer counseling
Participation in grievance resolution
Security advisory council
School-safety committee

TABLE 1.3. (continued)

II. TEACHER ORIENTED

Aggression-management training for teachers
Increased teacher-student nonclass contact
Teacher-student-administration group discussions
Low teacher-pupil ratio
Firm, fair, consistent teacher discipline
Self-defense training
Carrying of weapons by teachers
Legalization of teacher use of force
Compensation for aggression-related expenses
Individualized teaching strategies
Enhanced teacher knowledge of student ethnic milieu
Increased teacher-parent interaction

III. CURRICULUM

Art and music courses
Law courses
Police courses
Courses dealing with practical aspects of adult life
Prescriptively tailored course sequences
Work-study programs
Equivalency diplomas
Schools without walls
Schools within schools
Learning centers (magnet schools, educational parks)
Continuation centers (street academies, evening high schools)
Minischools
Self-paced instruction
Idiographic grading

IV. ADMINISTRATIVE

Use of skilled conflict negotiators
Twenty-four hour custodial service
Clear lines of responsibility and authority among administrators
School-safety committee
School administration-police coordination
Legal-rights handbook
School-procedures manual
Written codes of rights and responsibilities
Aggression-management training for administrators
Democratized school governance
Human-relations courses
Effective intelligence network
Principal visibility and availability
Relaxation of arbitrary rules (re smoking, dressing, absences, etc.)

TABLE 1.3. (continued)

V. PHYSICAL SCHOOL ALTERATIONS

Extensive lighting program
Blackout of all lighting
Reduction of school size
Reduction of class size
Close off isolated areas
Increase staff supervision
Implement rapid repair of vandalism targets
Electronic monitoring for weapons detection
Safety corridors (school to street)
Removal of tempting vandalism targets
Recess fixtures where possible
Install graffiti boards
Encourage student-drawn murals
Paint lockers bright colors
Use ceramic-type, hard-surface paints
Sponsor clean-up, pick-up, fix-up days
Pave or asphalt graveled parking areas
Use plexiglass or polycarbon windows
Install decorative grillwork over windows
Mark all school property for identification
Use intruder detectors (microwave, ultrasonic, infrared, audio, video, mechanical)
Employ personal alarm systems
Alter isolated areas to attract people traffic

VI. PARENT ORIENTED

Telephone campaigns to encourage PTA attendance
Antitruancy committee (parent, counselor, student)
Parenting-skills training
Parents as guest speakers
Parents as apprenticeship resources
Parents as work-study contacts
Increased parent legal responsibility for their children's behavior
Family education centers

VII. SECURITY PERSONNEL

Police-K-9 patrol units
Police helicopter surveillance
Use of security personnel for patrol
Use of security personnel for crowd control
Use of security personnel for intelligence gathering
Use of security personnel for record keeping
Use of security personnel for teaching (e.g., law)
Use of security personnel for counseling
Use of security personnel for home visits
Development of school security manuals

TABLE 1.3. (continued)

VIII. COMMUNITY ORIENTED

Helping-hand programs
Restitution programs
Adopt-a-school programs
Vandalism-prevention education
Mass-media publication of cost of vandalism
Open school to community use after hours
Improved school-juvenile court liaison
Family back-to-school week
Neighborhood Day
Vandalism watch on or near school grounds via mobile homes
Encourage reporting by CB users of observed vandalism
Community-education programs
More and better programs for disruptive/disturbed youngsters

IX. STATE AND FEDERAL ORIENTED

Establish uniform violence and vandalism reporting system
Establish state antiviolence advisory committee
Stronger gun-control legislation
Enhanced national moral leadership
Better coordination of relevant federal, state, community agencies
Stronger antitrespass legislation
More prosocial television programs
Less restrictive child-labor laws

---

shows us, equally clearly, that the response of the American educational establishment to this painful and costly trend has been energetic, constructive, and, as we shall see in the case of at least a few programs, demonstrably successful. Such initial success at controlling, reducing, or even preventing school violence may be enhanced considerably, we believe, when the techniques thus identified are not only refined and systematically implemented, but also when they are used in optimal combinations. This will be especially true, we feel, when these combinations of singly succesful interventions are simultaneously targeted toward the different sources immediately or implicitly responsible for school violence—the youngsters themselves, the teachers, the schools, the larger community. We now turn to specific aggression-relevant interventions at these various levels of application.

REFERENCES

BAN, J. R., & CIMINILLO, L. M. *Violence and vandalism in public education.* Danville, Ill.: The Interstate Printers & Publishers, Inc., 1977.
BATES, W. Caste, class and vandalism. *Social Problems,* 1962, *9,* 348–353.

BAYH, B. *Our nation's schools—A report card: "A" in school violence and vandalism.* Washington, D.C.: Preliminary report of the subcommittee to investigate juvenile delinquency, U.S. Senate, April 1975.

BAYH, B. School violence and vandalism: Problems and solutions. *Journal of Research and Development in Education,* 1978, *11,* 5–9.

BLOCK, A. The battered teacher. *Today's Education,* 1977, *66,* 58–62.

CASSERLY, M. D., BASS, S. A., & GARRETT, J. R. *School vandalism: Strategies for prevention.* Lexington, Mass.: Lexington Books, 1980.

CLINARD, M. B., & WADE, A. L. Toward the delineation of vandalism as a subtype in juvenile delinquency. *Journal of Criminal Law, Criminology and Police Science,* 1958, *48,* 493–499.

COHEN, S. Direction for research on adolescent school violence and vandalism. *British Journal of Criminology,* 1971, *9,* 319–340.

ELLISON, W. S. School vandalism: 100 million dollar challenge. *Community Education Journal,* 1973, *3,* 27–33.

FELDMAN, M. P. *Criminal behavior: A psychological analysis.* New York: Wiley, 1977.

GOLDMAN, N. A socio-psychological study of school vandalism. *Crime and Delinquency,* 1961, *7,* 221–230.

GOLDMEIR, H. Vandalism: The effects of unmanageable confrontations. *Adolescence,* 1974, *9,* 49–56.

GREENBERG, B. *School vandalism: A national dilemma.* Menlo Park, Calif.: Stanford Research Institute, 1969.

GREENBERG, B. School vandalism: Its effects and paradoxical solutions. *Crime Prevention Review,* 1974, *1,* 11–18.

HOWARD, J. L. Factors in school vandalism. *Journal of Research and Development in Education.* 1978, *11,* 13–18.

IANNI, F. A. J. The social organization of the high school: School-specific aspects of school crime. In E. Wenk & N. Harlow (Eds.), *School crime and disruption.* Davis, Calif.: Responsible Action, 1978.

INCIARDI, J. A., & POTTIEGER, A. E. (Eds.). *Violent crime: Historical and contemporary issues.* Beverly Hills: Sage Publications, 1978.

KUSHLER, M. G., & DAVIDSON, W. S. Community and organizational level change. In A. P. Goldstein, E. G. Carr, W. S. Davidson, & P. Wehr (Eds.), *In response to aggression.* New York: Pergamon Press, 1981.

LEFTWICH, D. *A study of vandalism in selected public schools in Alabama.* Doctoral dissertation, University of Alabama, 1977.

MARTIN, J. M. *Juvenile vandalism: A study of its nature and prevention.* Springfield, Ill.: Charles C Thomas, 1961.

McDERMOTT, M. J. *Criminal victimization in urban schools.* Albany, N.Y.: Criminal Justice Research Center, 1979.

NATIONAL EDUCATION ASSOCIATION. Teacher opinion on pupil behavior, 1955–1956. Washington, D.C.: *Research Bulletin of the National Education Association,* 1956, *34,* No. 2.

NATIONAL EDUCATION ASSOCIATION. *Danger—school ahead: Violence in the public schools.* Washington, D.C.: National Education Association, 1977.

NEILL, S. B. *Violence and vandalism: Current trends in school policies and programs.* Arlington, Va.: National School Public Relations Association, 1977.

NIETZEL, M. T. *Crime and its modification.* New York: Pergamon Press, 1979.

NOWAKOWSKI, R. *Vandals and vandalism in the schools: An analysis of vandalism in large school systems and a description of 93 vandals in Dade County schools.* Doctoral dissertation, University of Miami, 1966.

RICHARDS, P. *Patterns of middle class vandalism: A case study of suburban adolescence.* Doctoral dissertation, Northwestern University, 1976.
RUBEL, R. J. *Unruly school: Disorders, disruptions, and crimes.* Lexington, Mass.: D. C. Heath, 1977.
YANKELOVICH, D. How students control their drug crisis. *Psychology Today,* 1975, *9,* 39–42.

2

The Teacher
As Decision Maker

... teachers must decide whether their role in classroom discipline is passive or participatory. Do teachers have a role in achieving discipline in their rooms or are their students expected to enter their rooms quietly, to be seated quietly, and quietly await their teacher's lessons? (Foster, 1974, p. 237)

Given that all the teachers in this study had at least three years of experience and *had been recommended as either average or outstanding at dealing with problem students by their principals,* the data suggest *widespread knowledge and skill deficiencies* in these areas. Relatively few teachers had specific knowledge, let alone training, in behavior modification, mental health consultation, or other strategies for dealing with problem students. Many teachers complained of this and stated a desire for such training, but *many others stated that their job was to teach and not to act as therapists for students with personality or behavior problems.* (Brophy & Rohrkemper, 1980a, p. 72 italics added)

Schooling can get better only classroom by classroom, teacher by teacher. The teacher's role in the reduction of school violence and aggression is obviously crucial. Just as obviously, the teacher is not the only factor involved—parents, the administration of the school, the community at large all play a part. But the teacher is the person at the forefront of any effort to cope successfully with the problem.

The stance taken in this chapter regarding the teacher's role with respect to the aggressive youngster views teaching as involving a series of decisions not all of which are necessarily made consciously, but which nonetheless take place and must be understood if the complexities surrounding the disruptive student in the classroom are to be unraveled. If the teacher chooses a priori to define teaching in such a way as to exclude dealing with disruptions and violence in the classroom or school, the consequences of such a definition would result (1) in a severely circumscribed and limited role for teachers, a role which in most modern postindustrial societies has been expanding rather than contracting; and (2) in such an action becoming in effect a nondecision or at least the forfeit of a decision, because sooner or later every teacher will be involved with some aspect of violence and disruption in school settings.

It may be that some teachers regard dealing with violence in schools as the province of police or as the lowering of their status with students (Edgerton, 1977; Foster, 1974). Whatever the reasons, the teacher's role in school violence is not going to diminish even when the teachers' union brings the issue to the bargaining table, as it did in 1968 in New York City. The question of how students' aggressive behaviors will be handled will continue to be an increasing concern in contract negotiations (Foster, 1968), but the individual teacher's skill and knowledge regarding these students will remain a crucial element in the amelioration of this problem. If we can accept the Brophy and Rohrkemper (1980a) findings indicating widespread teacher unpreparedness for dealing effectively with aggression with students as representative of the current state of affairs regarding classroom teachers in America, then the remaining chapters in this book offer a beginning answer by providing the teacher with useful knowledge of and strategies for aggression reduction and aggression alternatives. In this chapter we first consider teaching as decision making from a number of perspectives and then some of the more specific aspects of decision making as they bear upon the school-violence problem in America's schools.

THE DECISION-MAKING
PERSPECTIVE OF TEACHING

How do teachers plan, implement, and evaluate the tasks and activities that describe instruction in their classrooms, particularly those tasks and activities that focus on the reduction of disruptive behaviors by their pupils? In planning, implementing, and evaluating instruction, teachers may be confronted with hundreds, if not thousands, of decisions (Hunt, 1976; Jackson, 1968). The planning or preactive phase of teaching has been given considerable, if not the major, attention of teacher-preparation programs for some time, as has the evaluative phase. More recently, attention has focused on the implementation or interactive phase of teaching and the moment-to-moment decisions required of the teachers. In Hunt's (1976) words:

> Teachers' adaptation to students is the heart of the teaching learning process, yet it remains poorly understood. It refers to the moment-to-moment shifts in teacher behavior in response to an individual student, a group of students, or an entire class, as well as shifts over a longer period of time. Such adaptation has been called spontaneous, intuitive, implicit or interactive. (p. 268)

Not only is our knowledge about interactive decisions less than clear, but the relationship between the planning and implementing of instruction has remained murky and largely speculative or intuitive (Shavelson & Stern, 1981). Although the paucity of evidence about this relationship was noted some time ago (Harootunian,

1966), recent research findings, tentative though they are, suggest that teachers construct mental scripts or images for interactive teaching. These mental pictures of the class describe routines which the teacher monitors automatically by looking for cues that confirm the established procedure. When these cues fall outside the limits of tolerance, the teacher must decide what course of action to take (Joyce, 1978-1979; Morine-Dershimer, 1978-1979). Thus, what evidence there is indicates that teachers resist changing or interrupting the flow of activity during a lesson. To do so "drastically increases the information processing demands on the teacher and increases the probability of classroom management problems" (Shavelson & Stern, 1981, p. 484). At the same time, student aggressive behavior constitutes one of the most serious disruptions of the interactive teaching routine and confronts the teacher with the necessity of making a decision. In other words, the evidence suggests that once teachers plan a routine or course of action, they guard against anything that involves drastic change, because such change complicates the classroom routine and makes a successful lesson problematic. If this view of interactive teaching is accurate, the response to student violence in all likelihood involves all of the critical decision-making skills a teacher possesses. The rest of this chapter focuses on identifying those factors which may affect the teacher's planning, interactive, and evaluative decisions about classroom aggression.

PROCESSES AND FACTORS
IN TEACHER DECISION MAKING

Although a number of individuals over the years have presented various views of teachers as decision makers or problem solvers (Bishop & Whitfield, 1972; Clark & Yinger, 1977; Coladarci, 1959; Joyce & Harootunian, 1967, 1967; McDonald, 1965; Shulman & Elstein, 1975), Richard Shavelson (1973, 1976; Shavelson & Stern, 1981) has probably been the person who has developed the most extensive perspective of the teacher's decision making. Shavelson (1976) has developed a model of teaching derived from statistical decision theory. He views his model as a heuristic for research on teaching rather than one that has immediate application to the classroom because he states that its purpose is to stimulate interest and inquiry about teaching from a decision-making approach (Shavelson, 1976).

As shown in Figure 2.1, Shavelson has identified five tasks for teachers in making decisions. These are: (1) the alternative courses of action available to the teacher; (2) the states of nature or environmental conditions over which the teacher has no direct control, such as the background of the students; (3) the outcome; (4) the utility for the teacher of a particular course of action taken for a particular set of environmental conditions; and (5) the goal or set of goals the decision maker hopes to attain. In this model it is assumed that teacher decisions are made to optimize student outcomes. The model can be further elaborated using statistical decision theory, and in this brief space we cannot do it justice. The reader is urged to study it in detail in its original form.

ALTERNATIVE COURSES OF ACTION

1. **Teaching Acts**
   Questioning
   Reinforcing
   Probing
   Explaining
   Surprising

2. **Microteaching Methods** (sequencing of teaching acts)
   Lower- to higher-order questions
   Rule-example-rule

3. **Macroteaching Methods**
   Lecture
   Discussion
   Discourse

STATES OF NATURE

1. **Student Cognitive States**
   Unlearned
   Transition

2. **Student Affective States**
   Uninterested
   Interested

3. **Administrative**
   Unpredicted assembly
   Fire drill
   Discipline

4. **Other**
   Football game
   Health
   Home

OUTCOMES/UTILITIES

1. **Student Cognitive Outcome/Utility**
   Learned/high
   Confused/low

2. **Student Affective Outcome/Utility**
   Motivated/high
   Unmotivated/low

3. **Student Social Outcome/Utility**
   Social/high
   Antisocial/low

GOALS FOR STUDENTS

1. **Cognitive**
   Learning
   Structure of discipline
   Learning to learn

2. **Affective**
   Motivation to learn
   Positive self-concept
   Internal locus of control

3. **Social**
   Positive interpersonal relations
   Behavioral self-control

FIGURE 2.1. Schematic representation of the elements in a decision. (Shavelson, R. J. Teacher decision making. In N. L. Gage (Ed.) *The psychology of teaching methods. The seventy-fifth yearbook of the National Society for the Study of Education*, Part 1. Chicago: University of Chicago Press, 1976.)

Since its original presentation, the model has been enhanced by the identification of a number of factors which contribute or influence teachers' pedagogical decisions and judgments. These factors are depicted in Figure 2.2. Taken together, the information in Figures 2.1 and 2.2 present a view of teachers as follows:

> Teachers are seen as active agents with many instructional techniques at their disposal to help students reach some goal. In order to choose from this repertoire, they must integrate a large amount of information about students from a variety of sources. And this information must somehow be combined with their own beliefs and goals, the nature of the instructional task, the constraints of the situation, and so on. (Shavelson & Stern, 1981, p. 472)

What may not be immediately apparent from either figure or our comments on them is that several alternative decisions are feasible. *There is not necessarily one correct decision.* Consequently, various teachers who might teach quite differently, but who are equal in decision-making skill, might achieve the same goals.

FIGURE 2.2.   Some factors in teachers' pedagogical decisions and judgments. (Shavelson, R. J. & Stern, P., "Research on Teacher's Pedagogical Thoughts, Judgments, Decisions and Behavior." *Review of Educational Research,* 1981, p. 472. Copyright 1981, American Educational Research Association, Washington, D.C.)

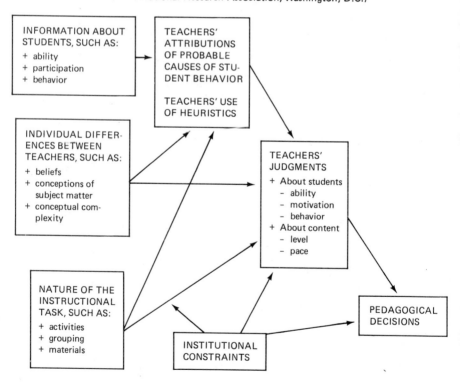

Shavelson's priority has been to provide direction for and to do research on teaching rather than to be concerned with classroom applications. Although many of his findings and those of his colleagues are noteworthy, and some can even be implemented by teachers, at present his approach is not readily translatable into the language of classroom teachers. For a perspective that can be of more immediate help, we have to depend on the thinking of David Hunt, whose approach to the study of teaching provides a framework for educational practice as well as theory and research. Hunt's thinking, though not cast in formal decision-making terms, has developed out of an information-processing perspective. What might be interesting to the reader is to note the great similarity between Hunt's intuitively derived teacher model (Hunt, 1976) and Shavelson's more formal depictions. Let us examine Hunt's approach and see how it can be applied by teachers involved with disruptive students.

APPLICATIONS
IN THE CLASSROOM

David Hunt points out that the three salient features of the educational experience are: (1) a student; (2) experiencing an educational approach; with (3) some kind of consequence. Hunt casts these three features into Kurt Lewin's formulation $B = f$ (P, E); *B*ehavior (educational outcome or consequence) results from the interaction of the *P*erson (student) and *E*nvironment (educational approach). For the teacher, particularly the teacher of disruptive students, the formula becomes $E: P \rightarrow B$ (or what teaching approach with these students will likely bring about the desired outcomes) (Hunt, 1976, 1977).

Merely listing the outcomes (B), student characteristics (P), and educational approaches (E) is insufficient for understanding the teaching-learning process. The arrangement of these different aspects is what the teacher has to think and make decisions about. Hunt has proposed that at least four features characterize his approach:

> (1) it should be *interactive* not only in coordinating person-environment interaction, but in accommodating differential behavioral effects; (2) it should view the person in *developmental* perspective so that differential effects of environmental influence may be seen developmentally as well as contemporaneously; (3) it should consider person-environment interaction in *reciprocal* terms that view the effect of the person on the environment as well as the effect of the environment on the person; and (4) it should consider the *practical* implications of such interactions so that conceptions can be enriched by application. (Hunt, 1975a, p. 218)

An interactive approach means that any decision involving alternative courses of action needs to be made in conjunction with the characteristics of the students involved. The teaching acts or methods have to be congruent with the nature of the learners. Viewing the person developmentally, as well as contemporaneously, requires the teacher not to lose sight of long-term student development in addition to immediate learning. The reciprocal features stress explicitly the idea that while the environment affects the students, the students affect the environment and can influence or pull the teacher in different directions. Finally, the practicality of *B-P-E* interactions refers to how translatable are any of the three previous features to the real world of the classroom.

To implement a *B-P-E* way of making decisions, Hunt (1977) looks at the process from the teacher's perspective. As noted in Table 2.1, communicating with a student, the teacher usually (1) begins with an intention (*B*); (2) perceives the student (*P*); (3) communicates or acts (*E*); and (4) checks on the effects (*B*). The sequence in teaching may be described as intention-perception-action-evaluation and with the addition of one more step—the teacher's implicit theory or central understanding about the teaching-learning process—between perception and action, the Hunt model is complete. As shown in Table 2.1, the Hunt sequence may be usefully compared with those used by program developers. The comparison of the activities describing the two approaches allows the reader to judge the similarities and differences. The teacher sequence depicted in Table 2.1 can take place in a brief time and then be repeated with readjustments resulting whenever there is a lack of congruity between intention and evaluation.

In the chapters that follow this one, we present and develop a number of programs based upon explicit theories or conceptualizations of learning and behavior. In comparing the two sequences depicted in Table 2.1, it is therefore important that the teacher know how and where the two diverge and converge because as Hunt (1976) notes

> ... the effect of these [research] results will depend on their congruence with teacher's concepts, and how well the findings can serve as guiding patterns. This is a radical change in our traditional theory-to-practice thinking, and is bound to be initially disturbing. (p. 274)

TABLE 2.1. Sequence of Steps Used by Teacher Model and Program-Development Model

	MODEL	
STEPS IN SEQUENCE	TEACHER	PROGRAM DEVELOPER
State objective (*B*)	Intention	Specify objectives
Characterize student (*P*)	Perception	Test students and assign
Translate to action	Implicit theory	Explicit theory
Provide environment (*E*)	Action	Prescribe approaches
Evaluate (*B*)	Check effects	Evaluate effects

Note: Based on D. E. Hunt. Teacher's adaptation: Reading and flexing to students. Journal of Teacher Education, 1976, 27, p. 274.

Let us try to understand the teacher sequence in Table 2.1 by applying it to the vignette sketched out here:

> The teacher is talking quietly with Mary when Don leaves his seat and goes over to Bob's desk, where he begins shouting at Bob, followed quickly by punching him. Bob is not fighting back as much as he is shielding himself from getting injured. The teacher shouts, "Stop!" The fighting continues. The teacher moves closer to Don, grabs his arms, and then removes him to a desk in the corner of the room away from the rest of the class. Don can watch the activities in the class, but there is no interaction with him by the teacher or by any of the other students during the remainder of the time the class is in session that day.

The preceding vignette probably represents an event similar to what has taken place in various classrooms for a long time. The difference between a decision-making perspective and an ordinary one may be seen as we consider each step in Table 2.1 in greater detail.

State Objective (B)—Intention

Adaptation of teaching approach to a student engaged in fighting must be viewed in the context of the teacher's goals or intent. The teacher first of all has to be able to discriminate and recognize the behaviors that are congruent with the intended outcomes. What this means is that the teacher's intentions have to be explicit. The teacher's intent in response to Don's fighting with Bob can be looked at on several levels. The immediate objective is to stop the violence, but beyond that what is the teacher's goal? It may be to help Don learn self-control; it may be to teach Don socially acceptable ways of expressing disagreement and disapproval; or it may be simply to remove Don from interaction with peers for a period of time. These different intentions may initially require similar kinds of teacher responses, but depending on where the teacher wants to go, different kinds of decisions will be necessary in each case. The last instance may simply exemplify one of the cease-and-desist techniques which teachers routinely use with disruptive students. But Don's separation from the rest of the class may reflect a conscious decision by the teacher to use nonexclusion time out (see pages 56 to 59) as the first phase in a behavior-modification sequence. If the goal is for Don to be able to be in greater control of his own behavior, the teacher may choose from among the behavior-modification techniques described in Chapter 3. If the teacher views the problem in terms of Don's learning prosocial expressions of behavior, then the subsequent decisions may involve the modeling and role-playing sequences detailed in Chapter 6.

When the teacher's intent is clear to the teacher and to others, the other steps in the sequence of decisions can be evaluated by the teacher and others. Moreover, when the intent is explicit it becomes possible to differentiate among the various intentions and to match them with the appropriate theoretical orientations. The specification of intentions is a skill that can be developed (Hunt, 1970). Teacher skills involve discriminating among different intentions and being able to state them explicitly. But specifying and distinguishing objectives is only one step in the sequence and by itself would be inadequate for coping with student aggression.

Characterize Student (P)—Perception

The teacher's perception of the student determines to a considerable extent what course of action the teacher will follow with that student or group of students. There is some recent evidence, for example, that some teachers believe that students like Don who are disruptive and engage in aggressive behavior can *control* their actions and are willfully misbehaving. As a consequence, these teachers have low expectations for promoting stable and global change with these youngsters and use teaching strategies that may be "characterized by a higher frequency of punishment, restricted language, and minimizing of long-term mental health goals in favor of short-term control or desist attempts" (Brophy & Rohrkemper, 1980a, p. 28).

David Hunt and his associates (Hunt, 1970, 1976, 1977) have done a great deal of research on how teachers process information about their students. One way they have studied this problem is by confronting the teacher with a teaching task which requires the teacher to respond to obstacles presented by role-playing students. The results reveal considerable variation among teachers' responses and their sensitivity to cues being signaled by the "students." According to Hunt (1976), the teacher's perception or "reading" of the student is the priority skill a teacher must have if what follows is to be successful. In the following chapters of this book, we provide the details of a number of very different kinds of interventions or approaches a teacher might employ with a student like Don. Regardless of which approach the teacher chooses, a "reading" of the student is a fundamental aspect of all of them. Knowledge of the aggressive student is an essential ingredient of the psychodynamic and humanistic approaches. For the teacher using behavior-modification methods, the issue of what constitutes positive or negative reinforcement for any given student cannot be made without knowledge of that disruptive student. The simplistic notion that teacher praise and attention function as all-purpose positive reinforcers ignores the fact that for some students, including violent ones, these teacher behaviors may not only be embarrassing, but threatening (Good & Brophy, 1978).

Flavell (1974) has studied the processes by which individuals make inferences about others. Although he has not studied teachers specifically, his results are worth noting. He has identified four features as crucial in communicating between persons: (1) *existence,* in the present context, the teacher's knowledge that information about Don exists; (2) *need,* the teacher's awareness that the situation requires inferential activity; (3) *inference,* "reading the student;" and (4) *application,* responding with an appropriate action. The first two of these features obviously can occur without face-to-face contact with a particular disruptive individual, that is, during the planning or evaluating phases of teaching.

Earlier we noted that the disruptive youngster can be viewed from a contemporaneous and/or a developmental perspective (Hunt, 1971, 1975a, 1975b). Knowledge of the student from both perspectives is important, as is the distinction between the two. Decisions made on the basis of the contemporaneous resolution of the student's aggression address the immediate condition of the problem; they frequently involve the stop-and-desist techniques which Brophy and Rohrkemper (1980a) noted. Decisions made from a developmental perspective are future oriented and focus on what we expect of the student in terms of growth or change. Both the contemporaneous and developmental perspective are important, although the former more readily leads to decisions which can be applied to the priority concerns of classroom practice.

But developmental information about a student or group of students can put an aggression problem in a context that might provide a different perspective for the teacher. For example, in their four-year longitudinal study, Jessor and Jessor (1977) found that the adolescent who is likely to be a behavior problem is one who does not place much value on academic achievement, has low expectations of academic or school success, seeks independence, and looks at society and its institutions as in conflict with his or her interests. But Jessor and Jessor (1977) note that the descriptors that characterize problem adolescents are the same ones that characterize most youth during adolescence and conclude that the "normal course of developmental change in adolescence is in the direction of greater problem-proneness" (p. 238). Brophy and Evertson (1976) also present a developmental perspective for the teacher to consider. As the students progress through school, their personal and social development takes them through various stages from being adult-oriented and compliant to being peer-oriented and more difficult to control. The testing of norms and adult values per se does not make an overtly aggressive student and is normal, though most teachers would prefer these behaviors not to occur.

It is problematic at this juncture whether a teacher with knowledge of the developmental aspects of students views disruptive and aggressive behavior differently than one who is naive in this respect. There is evidence that suggests that knowledge per se may be a necessary but insufficient prerequisite to competence in making decisions (Glaser, 1981). The fact is that we do not have enough information on teachers' decision making and can only get at it indirectly. Before considering some of this evidence, two quotations,* one by Dewey and one by Maslow, are relevant:

> Of what use, educationally speaking, is it to be able to see the end in the beginning? How does it assist us in dealing with the early stages of growth to be

---

*David Hunt first brought these to our attention, and we acknowledge our debt to him.

able to anticipate its later phases? To see the outcome is to know in what direction the present experience is moving, provided it moves normally and soundly. The far away point, which is of no significance to us simply as far away, becomes of huge importance the moment we take it as defining a present direction of movement. Taken in this way, it is no remote and distant result to be achieved, but a guiding method in dealing with the present . . . . (Dewey, 1902, pp. 12–13)

This is a ticklish task, for it implies simultaneously that we know what is best for him (since we do not beckon him on in a direction we choose), and also that only he knows what is best for himself in the long run. This means that we must offer only, and rarely force. We must be quite ready, not only to beckon forward, but to respect retreat to lick wounds, to recover strength, to look over the situation from a safe vantage point, or even to regress to a previous mastery or a "lower" delight, so that courage for growth can be regained. (Maslow, 1968, pp. 54–55)

Let us return to our student Don. We have already mentioned some possible course of immediate action that may be appropriate to match the teacher's contemporaneous view of him, such as use of time out (see pages 56 to 59). But what assumptions can we or the teacher make about his developmental level? For example, can we assume that Don has in his behavior repertoire alternative ways of coping with the problem that gave vent to his aggression? Do we know what his value system is and what his subculture or reference group consider most important? For example, Foster (1974) makes the point that much of what is perceived by the teacher as threatening and illegitimate violence by lower-class children is often nothing more than the testing of the teacher's ability to control and set limits. Of course, Don's aggression has been directed toward another student and must be stopped, but what strategy or teaching act would be an appropriate follow-up depends to a considerable extent on the teacher's "reading" of Don. Again, the feature that Flavell (1974) identified as the first step in the processes used in making inferences about another person is the existence of information. The absence of a developmental perspective in a teacher, particularly with an aggressive student, increases the likelihood of failure with that student.

The teacher may well note, at this juncture, that there are a great many ways that individual differences among students can be viewed. Which characteristics of the individual are most relevant? One of the reasons why Hunt's approach may be of particular value to the teacher is his strategy for identifying student differences that make a difference. In order for a characteristic to be relevant to the practice of teaching, it needs to indicate a student's susceptibility to different educational environments or ways of teaching. Hunt (1971) has described these student differences as "accessibility characteristics" to which a teacher can "tune in" by implementing different approaches. In other words, the student characteristics that are important are the ones that not only tell a teacher what to look for but what to do as well. The four accessibility channels that Hunt (1971) has identified as most relevant are the student's (1) cognitive orientation, which is linked to the degree of structure in the environment; (2) motivational orientation which suggests to the teacher the form of feedback and positive reinforcement for the student; (3) value orientation, which identifies the range or context of the values currently acceptable to the student; and (4) sensory orientation, which refers to the sense modalities available to the student.

In the case of Don, the boy fighting in the vignette, Hunt would say that to describe him as a "hostile underachiever" does not provide the teacher with the information about how best to approach him. To characterize Don in terms of his I.Q. is also not very helpful, because the I.Q. is based on a psychometric view of individual differences based on consistency and stability of measurement. In other words, the I.Q. was developed to resist change and environmental influence so that it per se is a poor index of changes in a student when they occur. Knowing that a violent student or group of students have low I.Q.s does not tell the teacher what to do about the violence. Similarly, the student's ethnicity is not an accessibility characteristic because in itself it does not say anything about a student's needs, but ethnicity's relation to the functional characteristics of language comprehension or value priorities would provide accessibility information (Foster, 1974). Glaser (1972, 1981) has labeled such relevant characteristics as "the new aptitudes" and has urged their study and identification for payoff in classrooms. In Glaser's (1981) words, "Teachers and schools need information on individuals that is oriented toward instructional decision rather than prediction" (p. 924).

In the final analysis, it is the teacher who must make the decisions regarding an aggressive youngster. Before considering how the teacher's implicit theory of teaching operates, we present the following questions, the first five of which were originally raised by Ossorio (1973) and supplemented by Hunt (1977) as a guide for making decisions about the student explicit:

1. Who is the person? (identify)
2. What does the person want? (intention)
3. What does the person know? (knowledge)
4. What does the person know how to do? (competence)
5. What is the person trying to do? (action)
6. How is the person trying to do it? (style)

Answers to these questions enable the teacher to "read" the disruptive student and proceed to the next decision. Even though all of the questions may not be answered or answerable in the context of a specific teaching decision, the important aspect is the realization that "reading" a student, particularly a disruptive one, involves knowing the various dimensions involved and the relations between these dimensions that describe a whole person. The way a teacher does this is not through a battery of tests and test profiles, although test scores are part of the information, but by questioning, observing, listening, and oftentimes letting the student tell what the problem is. The task is not an easy one in light of the student diversity that occurs in most classrooms, but it may be made more manageable by applying Hunt's (1977) translation of Kluckhohn and Murray's (1949) observation that:

Every student is:

1. Like *all* other students in some ways,
2. Like *some* other students in some ways, and
3. Like *no* other students in some ways. (p. 34)

These three statements enable the teacher to sometimes teach and adapt the teaching to an entire class, sometimes to smaller groups within a class, and sometimes to an individual student. For most teachers, these three levels reflect what they do intuitively; the difference once again has to do with conscious decisions on the part of the teacher, more so when those decisions focus on the aggressive or disruptive student. Adaptation to individual differences becomes feasible once the teacher decides at what level it is going to occur. Even if it takes place only at the second level, such adaptation provides an initial response to *some* of the student's uniqueness. Let us now consider the process by which teachers decide to implement action, a process which may occur simultaneously with the "reading" of the student.

Translate to Action—Implicit Theory

In 1962 Travers concluded that "teachers do not change their ways of behaving simply by being told that learning would proceed with greater efficiency if they behaved differently" (p. 557). More recently Fenstermacher (1979) has presented what he has termed an "intentionalist" critique of research on teaching. According to this view, "because the beliefs of teachers are not taken into account, any attempt at converting the results of research to rules for effective teaching is essentially 'miseducative'" (p. 20). Harré and Secord (1972) have developed an argument which parallels Fenstermacher's. They believe that "the things that people say about themselves and other people should be taken as seriously as reports of data relevant to phenomena that really exist and which are relevant to the explanation of behavior" (p. 117).

Jackson (1968) has criticized the view of the teacher as a rational decision maker as essentially unrealistic. For Jackson, teaching is an opportunistic process in which the teacher is ultimately concerned about the pupils' learning, but primarily the teacher's attention is on the activities and tasks that achieve and maintain student involvement. According to Jackson (1968) teachers focus on the "stylistic qualities of their performance as much as on whether specific goals and objectives are accomplished" (p. 192). More recently, Doyle (1979) has presented a similar argument and maintains that the teacher's decision priorities revolve around gaining and maintaining cooperation in classroom activities. Doyle has developed a model of teacher decision making based on this perspective which is very worthy of study. Its importance to the discussion at hand can be seen from the following quotation:

> . . . the analysis of information processing in response to the demands of the classroom underscores the pervasive role of classroom knowledge in teachers' decision making. Understanding the situationally defined task of teaching and the character of the environment in which that task is accomplished enables a

teacher to select activities, interpret events, anticipate consequences, and monitor a system with maximum efficiency. . . . *The present framework, which defines the content of the implicit theories of teachers in terms of cooperation, would seem to offer an appropriate beginning for the study of classroom knowledge.* (Doyle, 1979, pp. 70–71, italics added)

Thus, in Doyle's approach to understanding teaching, the central feature revolves around the teacher's implicit theory of teaching. Moreover, in the case of the disruptive student, the teacher's automatic or routine information processing and attending are interfered with, particularly if the disruption is emotion laden (Doyle, 1979). Cone's (1978) findings support Doyle's approach in identifying the implicit theories of the teacher. Cone found that deviant behavior was perceived to be more disruptive in the whole-class grouping rather than in smaller groupings. Teachers were able to provide elaborate and detailed explanations and suggestions about classroom management and cooperation. These results are consistent with those of Harootunian (1980; Harootunian & Yarger, 1981), who reported that teachers define their success in the classroom not in terms of learning but in terms of the involvement of their students. Student aggression or disruptive behavior was a factor in lack of success for these teachers, but absence of such behaviors did not define success. Thus, student violence plays a very negative role in teachers' self-appraisal and probably is an integral aspect of their implicit theories. As teachers gain in experience, they view success as (1) increased focus on individual students and less on the group as a whole; (2) an increased repertoire of teaching skills; and (3) greater self-confidence, flexibility, and sensitivity (Harootunian & Yarger, 1981). This last set of findings is in agreement with Doyle's (1979) contention that "beginning teachers are, in effect, simultaneously required to construct classroom knowledge *and* respond to tests of their managerial skill. It is likely, therefore, that classroom demands for beginning teachers are especially intense" (p. 65). Foster (1974) identifies the new teachers' four-phase rites of passage vis-à-vis inner-city youngsters as (1) friends; (2) rejection and chaos; (3) discipline; and (4) humanization. The not-uncommon practice in some schools of the new teacher's ending up with the most disruptive individuals simply exacerbates the problem.

Brophy and Rohrkemper (1980a, 1980b) believe that the teacher's implicit theories involve the teacher's attribution patterns which "form important links in the process that teachers use to construct strategies for coping with problem students, especially when initiating or changing strategies" (Brophy & Rohrkemper, 1980b, p. 76) (that is, especially when engaging in active decision making rather than merely responding habitually). They found that teachers' attributions about the motivations and other causal factors underlying simulated problem student behavior are related to their expectations about what they can do to resolve the problem. These expectations also influence the goals that teachers set and the strategies they implement in striving to effect those goals. The reader will recall that Brophy and Rohrkemper (1980b) found that some teachers believed that students engaged in violent behavior were doing so intentionally and could control such behavior if they wished. Moreover, these teachers had low expectations for being able to promote stable and global change in such students and engaged in strategies involving a higher frequency of punishment, restricted language, and "minimizing of long-term mental-health goals in favor of short-term control or desist attempts" (p. 28).

Hunt (1976) believes that one of the reasons for inconsistent findings in the study of teacher awareness and its influence on teacher behavior has been the failure to allow teachers to use their own terms in expressing themselves about the teaching-learning process. According to Hunt (1975a), to understand which concepts teachers use to view their students, we need to know the content, structure, and maleability of these concepts. For example, the content for Brophy and Rohr-kemper's (1980a) teachers regarding disruptive students was largely in terms of controllability and intentionality. Others (Hofer, 1978; Weiner, 1979) have described the dimensions of teacher constructs in terms of ability and effort. Hunt's (1976, 1980) own research has found that teachers define their teaching most frequently in such categories as the student's ability, sociability, motivation, and self-concept.

Teachers' various content categories can be organized in a number of patterns varying in structure from simple to complex. The simplest can be classified into a good-bad dichotomy, whereas the most complex can be arranged in hierarchical, interrelated patterns. A system devised by Schroder, Karlins, and Phares (1973) to classify the organization of teachers' concepts of students uses three structural features: number of dimensions, degree of discrimination, and combinatory rules.

Maleability of teachers' dimensions refers to how readily teachers may incorporate an espoused perspective or theory of teaching-learning into their interactions with students. Teachers, like others (Argyris & Schön, 1976) are able to espouse and list more concepts than they practice. Some teachers, for example, espouse humanistic ideals but are unable to implement these views in their teaching when dealing with aggressive youngsters (Foster, 1974).

To help teachers make their theories of teaching explicit, Hunt (1976, 1980) has used an adaptation of Kelly's (1955) Role Concept Repertory or REP Test. Figure 2.3 presents a miniature version of the steps required in the REP Test. What we cannot provide is the follow-up discussion of readers' responses, which readers will have to gain for themselves, preferably with a group of other teachers who have also gone through the steps listed in Figure 2.3.

What is presented in Figure 2.3 is but one way of making explicit the teacher's theory of teaching. There are other exercises that might be applied. For example, Morine-Dershimer (1978-1979) asks teachers to put the names of all of their students on cards and then to group them in as many or as few groups as desired. After completing the sort, the teacher is asked to describe each group's characteristics and explain the similarities within the group and the differences between groups.

Making explicit the teacher's view of learners is particularly important with disruptive students. In our example, what teachers believe about Don may determine to a considerable extent how they approach him pedagogically. There is evidence that teachers, when provided with knowledge and skills to deal with class-

You need two sheets of paper, six 3 x 5 cards (or similar-sized paper), and something to write with. Here's what to do:

Step 1. At the top of the first sheet, write "About my teaching," and then imagine you are writing to another teacher, someone with whom you feel comfortable. You want to communicate about your teaching so that this teacher will understand how you teach and what is most important in your teaching. Next, write what came to your mind, stopping after five minutes, frustrating as this may be, and turn over the sheet.

Step 2. Turn the second sheet lengthwise, and label three column headings: "Student characteristics" (P), "Objectives" (B), and "Approaches" (E). On the left far side and below the first heading, write 1-2-3 and below this write 4-5-6.

Step 3. After numbering the cards from 1 to 6, write the name (or initials) of six students, one on each card. Select six students who are fairly representative of all your students.

Step 4. Look at cards 1, 2, and 3. "Which *two* of these three students are most alike in some important way and different from the third?" Circle these two numbers on your recording sheet. Next: "How are these two students alike and different from the third?" Write how they are alike as students in a word or phrase under "Student characteristics" (P). Repeat procedure for 4, 5, and 6.

Step 5. Consider those two students circled in the first triad: "How are these two alike in terms of objectives I would have for them?" Record this in the "Objectives" (B) column, and repeat for second pair of circled students.

Step 6. Consider the first pair again: "How are these two students alike in terms of how I would work with them?" Record this in the "Approaches" (E) column, and repeat for the second pair.

Step 7. Look over the three P-B-E entries for the top row (1-2-3). "How are these three features related to one another, i.e., in what way is P related to B and E?" Record below, and repeat for the second row. This requires some time and thought. When you are finished, keep your exercise sheets handy to compare your responses to those of others.

FIGURE 2.3.   Steps in making explicit a teacher's implicit theory of teaching and learning. (Hunt, D. E. How to be your own best theorist. *Theory into Practice.* College of Education, The Ohio State University, 1980, 19, pp. 287-288).

room disruptions, can reduce aggression in the classroom (Borg & Ascione, 1979, 1982; Thomas, Becker, & Armstrong, 1968).

Whatever exercises or means are used to identify the concepts which underlie classroom practice, the teacher has to decide which approach or strategy is most appropriate to implement. There are a number of alternatives available to the teacher, so let us now look at some of them.

Provide Environment (E)—Action

In considering the alternative courses of action which the teacher might utilize, we need to differentiate more specifically the various levels at which an action may be planned and implemented. The teacher may engage in (1) a specific teaching act; (2) a sequence of teaching acts; or (3) macroteaching methods. For the behavior problem depicted in the vignette earlier, the specific teaching acts include restraining Don and removing him from the group to a time-out location in the class; the sequence of acts may include ignoring (see pages 54 to 56), time out (see pages 56 to 59), and response cost (see pages 60 to 63); and the macroteaching methods or strategies might engage him in the series of structured learning activities (outlined in Chapter 6) whose aim is to teach Don prosocial behaviors and which are based on a particular model of teaching and learning. Each higher level may subsume the courses of action listed below it.

Hunt (1976) refers to the step of providing environments as "flexing." Thus, "reading" and "flexing" are the essential features of teaching. Flexing may occur over a brief period and then be repeated with changes required by the information the teacher has "read." These moment-to-moment multiple teaching transactions are microadaptations whereas the various approaches we have presented in Chapters 3 through 6 are macroadaptations. The important point about the latter is that they serve in one sense as an algorithm which the teacher may use to derive the microadaptations or decisions. In other words, if a teacher consciously makes a decision to work within the framework of a particular approach, then many moment-to-moment decisions have to be carried out consistently with a specific direction; otherwise the macroteaching method becomes moot. The conscious choice of a macrostrategy also will make the teacher aware of, and perhaps facilitate, the teacher's planning, interactive, and evaluative options about the disruptive student.

Although the evidence is not overwhelming, what there is suggests that teachers vary considerably in their consideration of and ability to implement alternatives. For example, Joyce (1978-1979) found that a teacher's plans may considerably affect what options are available to implement: *"In effect the selection of materials and the subsequent activity flow establishes the 'problem frame'—the boundaries within which decision making will be carried on"* (p. 75, italics in original).

The question remains how the teacher might develop expertise in responding rapidly and without much conscious deliberation to the problems of violent and disruptive students. Perhaps, by extrapolating from studies of expertise in other areas (Chase & Simon, 1973; Glaser, 1981; Larkin, McDermott, Simon & Simon, 1980), we can say that expert teachers need to develop a large repertoire of specific "reading" and "flexing" patterns that can be accessed in their memory and quickly recognized. Expert teachers would organize their knowledge of disruption and violence around the central principles explicated in the rest of this book. As Glaser (1981) notes:

In general, then, the learning and experience of the competent individual results in knowledge and in an organization of that knowledge into a fast-access pattern recognition or encoding system that greatly reduces the mental processing load. Understanding appears to result from these acquired knowledge patterns that enable an individual to form a particular representation of a problem situation. Novices have systematic knowledge structures at a qualitatively different level than do experts, and the relative adequacy of the initial representation of a situation (which is determined by acquired knowledge structures) appears to be an index of developing competence. (p. 932)

We started this chapter with a quotation from Brophy and Rohrkemper (1980a), who found that few of their teachers, irrespective of their experience, were able to deal adequately with aggressive students even though the knowledge and information for helping and dealing with such students are available. Whether possession of that information would develop teacher expertise on the violent student is problematic, but without such knowledge, the teachers' role in addressing the difficulties with disruptive individuals in school will continue to be quixotic.

Evaluation (B)—Check Effects

The teacher's adaptation to students is a dynamic process. This simply means that teachers monitor and adapt their activities on a continuing basis. Adaptation cannot be a static, one-shot process that responds to the student inflexibly. The teacher's evaluation of the effects of responses to a disruptive incident is the last phase of one teaching act and the beginning of another. Figure 2.4 depicts these steps. The sequence that ends with the evaluation phase of the decision process may occur in a brief time period or it may take place over a longer interval. Each of the diamond-shaped items in Figure 2.4 represents a decision requiring evaluative activity by the teacher. The sequence is repeated with the appropriate readjustments imposed by the disparity between intention and evaluation. Going back to Don, our fighting student, whether the time-out strategy is the way to deal with him will depend on his responses to the intervention. If he is unresponsive in terms of controlling his immediate aggression, more restrictive steps might be taken. The long-term strategy with respect to Don and others like him will similarly be evaluated in terms of their specific behavioral consequences.

TEACHERS AS PEOPLE:
PRACTICAL CONSIDERATIONS

No theory or account in a book can ever provide a comprehensive picture of the classroom experience. In this chapter we have focused on the teacher's decisions about disruptive, violent students as if these decisions take place in a logical sequence. Of course, in the real world of teaching, many of these decisions are made in microseconds, and we do not know whether the sequence is as we have depicted it. Until the development of an alternative decision sequence that fits the real world

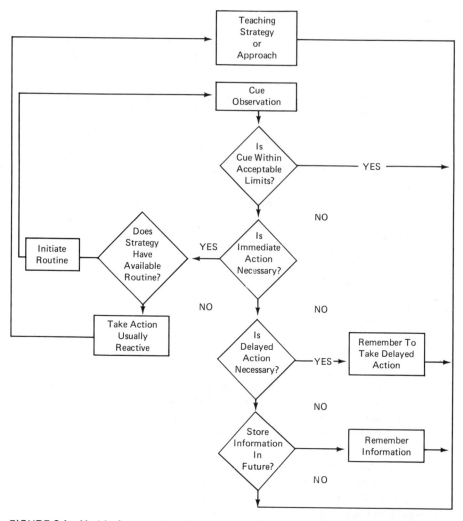

FIGURE 2.4. Model of teachers' decision making during teaching. (Shavelson, R. J. & Stern, P., "Research on Teacher's Pedagogical Thoughts, Judgments, Decisions and Behavior." *Review of Educational Research,* 1981, p. 483. Copyright 1981, American Educational Research Association, Washington, D.C.)

better, however, we think our depiction is helpful to those who would improve in their working with youngsters who manifest overt aggression. We have looked at the tasks and activities of teaching without venturing at all into the nature of schools or the context of the community in which a school is located, because we address these facets in later chapters. What we want to stress at this juncture is that teachers are persons who represent a good portion of the range of human strengths and foibles. Like everyone else, teachers have needs and concerns, and paramount among them, as consistently revealed by recent Gallup Polls, has been the question of discipline.

Even though the school may stress that teaching basic skills and subject matter is its primary task, a secondary goal has always been the development of responsible and social behavior. For teachers these priorities are reversed because, confronted with hostility and aggression, the teacher knows that if these antisocial behaviors are not ameliorated, the first set of priorities becomes moot.

The teacher is not "Superman." There are individuals in the class who need more help than the teacher alone can provide. There are various consultative services (e.g., resource teachers, school psychologists, school social workers) available to the teacher, and they can provide assistance to the student, the student's family, and the teacher.* The problem is that teachers usually wait until the antisocial behaviors have become well established in the youngster before responding. Longitudinal studies of disruptive youngsters indicate that teachers' assessments of antisocial behavior can predict these behaviors in children up to nine years after the original assessment (Feldhusen, Roeser, & Thurston, 1977). Awareness of a problem is only the first step in any problem-solving process, but it is the crucial one. We have attempted in this volume to help the teacher with some of the other steps.

Dealing with aggression in the classroom is one of the most difficult tasks with which the teacher will be confronted. It requires both strength and sensitivity on the part of the teacher, two qualities which apparently are independent of one another (Hunt, 1970). Strength is determined by how well a teacher can control and regulate disruptive students, whereas sensitivity is reflected in the teacher's adaptability to the cues signaled by these students. The teacher's acquisition of these characteristics is what this book is all about. Of course, there are other qualities or characteristics that would help the teacher, but we must be careful in listing them so that we do not end up with a list of characteristics describing the ideal human being rather than those that are particularly relevant to teachers—characteristics like friendliness, emotional maturity, sincerity, and so on. The personal qualities which seem to be of special importance to the role of teacher as decision maker would likely involve the ability to (1) remain calm in crisis situations; (2) listen actively and not become defensive or authoritarian; (3) avoid win-lose situations; and (4) "maintain a problem-solving orientation rather than resort to withdrawal, blaming, or hysteria, or other emotional overreactions" (Brophy & Putnam, 1979).

Like most skills, decision-making skills in teaching require practice or experience for improvement. There is a growing body of evidence (Fuller & Bown, 1975; Harootunian & Yarger, 1981; Katz, 1972) that teachers go through various developmental stages with respect to their teaching. The facility with which decisions about violent behavior are made will reflect in part a teacher's particular developmental status. Of course, no two teachers, classrooms, and contexts of violence and aggression can ever be precisely the same. But paraphrasing an earlier quotation from Hunt, we point out that every teacher is:

---

*For a look at a shoestring program that attempted to work with children usually considered too hostile for regular classrooms, the reader might consult the BRIDGE Program Final Report (Apter, Apter, Trief, Cohen, Woodlock, & Harootunian, 1978).

1. Like all other teachers in some decisions.
2. Like some teachers in some decisions.
3. Like no other teachers in some decisions.

Conscious decision making requires more thoughtful teaching and is hard work. No one claims it will be easy.

REFERENCES

APTER, S., APTER, D., TRIEF, P., COHEN, N., WOODLOCK, D., & HAROOT-UNIAN, B. *The Bridge program.* A report published by the Bridge Program, Syracuse, New York, 1978.
ARGYRIS, C., & SCHÖN, D. A. *Theory in practice.* San Francisco: Jossey-Bass, 1976.
BISHOP, A. J., & WHITFIELD, R. C. *Situations in teaching.* Maidenhead, United Kingdom: McGraw-Hill, 1972.
BORG, W. R., & ASCIONE, F. R. Changing on-task, off-task, and disruptive pupil behavior in elementary mainstreaming classrooms. *Journal of Educational Research,* 1979, *72,* 243–252.
BORG, W. R., & ASCIONE, F. R. Classroom management in elementary mainstreaming classrooms. *Journal of Educational Psychology,* 1982, *74,* 85–95.
BROPHY, J. E., & EVERTSON, C. M. *Learning from teaching: A developmental perspective.* Boston: Allyn & Bacon, 1976.
BROPHY, J. E., & PUTNAM, J. G. Classroom management in the elementary grades. In D. L. Duke (Ed.), *Classroom management, The seventy-eighth yearbook of the National Society for the Study of Education, Part II.* Chicago: University of Chicago Press, 1979.
BROPHY, J. E., & ROHRKEMPER, M. M. *The influence of problem ownership on teachers' perceptions of and strategies for coping with problem students* (Research Series No. 84). East Lansing, Mich.: Institute for Research on Teaching, Michigan State University, 1980(a).
BROPHY, J. E., & ROHRKEMPER, M. M. *Teachers' specific strategies for dealing with hostile aggressive students* (Research Series No. 86). East Lansing, Mich.: Institute for Research on Teaching, Michigan State University, 1980(b).
CHASE, W. G., & SIMON, H. A. Perception in chess. *Cognitive Psychology,* 1973, *1,* 53–81.
CLARK, C., & YINGER, R. J. Research on teacher thinking. *Curriculum Inquiry,* 1977, *7,* 280–303.
COLADARCI, A. P. The teacher as hypothesis-maker. *California Journal for Instructional Improvement,* 1959, *2,* 3–6.
CONE, R. *Teachers' decisions in managing student behavior: A laboratory simulation of interactive decision making by teachers.* Paper presented at the annual meeting of the American Educational Research Association, Toronto, 1978.
DEWEY, J. *The child and the curriculum.* Chicago: University of Chicago Press, 1902.
DOYLE, W. Making managerial decisions in classrooms. In D. L. Duke (Ed.), *Classroom management. The seventy-eighth yearbook of the National Society for the Study of Education, Part II.* Chicago: University of Chicago Press, 1979.

EDGERTON, S. K. Teachers in role conflict: The hidden dilemma. *Phi Delta Kappan,* 1977, *59,* 120–122.
FELDHUSEN, J. F., ROESER, T. D., & THURSTON, J. R. Prediction of social adjustment over a period of six or nine years. *Journal of Special Education,* 1977, *11,* 29–36.
FENSTERMACHER, G. D. A philosophical consideration of recent research on teacher effectiveness. In L. S. Shulman (Ed.), *Review of research in education* (No. 6). Itasca, Ill.: Peacock, 1979.
FLAVELL, J. H. The development of inferences about others. In T. Mischel (Ed.), *Understanding other persons.* Oxford, United Kingdom: Blackwell, Basil & Mott, 1974.
FOSTER, H. J. The inner-city teacher and violence: Suggestions for action research. *Phi Delta Kappan,* 1968, *50,* 172–175.
FOSTER, H. J. *Ribbin', jivin', and playin' the dozens.* Cambridge, Mass.: Ballinger Publishing, 1974.
FULLER, F. F., & BOWN, O. H. Becoming a teacher. In K. Ryan (Ed.), *Teacher education. The seventy-fourth yearbook of the National Society for the Study of Education, Part II.* Chicago: University of Chicago Press, 1975.
GLASER, R. Individuals and learning: The new aptitudes. *Educational Researcher,* 1972, *1,* 5–12.
GLASER, R. The future of testing: A research agenda for cognitive psychology and psychometrics. *American Psychologist,* 1981, *36,* 923–936.
GOOD, T. L., & BROPHY, J. E. *Looking in classrooms.* New York: Harper & Row, 1978.
HAROOTUNIAN, B. *The teacher as problem-solver: Extraclass decision making.* Paper presented at the annual meeting of the American Educational Research Association, Chicago, 1966.
HAROOTUNIAN, B. Teacher effectiveness: The view from within. *Theory into Practice,* 1980, *19,* 266–270.
HAROOTUNIAN, B., & YARGER, G. *Teachers' conceptions of their own success.* Washington, D.C.: ERIC Clearinghouse on Teacher Education, 1981.
HARRÉ, R., & SECORD, P. F. *The explanation of social behaviour.* Oxford, United Kingdom: Basil Blackwell, 1972.
HOFER, M. *Implicit personality theory of teachers, causal attribution, and their perception of students.* Paper presented at the annual meeting of the American Educational Research Association, Toronto, 1978.
HUNT, D. E. Adaptability in interpersonal communication among training agents. *Merrill Palmer Quarterly,* 1970, *16,* 324–344.
HUNT, D. E. *Matching models in education.* Toronto: Ontario Institute for Studies in Education, 1971.
HUNT, D. E. Person-environment interaction: A challenge found wanting before it was tried. *Review of Educational Research,* 1975, *45,* 209–230(a).
HUNT, D. E. Teachers' adaptation to students: From implicit to explicit matching. Stanford, Calif.: Research and Development Memorandum No. 139, SCRDT, 1975(b).
HUNT, D. E. Teachers' adaptation: 'Reading' and 'flexing' to students. *Journal of Teacher Education,* 1976, *27,* 268–275.
HUNT, D. E. Theory to practice as persons-in-relation. *Ontario Psychologist,* 1977, *9,* 52–62.
HUNT, D. E. How to be your own best theorist. *Theory into Practice,* 1980, *19,* 287–293.
JACKSON, P. *Life in classrooms.* New York: Holt, Rinehart & Winston, 1968.

JESSOR, R. J., & JESSOR, S. L. *Problem behavior and psychosocial development.* New York: Academic Press, 1977.

JOYCE, B. Toward a theory of information processing in teaching. *Educational Research Quarterly,* 1978-1979, *3,* 66-67.

JOYCE, B. R., & HAROOTUNIAN, B. *The structure of teaching.* Chicago: Science Research Associates, 1967.

KATZ, L. Developmental stages of preschool teachers. *Elementary School Journal,* 1972, *7,* 50-54.

KELLY, G. A. *The psychology of personal constructs* (Vol. 1). New York: Norton, 1955.

KLUCKHOHN, C., & MURRAY, H. A. (Ed.). *Personality in nature, society, and culture.* New York: Knopf, 1949.

LARKIN, J., McDERMOTT, J., SIMON, D. P., & SIMON, H. A. Expert and novice performance in solving physics problems. *Science,* 1980, *208,* 1335-1342.

MASLOW, A. H. *Toward a psychology of being.* New York: Van Nostrand, 1968.

McDONALD, E. J. *Educational psychology.* Belmont, Calif.: Wadsworth, 1965.

MORINE-DERSHIMER, G. Planning in classroom reality, an in depth look. *Educational Research Quarterly,* 1978-1979, *3,* 83-99.

OSSORIO, P. Never smile at a crocodile. *Journal of Theory of Social Behaviour,* 1973, *3,* 121-140.

SCHRODER, H. M., KARLINS, M., & PHARES, J. *Education for freedom.* New York: Wiley, 1973.

SHAVELSON, R. J. What is the basic teaching skill? *Journal of Teacher Education,* 1973, *24,* 144-147.

SHAVELSON, R. J. Teachers' decision making. In N. L. Gage (Ed.), *The psychology of teaching methods. The seventy-fifth yearbook of the National Society for the Study of Education, Part I.* Chicago: University of Chicago Press, 1976.

SHAVELSON, R. J., & STERN, P. Research on teachers' pedagogical thoughts, judgments, decisions, and behavior. *Review of Educational Research,* 1981, *51,* 455-498.

SHULMAN, L. A., & ELSTEIN, A. S. Studies of problem solving, judgment, and decision making: Implications for educational research. In F. N. Kerlinger (Ed.), *Review of research in education* (Vol. 3). Itasca, Ill.: Peacock, 1975.

THOMAS, D. R., BECKER, W. C., & ARMSTRONG, M. Production and elimination of disruptive classroom behavior by systematically varying teacher's behavior. *Journal of Applied Behavior Analysis,* 1968, *1,* 35-45.

TRAVERS, R. M. W. A study of the relationship of psychological research to educational practice. In R. Glaser (Ed.), *Training, research and education.* Pittsburgh: University of Pittsburgh, 1962.

WEINER, B. A theory of motivation for some classroom experiences. *Journal of Educational Psychology,* 1979, *71,* 3-25.

3
Behavior-Modification Techniques

In sum, the results of a decade or so of research have documented the effectiveness of the behavior modification approach in a wide variety of settings with very diverse child populations. . . . [T]he behavior of children in classroom settings has been repeatedly altered by a variety of different procedures used by a number of investigators. In contrast to a host of other approaches applied to educational problems, most behavioral principles . . . were first documented in laboratory settings, and thus there is evidence from both basic and applied research of the efficacy of such principles. (Reprinted with permission from *Classroom Management* by K. D. O'Leary and S. G. O'Leary, copyright 1980, Pergamon Press.)

If chapters may appropriately begin with a quotation reflecting the central underpinning of the content which is to follow, we have just done so for the present chapter. Though the bulk of this chapter consists of a presentation and examination of behavior-modification *techniques* of demonstrated effectiveness with aggressive youngsters, their sound empirical bases are an overriding consideration for both understanding the development of these techniques, and for making decisions about their adoption and implementation. As is clarified throughout this chapter, the technology of behavior modification indeed rests upon a firm experimental foundation.

There are further important reasons for our inclusion in this book of a chapter on behavior modification, beyond the repeated demonstration that "it works." Behavior-modification techniques are relatively easy to learn and utilize; may be teacher, peer, parent, and/or self-administered; are generally cost effective; yield typically unambiguous behavior-change results; have a long history of successful application with aggressive youngsters in particular; and, for these several reasons, can maximize the opportunity in both available time and student accessibility for teachers to do most what teachers do best . . . teach!

That, as the expression goes, is the good news. Many persons see a darker, much less positive side to the behavior-modification coin. Some of its constituent techniques are viewed as bribery, and as likely to increase the contagion throughout a class of disruptive behaviors as nondisruptive youngsters see their more aggressive peers receive rewards for reducing their levels of disruptiveness. All behavior-modification techniques, its critics hold further, are unfair, highly manipulative, mechanistic, overly simplistic, demanding of extra teacher effort, and, more generally, promoting of a view of people as objects to be acted upon. We address these serious ethical and philosophical reservations and objections later in this chapter. At this point, however, it is appropriate that we turn directly to the methodological substance of behavior modification. We wish to briefly sketch the historical development of behavior modification, and define and describe its major behavior-change procedures and the rules which optimally govern their utilization, especially as aggression-reducing and prosocial-enhancing interventions.

BEHAVIOR-MODIFICATION
DEFINITIONS

Behavior modification is a set of techniques, derived from formal learning theory, systematically applied in an effort to change observable behavior, and rigorously evaluated by experimental research. Almost all of its constituent techniques derive from the basic premise developed by Skinner and his followers (Ferster & Skinner, 1957; Skinner, 1938, 1953) that behavior is largely determined by its environmental consequences. In a broad operational sense, this premise has found expression in techniques which by one means or another contingently present or withdraw rewards or punishments (e.g., environmental consequences) to alter the behavior which precedes these consequences. It is this contingent quality which has led to the use of the term *contingency management* to describe most of the activities in which the behavior modifier engages. Specifically, if one's goal is to increase the likelihood that a given (e.g., prosocial) behavior will occur, one follows instances of its occurrence with positive consequences—that is, by means of one or another technique for presenting a reward or removing an aversive event. In a directly analogous management of contingencies, if one's goal is to decrease the likelihood that a given (e.g., antisocial) behavior will occur, one follows instances of its occurrence with negative consequences—that is, by means of one or another behavior-modification technique for presenting an aversive event or removing a rewarding event. To decrease the disruptiveness, aggression, or acting-out behavior of a given youngster, and simultaneously increase the chances that he or she will behave in a constructive, attending, prosocial manner, the skilled behavior modifier will often use a combination of aversive or reward-withdrawing (for the aggression) and aversiveness-reducing or reward-providing (for the constructive behaviors) techniques. A few formal definitions here help clarify further the substance of the contingency-management process.

A *reinforcer* is an event which increases the subsequent frequency of any behavior which it follows. When the presentation of an event following a behavior increases its frequency, the event is referred to as a *positive reinforcer*. Praise, special privileges, tokens or points exchangeable for toys, or snacks are a few examples of positive reinforcers. When the removal of an event following a behavior increases the subsequent frequency of the behavior, the event is referred to as a *negative reinforcer*. When a youngster ceases to behave in a disruptive manner following his or her teacher's yelling at him or her to do so, we may say that the youngster has negatively reinforced, and thus increased the future likelihood of, teacher yelling. When the presentation of an event following a behavior decreases its subsequent frequency, the event is referred to as a *punisher*. In the preceding example, the teacher's yelling, which was negatively reinforced by the student's decrease in disruptive behavior, functions as a punishment to the student to the extent that it decreases the likelihood of subsequent student disruptiveness. A second way of decreasing the probability of a given behavior is by *removing positive reinforcers* each time that the behavior occurs. Ignoring the behavior or removing the reinforcer of attention (i.e., extinction), physically removing the person from important sources of reinforcement (i.e., time out), and removing the reinforcers from the person (i.e., response cost) are three means of contingently managing behavior by removing positive reinforcers. To repeat, these four groups of techniques—positive reinforcement, negative reinforcement, punishment, and the removal of positive reinforcers—constitute the core general methods of contingency management, from which grew all the specific contingency-management techniques described later in this chapter.

It will aid further in understanding the relationship between these four procedures, as well as their characteristic implementation in classroom settings, to point out that they are all means for either presenting or removing positive reinforcers or presenting or removing aversive stimuli. The various procedures for presenting or removing positive reinforcement are by far the more common uses of contingency management in school contexts. We examine these two sets of procedures first, and in considerable depth. Procedures for the presentation of aversive stimuli (i.e., punishment) or for their removal (i.e., negative reinforcement) are appropriately employed less frequently in school settings, and we examine them more briefly following our consideration of positive reinforcement.

NONCLASSROOM APPLICATIONS

Though much of the basic thinking relevant to the contingency-management approach to human behavior was available for a number of years (Mowrer & Mowrer, 1938; Skinner, 1938; Watson & Rayner, 1920), it was not until the 1950s that it began to find substantial, overt implementation in hospitals, clinics, schools, and other institutions in which one found disturbed or disturbing youngsters. Skinner's (1953) book *Science and Human Behavior* was a significant stimulus to this growth, as were a large number of investigations conducted during the 1950s and 1960s in the contexts just noted, all of which successfully demonstrated the behavior-change effectiveness of contingency management. Much of this research sought to alter the highly aggressive or otherwise severely deviant behavior of institutionalized emotionally disturbed, autistic, or developmentally disabled children and adolescents, and did so with considerable levels of success (Ayllon & Michael, 1959; Ferster & DeMyer, 1962; Lovaas, Schaeffer, & Simmons, 1965; Wolf, Risley, & Mees, 1964). In outpatient clinic and laboratory settings, successful use of contingency management was reported with such diverse behaviors as delinquency rates (Patterson, Ray, & Shaw, 1968; Schwitzgebel, 1964), social withdrawal (Allen, Hart, Buell, Harris, & Wolf, 1964; Lovaas, Koegel, Simmons, & Long, 1973), fearfulness (Lazarus & Rachman, 1967; Patterson, 1965), hyperactivity (Allen, Kenke, Harris, Baer, & Reynolds, 1967; Hall, Lund, & Jackson, 1968); depression (Wahler & Pollio, 1968); anorexia (Bachrach, Erwin, & Mohr, 1965; Leitenberg, Agras, & Thomson, 1968), mutism (Sherman, 1965; Straughan, 1968), and dozens of other diverse deviant behaviors involving hundreds of youngsters. As is made explicit throughout this chapter, the general success of this orientation to behavior change has flowered further in the 1970s and 1980s, finding still wider application across many, many behaviors and settings. It is not surprising, given the breadth and depth of this successful demonstration of behavior-change effectiveness, that numerous studies evaluating the classroom application of contingency management were also forthcoming. We briefly refer to a number of these studies later, in the context of the particular contingency-management technique to which they pertain.

CONTINGENCY-MANAGEMENT PROCEDURES

Classroom use of contingency management optimally begins with (1) selecting behavioral *goals*; (2) informing the class of the behavioral *rules* ideally followed in order to reach such goals; (3) observing and recording current (base-rate) classroom behavior; and then (4) applying one or a combination of behavior-change procedures (the presentation or removal of positive reinforcement or the presentation of removal of aversive stimuli) in order to alter undesirable current behaviors in desirable goal directions. Let us examine each step in this process in detail.

Selecting Behavioral Goals

What will be the behavioral climate of the classroom? What student behaviors will be defined by the teacher as truly disruptive and as impediments to learning, and which will be tolerated and perhaps even welcomed as normative and maybe even facilitative of the learning process? Behavior-change goal selection should concern itself with reducing those aggressive, disruptive, acting-out behaviors which interfere with the learning process but it must also be acutely responsive to normal student-developmental stages, examined to the extent possible in collaboration with the students themselves. Behavior modification should also be appropriately but not overly responsive to both teacher needs and the influence of overall school climate and policy on decisions about classroom decorum. Each reader, we feel, must make his or her own decisions in this regard, but our position vis-à-vis behavioral goal setting is that it is better to err slightly on the side of permissiveness and underregulation than risk an overly conforming, perhaps rigid classroom climate that is likely to be more inhibiting of *both* aggression and enduring learning. Sarason, Glaser, and Fargo (1972) reflect this sentiment well in their statement:

> Disruptive children can be managed, but if behavior modification is used to make children conform to a rigid idea of goodness or to squelch creativity or to force sterile compliance, the cost of an orderly classroom may be too high. Behavior modification is not intended to serve as a new type of tranquilizer. It is intended to serve as a means of facilitating efforts to bring about meaningful learning. (p. 13)

In addition to student, school-policy, and community influences (see Chapters 7 and 8) on the teacher's decisions about behavioral goals for the classroom, such goal selection can meaningfully follow from the teacher's thoughtful answers to such questions as:

1. What kind of student behavior interferes with the learning of the rest of the class, and what is perhaps annoying to you, but essentially harmless to the learner and his peers?
2. How much classroom freedom can be permitted without interfering with the rights of other students? On the other side of this coin, what are your responsibilities and the responsibilities of the students?
3. Should silence be maintained while children are working, or should reasonable communication among students be permitted, such as is encouraged in the "open classroom"?
4. Are your classroom regulations really for the benefit of the students . . . or primarily for your own comfort and convenience?
5. Are you thinking about how the disruptive child can be helped to learn better, not just how his disruptive behavior can be decreased?
6. Have you been able to maintain an attitude of openness to new ideas and approaches which can benefit children even though they do not coincide with your personal biases?
7. Have you considered the attitudes and standards of the child and his family in setting standards for the child? Are your standards in conflict with theirs?
8. Have you discussed your goals for the class with the class?
9. Have you discussed your goals for the child with the child and his parents? (Sarason et al., 1972, p. 23)

These are not often easy questions to answer, but they reflect the fact that the teacher is primary among the several determiners of classroom behavior. Given this, we are urging that such goals be selected in a careful, thoughtful, ethical manner in which conduciveness to learning is the central criterion.

Communicating Behavioral Rules

Having decided (hopefully, *with* the class) the behavioral directions in which . the teacher wishes the class to head, particularly with regard to reducing aggressive and disruptive behaviors and increasing positive behaviors, the teacher's next task is to clearly communicate to the students the rules and procedures they are to follow in order to attain these goals. A number of effective "rules for use of rules" have emerged in the contingency-management literature (Greenwood, Hops, Delquadri, & Guild, 1974; Sarason et al., 1972; Walker, 1979), and include:

1. Define and communicate rules for student behavior in clear, specific, and, especially, behavioral terms. As Walker (1979) notes, it is better (more concrete and behavioral) to say "Raise your hand before asking a question." than "Be considerate of others." Similarly, "Listen carefully to teacher instructions." or "Pay attention to the assignment and complete your work." are more likely to serve as rules which actually find expression in student behavior than the more ambiguous "Behave in class." or "Do what you are told."
2. It is more effective to tell students what to do, rather than what not to do. This accentuating of the positive would, for example, find expression in rules about taking turns, or talking over disagreements, or working quietly, rather than in rules directing students not to jump in or not to fight or not to speak out.
3. Rules should be communicated in such a manner that students are aided in memorizing them. Depending on the age of the students, and the complexity and difficulty of enactment of the rules the teacher is presenting, such memorization aides may include (a) keeping the rules short; (b) keeping the rules few in number; (c) repeating your presentation of the rules several times; and (d) posting the rules in written form where they can readily be seen.
4. Rule adherence is likely to be more effective when students have had a substantial role in their development, modification, and implementation. This sense of participation may be brought about by (a) explicit student involvement in rule development; (b) thorough discussion of rules with the entire class; (c) having selected students explain to the class the specific meaning of each rule; and (d) student role play of the behaviors identified by the rule.
5. In addition to the foregoing, further effective rules for rules are that they be developed at the start of the school year, before other less useful and less explicit rules emerge; that they be fair, reasonable, and within the student's capacity to follow them; that all members of the class understand them; and that they be applied equally and evenly to all class members.

Observing and Recording Behavior

The teacher and the class have set behavioral goals to be worked toward, and the rules which are the paths to be followed in getting there. The teacher's attention can now turn to the particular students displaying those aggressive, disruptive, rule-breaking, or goal-avoiding behaviors he or she wishes to modify. In doing so, the first task is to identify as concretely as possible the specific behaviors to be changed. Stated otherwise, the beginning stages of behavior modification include specification of desirable or appropriate behaviors (goal behaviors), specification of behavioral means to reach these goals (rule behaviors), and specification of the undesirable or inappropriate behaviors to be altered. This specification of undesirable behaviors (in the case of this book, mostly aggressive behaviors) ideally proceeds by means of *systematic* observation and recording. There are a number of purposes that are served by this process.

First, systematic observation and recording seek to identify not only which behaviors are undesirable, and thus possibly to be changed, but also the rate or frequency of such behaviors. This establishment of a *base rate* permits the teacher to determine later (against the base rate) whether the behavior is remaining constant, increasing in rate or frequency, or, as is hoped, actually decreasing. This *monitoring* of change in the behavior over time is, then, the second purpose of systematic observation and recording. Finally, because it is suggested that after the establishment of a base-rate level the teacher intervene with one or more contingency-management procedures, the third purpose of observation and recording is to *evaluate* the success or failure of the completed intervention. At all three stages of this process—establishment of a base rate, monitoring, evaluation of outcome—it is crucial that observation and recording be conducted in a *systematic* manner. Many authorities on classroom contingency management have commented that teacher guesses regarding the rate or frequency of a given student's aggressive, disruptive, or acting-out behavior are very often erroneously high. It is as if a small number of perhaps seriously disruptive behaviors by a student leads to a teacher's global impression of the student as "a troublemaker" or as "chronically aggressive," an impression or label which often clouds the fact that by far most of the time that youngster is engaged in appropriate behaviors. Thus, for these reasons, it is crucial to obtain an accurate accounting of how often or how long the student engages in problematic behaviors.

Who shall the observer be, especially given the obvious fact that the teacher faces daily, and must strive to teach, a full classroom of youngsters, and not only those relative few who on occasion behave aggressively? The contingency-management literature contains numerous examples not only of teachers as observer-recorders, but also of teacher aides, parents, peers, and the target youngsters themselves. Whoever serves in this capacity, the task is greatly facilitated by the attempt to observe and record by means preprepared explicitly for such purposes. Recording sheets, special classroom behavior charts, wrist counters, and other similar means exist as aides to observer-recorders in systematically identifying and noting representative samples of the frequency or rate of student inappropriate behaviors (see Jackson, Della-Piana, & Sloane, 1975; Morris, 1976; Sarason et al., 1972; Walker, 1979). We refer the interested reader to these sources for such operational information and materials.

We close our discussion of this phase of the contingency-management process with an excerpt from Walker (1979) which will help reiterate the all-important theme that at all phases of the process, the teacher optimally will think and act in strictly behavioral terms. Commenting on the observation-recording process, Walker (1979) notes:

> Pinpointing requires attention to the overt features of child behavior. Classroom behaviors that are capable of being pinpointed are characterized by being: (1) controllable, (2) repeatable, (3) containing movement, (4) possessing a starting and ending point. Instances and noninstances of classroom behaviors that qualify as behavioral pinpoints are listed below:

INSTANCES OF GOOD PINPOINTS

1. Argues
2. Steals
3. Does not comply with directions
4. Out of seat
5. Talks out
6. Has temper tantrums
7. Hits peers
8. Looks away from assigned tasks

NONINSTANCES OF GOOD PINPOINTS

1. Hyperactive
2. Lazy
3. Belligerent
4. Angry
5. Hostile
6. Frustrated
7. Unmotivated

Applying Behavior-Change Procedures
Identifying Positive Reinforcers

At this point in the contingency-management sequence, the teacher is aware of goals, rules, and specific inappropriate behaviors. Our overall purpose is to substitute appropriate for the inappropriate behaviors by means of skilled management of contingencies. As noted earlier, one major means for doing this is to present positive reinforcement to the student following and contingent upon the occurrence of an instance of his or her appropriate behaviors. Our earlier consideration of behavioral goals helped identify what constitutes appropriate behaviors. Before discussing optimal procedures for the actual *presentation* of positive reinforcers in the next section of this chapter, we must first consider the process of identifying—both for a given youngster and for youngsters in general—just what events may in fact function as positive reinforcers.

Classroom contingency managers have worked successfully with four types of positive reinforcers: material, social, activity, and token. *Material* or tangible reinforcers are actual desirable goods or objects presented to the individual contingent upon his or her enactment of appropriate behaviors. One especially important sub-category of material reinforcement, primary reinforcement, occurs when the contingent event presented satisfies a basic biological need. Food is one such primary reinforcer.

Social reinforcers, most often expressed in the form of attention, praise, or approval, are a particularly powerful and frequent classroom reinforcer. Both teacher lore and extensive experimental research testify to the potency of teacher-dispensed social reinforcement in influencing a broad array of personal, interpersonal, and academic student behaviors.

Activity reinforcers are those events in which the youngster freely chooses to engage when he or she has an opportunity to engage in several different activities. Given freedom to choose, many youngsters will watch television rather than complete their homework. The parent wishing to use this activity-reinforcer information will specify to the youngster that he or she may watch television for a given time period contingent upon the prior completion of the homework. Stated otherwise, the opportunity to perform a high-probability behavior (given free choice) can be used as a reinforcer for a lower-probability behavior.

Token reinforcers, usually employed when more easily implemented social reinforcers prove insufficient, are symbolic items or currency (chips, stars, points, etc.) provided to the youngster contingent upon the performance of appropriate or desirable behaviors. Tokens thus obtained are exchangeable for a wide range of material or activity reinforcers. The system by which specific numbers of tokens are contingently gained (or lost), and the procedures by which they may be exchanged for the backup material or activity reinforcers, is called a token economy.

In making decisions about which type of reinforcer to employ with a given youngster, the teacher should keep in mind that social reinforcement (e.g., teacher attention, praise, approval) is easiest to implement on a continuing basis, is most likely (for reasons discussed in the transfer and maintenance section later in this chapter) to lead to *enduring* behavior change, and is thus probably the type of reinforcement the teacher will wish to utilize most frequently. Unfortunately, in the initial stages of a behavior-change effort, especially when aggressive, disruptive, and other inappropriate behaviors are probably being richly rewarded by the social reinforcement of teacher and peer attention as well as by tangible reinforcers, heavier teacher reliance on material and activity reinforcers for desirable behaviors will likely be more appropriate. Alternatively, a token reinforcement system may prove most effective as the initial reinforcement strategy. Youngsters' reinforcement preferences change over time, and teacher views of the appropriate reward value of desirable behaviors also change over time; both variable factors are easily reflected in token-level adjustments. For these and related ease-of-administration and effectiveness-of-outcome reasons, the skilled contingency manager should be intimately acquainted with the full range of token-economy procedures (Ayllon & Azrin, 1968; Christopherson, Arnold, Hill, & Quilitch, 1972; Kazdin, 1975; Morris, 1976; Walker, Hops, & Fiegenbaum, 1976). Again, however, it is crucial to remember that with but a few exceptions, it is desirable that reliance on material, activity, or token reinforcement eventually give way to reliance upon more real-lifelike social reinforcement.

Table 3.1, excerpted from Safer and Allen (1976), lists specific examples of commonly used materials (edible and nonedible), social, activity, and token reinforcers.

Given this wide and nonexhaustive array of several types of potential reinforcers, and the fact that almost any event may serve as a reinforcer for one indi-

TABLE 3.1. Commonly Used Reinforcers

EDIBLE	NONEDIBLE	SOCIAL	ACTIVITY	TOKEN (POINTS)
Gum	Balloons	Attention	Gym time	(For general
Candy	Clothes	Public praise	Shop time	exchange)
M & M's	Scout uniform	Posting work in	Library time	
Popcorn	Shoes, etc.	school or at home	Driver's	
Cracker Jacks	Toys (dolls, cars)	Approval	license	
Sodas	Sports-related items	Access to privilege	Movies	
Cakes	Baseball cards	areas (e.g., black-	Concerts	
Pies	Baseball	board, lavatory,	(folk, rock,	
Ice cream (bars,	Sports equipment	parent's office,	ballet)	
etc.)	Records	den, T.V. room)	Field trips	
Hamburgers	Music equipment	Time off from school	Hobbies	
Nuts (peanuts)	Car parts	Hours for out-of-	Theater	
Raisins	(also motorcycle,	house	Ballet	
	etc., parts)	Private areas	Sports teams	
	Motorcycle, minibike,	Private times	Camping	
	bicycle	T.V. privileges	Travel	
	Furnishings for	Program choice	Day trips	
	room (T.V.,	Time watching	Overnight	
	posters, black	Dinner out	trips	
	lights, dolls)	Dinner time choice		
	Telephone	Friend's privileges		
		In house, at dinner		
		Overnight		
		Bedtime		
		Bath choices		
		Parties		
		Time with one parent		
		Special work		
		Collecting papers		
		Run recorders		
		Carrying messages		
		Telephone privilege		
		Hair length		
		Clothing choice		

Source: Safer, D. J. and Allen, R. P. *Hyperactive children.* Baltimore: University Park Press, 1976, pp. 154–155.

vidual but not another, how may the teacher or others decide which reinforcer(s) may be optimally utilized with a particular youngster at a given point in time? Most simply, the youngster can straightforwardly be asked which events he or she would like to earn. Often, however, this approach will not prove sufficient because youngsters are infrequently not fully aware of the range of reinforcers available to them or, when aware, may discount in advance the possibility that the given reinforcer will actually be forthcoming in a particular instance. When this is the case, other reinforcement-identification procedures must be employed. Carr (1981) and others have reported three procedures which typically have been used for this purpose.

Observing Effects. The teacher can often make an accurate determination whether a given event is in fact functioning as a reinforcer by carefully observing its impact on the youngster. It probably is if the youngster (1) asks that the event be repeated; (2) seems happy during the event's occurrence; (3) seems unhappy when the event ends; or (4) will work in order to earn the event. If one or more of these reactions is observed, the chances are good that the event is a positive reinforcer and that it can be contingently provided to strengthen appropriate, nonaggressive behaviors.

Observing Choices. As we noted earlier in connection with activity reinforcers, when a youngster is free to choose among several equally available activities, *which one* he or she chooses, and *how long* he or she engages in the chosen activity, are both readily observed, youngster-identified positive reinforcers.

Questionnaires. A small number of questionnaires exist which have been effectively utilized in identifying positive reinforcers. Tharp and Wetzel's (1969) Mediation-Reinforcer Incomplete Blank is one oft-used example. It consists of a series of incomplete sentences which the youngster must complete by specifying particular reinforcers—for example, "The thing I like to do best with my mother/ father is . . . " or "I will do almost anything to get . . . "* The response format of this questionnaire also asks the youngster to indicate his or her sense of the potency of the reinforcer written in for each item. Thus, this measure provides a self-report of *which* events are reinforcing for the youngster, when delivered or mediated by *whom,* as well as the youngster's perception of just *how reinforcing* each event is for him or for her.

A rather different type of questionnairelike instrument for identifying positive reinforcers, especially appropriate for younger children and children with limited verbal abilities, is Homme's (1971) Reinforcing Event Menu. This measure is

---

*Most of the Mediation-Reinforcer Incomplete Blank items help specify not only the nature of the events which the youngster perceives as positive reinforcers, but also who are the mediators of such reinforcers—highly important information in carrying out a contingency-management effort. Going to a ball game may be a powerful reinforcer if accompanied by peers, a weak one if taken there by one's teacher or mother. Praise from a respected teacher may be a potent reinforcing event, whereas the same praise delivered by a peer considered by the youngster as ignorant vis-à-vis the behavior involved may be totally lacking in potency.

essentially a collection of pictures portraying a variety of material and activity reinforcers, as well as pictures depicting a number of potential reinforcement mediators. It is the youngster's task to select from these pictures those for which he or she would most like to work.

This process of identifying positive reinforcers for given youngsters completes the series of preparatory steps a teacher or other contingency manager must undertake prior to the actual presentation of such events contingent upon the occurrence of appropriate behaviors.

Presenting Positive Reinforcers

The basic principle of contingency management is that the presentation of a reinforcing event contingent upon the occurrence of a given behavior will function to increase the likelihood of the reoccurrence of that behavior. Research has demonstrated a substantial number of considerations which influence the success of this reinforcement effort, and thus which optimally are reflected in its actual presentation when seeking to increase appropriate behaviors.

Be Contingent. Although this rule for reinforcer presentations may be largely obvious at this point, it is a crucial rule which is sometimes forgotten or inadequately implemented. The connection between the desirable behavior and the subsequent provision of reward should be made clear and explicit to the youngster. As is true for all aspects of a contingency-management effort, this teacher description should be behaviorally specific—that is, it is the connection between particular behavioral acts and reinforcement which is made clear, not behaviorally ambiguous comments about "good behavior," "being a good boy," "being well behaved," or the like.

Reinforce Immediately. Related to the communication of the behavior-reinforcement contingency, the more immediately the presentation of reinforcement occurs following the desirable behavior, the more likely is its effectiveness. Not only will rapid reinforcement augment the message that the immediately preceding behavior is desirable, but delayed reinforcer presentation runs the risk that a sequence will occur of (a) desirable behavior → (b) undesirable behavior → (c) reinforcement intended for (a) which in actuality reinforces (b).

Reinforce Consistently. The effects of positive reinforcement on altering behavior are usually gradual, not dramatic. It works to slowly strengthen behavior over a period of time. Thus it is important that positive reinforcement be presented consistently. Consistency here means not only that the teacher herself or himself must be consistent, but also that the teacher must make certain as best as he or she can that the reinforcement delivery efforts are matched by similar efforts from as many other important persons in the youngster's life as possible. Concretely, this means that when the youngster enacts the behavior to be reinforced, in school in the presence of other teachers, at home in the presence of parents or siblings, or at play in the presence of peers, such reinforcement ideally will be forthcoming.

Frequency of Reinforcement. When first trying to establish a new, appropriate behavior, the teacher should seek to reinforce all or almost all instances of that behavior. This high frequency of reinforcement is necessary initially to establish or firmly root the behavior in the individual's behavioral repertoire. Once it seems clear that the behavior has actually been acquired, it is appropriate for the teacher to thin the reinforcement schedule, decreasing the presentation of reinforcement so that only some of the youngster's desirable behaviors are followed by reinforcement. This thinner reinforcement by the teacher, known as a partial-reinforcement strategy, is an important contribution to the continued likelihood of the appropriate behavior because such a reinforcement schedule more closely parallels the sometimes-reinforced–sometimes-not reaction the youngster's appropriate behavior will elicit in other settings from other people. Teacher partial reinforcement of youngster's appropriate behaviors may be ón a fixed time schedule (e.g., at the end of each class), on a fixed number of responses schedule (e.g., every fifth instance of the appropriate behavior), or on variable time or number of response schedules. In any event, the basic strategy for reinforcement frequency remains: a rich level for initial learning; partial reinforcement to sustain performance.

Amount of Reinforcement. In our preceding discussion of frequency of reinforcement, we began to distinguish between learning—that is, acquiring knowledge about how to perform new behaviors—and actual performance—that is, overtly using these behaviors. The amount of reinforcement provided influences performance much more than learning. Youngsters will learn new, appropriate behaviors just about as fast for a small as a large reward, but they are more likely to perform the behaviors on a continuing basis when large rewards are involved. Yet, rewards can be too large, causing a satiation effect in which the youngster loses interest in seeking the given reinforcement because it is "too much of a good thing." Or, rewards can be too small—too little time on the playground, too few tokens, too thin a social-reinforcement schedule. The optimal amount can be determined empirically. If a youngster has in the past worked energetically to obtain a particular reinforcer but gradually slacks off and seems to lose interest in obtaining it, a satiation effect has probably occurred and the amount of reinforcement should be reduced. On the other hand, if a youngster seems unwilling to work for a reinforcer you believe he or she desires, try giving it to him or her once or twice for free—that is, not contingent on a specific desirable behavior. If the child seems to enjoy the reinforcer and even wishes more of the same, the amount you had been using may have been too little. Increase the amount, make it contingent, and observe whether it is yielding the desired, behavior-modification effect. If so, the amount of reinforcement you are offering is appropriate.

Variety of Reinforcement. In the preceding discussion, we mentioned a reinforcement satiation effect due to an excessive *amount* of reinforcement. There is a parallel type of satiation of reinforcement that occurs when the teacher uses the same approving phrase or other reward over and over again. Youngsters may perceive such reinforcement as taking on a mechanized quality, and they may thus lose interest in or responsiveness to it. By varying the content of the reinforcer presented, the teacher can maintain its potency. Thus, instead of repeating "nice job" four or five times, using a mix of comments—"I'm really proud of you." or "You're certainly doing fine." or "Well done."—is more likely to yield a sustained effect.

Pair with Praise. Our earlier statements about types of reinforcers emphasized that social reinforcement is most germaine to enduring behavior change, though there were circumstances under which an emphasis upon material, activity, or token reinforcers was (at least initially) more appropriate. To aid in the desired movement toward social reinforcement, the teacher should seek to pair all presentations of material, activity, or token reward with some expression of social reinforcement: an approving comment, a pat on the back, a wink, a smile, and so forth. A major benefit of this tactic is noted by Walker (1979):

> . . . by virtue of being consistently paired with reinforcement delivery, praise can take on the reinforcing properties of the actual reinforcer(s) used. This is especially important since teacher praise is not always initially effective with many deviant children. By systematically increasing the incentive value of praise though pairing, the teacher is in a position to gradually reduce the frequency of [material, activity, or token] reinforcement and to substitute praise. After systematic pairing, the teacher's praise may be much more effective in maintaining the child's appropriate behavior. (p. 108)

Shaping New Behaviors. Reinforcement cannot be presented contingent upon new behaviors when such behaviors are not part of the youngster's behavioral repertoire. A child cannot be rewarded at all for talking over disputes with other students at the proper frequency, amount, consistency, and so forth, if he or she never does so. Yet the teacher is not doomed here to perpetual waiting, reinforcers ready, for nonemergent desirable behaviors. Approximations to such desirable negotiating behaviors, even remote approximations, can be positively reinforced. Looking at the other disputant, walking towards him or her, discussing an irrelevant (to the dispute) topic are all reinforcable steps in the direction of the ultimately desired behaviors. By a process of such reinforcement of successively closer behaviors (to the final target behavior), coupled with successive withdrawal of such reinforcement for less good approximations, the behavior-change process can proceed in a stepwise fashion in which youngsters' behaviors are systematically shaped into ever-better approximations to the final target behavior.

These aforementioned rules for maximizing the effectiveness of the presentation of positive reinforcement are all essentially remedial in nature. They are efforts to substitute appropriate, prosocial behaviors for aggressive, disruptive, or antisocial behaviors which have already begun to be displayed by specific young-sters. It is also worth noting, however, that the presentation of positive reinforce-ment may also be used for preventive purposes. Sarason et al. (1972) urge teachers to openly present positive reinforcement to specific youngsters in such a manner that the entire class is aware of it. They comment:

> Positive reinforcements for productive activity for the whole group is a power-ful preventive technique. It can eliminate or reduce the great majority of be-havior problems in classrooms. Try to praise the children who are paying attention. Attend to those who are sitting in their seats, doing their work in a nondisruptive manner. "That's right, John, you're doing a good job." "You watched the board all the time I was presenting the problem. That's paying attention." . . . These responses not only reinforce the child to whom they are directed, but they also help to provide the rest of the class with an explicit idea of what you mean by paying attention and working hard. Young chil-dren, especially, . . . learn to model their actions after the positive examples established and noted by the teacher. (p. 18)

We wish to close this discussion of procedures for the presentation of positive reinforcement by suggesting additional sources for the reader wishing to pursue the substantial experimental evidence which exists in support of this dimension of contingency management. Especially comprehensive reviews include Bandura (1969), Gambrill (1977), Kazdin (1977), O'Leary and O'Leary (1976, 1980), and Walker (1979). Individual studies which seem to be particularly instructive of meth-ods and results involving these procedures as applied to youngsters displaying aggres-sive or disruptive behavior are those of Adams (1973), Becker, Madsen, Arnold, and Thomas (1967), Buys (1972), Hall, Panyan, Rabon, and Broden (1968), Kirschner and Levin (1975), Pinkston, Reese, LeBlanc, and Baer (1973), Sewell, McCoy, and Sewell (1973), and Ward and Baker (1968).

Removing Positive Reinforcers

The teacher's behavior-modification goal with youngsters displaying aggressive behaviors is, in a general sense, twofold. Both sides of the behavioral coin—appropriate and inappropriate, prosocial and antisocial, desirable and un-desirable—must be attended to. In a proper behavior-change effort, procedures are simultaneously or sequentially employed to reduce and eliminate the inappropriate, antisocial, or undesirable components of the youngster's behavioral repertoire, and to increase the quality and frequency of appropriate, prosocial, or desirable com-ponents. This latter task is served primarily by the contingent presentation of posi-tive reinforcement. Conversely, the contingent removal of positive reinforcement in response to aggressive, disruptive, or similar behaviors is the major behavior-modifi-cation strategy for reducing or eliminating such behaviors. Therefore, in conjunction with the procedures discussed previously for presenting positive reinforcement, the teacher should also simultaneously or consecutively employ one or more of the three positive reinforcer-removing techniques we now examine.

Extinction

KNOWING WHEN TO USE EXTINCTION

Extinction is the withdrawal or removal of positive reinforcement for aggressive or other undesirable behaviors which have been either deliberately or inadvertently reinforced in the past. Its use can be thought of prescriptively. It is the procedure of choice with milder forms of aggression, such as threats, swearing, or other forms of verbal aggression, or low-amplitude physical aggression. More generally, extinction should be used when other individuals are not in any serious physical danger from the aggression being displayed. When it is and is not appropriate to use extinction is, of course, in part a function of each teacher's tolerance for deviance and guiding classroom-management philosophy. Extinction is usually implemented by teachers and classroom peers seeking to ignore the ongoing inappropriate behavior. Each teacher will have to decide for herself or himself the range of undesirable behaviors that can be safely ignored. Taking a rather conservative stance, Walker (1979) suggests that extinction ". . . should be applied only to those inappropriate behaviors that are minimally disruptive to classroom atmosphere" (p. 40). Others are somewhat more liberal in its application—for example, Carr (1981). In any event, it is clear that the first step in applying extinction is knowing when to use it.

PROVIDING POSITIVE REINFORCEMENT
FOR APPROPRIATE BEHAVIORS

We mentioned this rule earlier, and wish to stress it here. Attempts to reduce inappropriate behavior by reinforcement withdrawal should always be accompanied by tandem efforts to increase appropriate behaviors by reinforcement provision. This combination of efforts will succeed especially well when the appropriate and inappropriate behaviors involved are opposite, or at least incompatible with one another—for example, reward in-seat behavior, ignore out-of-seat behavior; reward talking at conversational level, ignore yelling.

IDENTIFYING THE POSITIVE REINFORCERS
MAINTAINING INAPPROPRIATE BEHAVIORS

These are the reinforcers to be withheld. Using essentially the same observation and recording procedures described earlier (see pages 44 to 46) in conjunction with the identification of positive reinforcers maintaining appropriate behaviors, the teacher should discern what the youngster is working for, what are his or her payoffs, and what are the reinforcers being sought or earned by aggression, disruptiveness, and similar behaviors. Very often the answer will be attention. Laughing, looking, staring, yelling at, talking to, or turning toward are common teacher and peer reactions to a youngster's aggression. The withdrawal of such positive social reinforcement by ignoring the behaviors, by turning away, by not yelling or talking or laughing at the perpetrator are the teacher and classmate behaviors which constitute extinction. Ignoring someone one would normally attend to is itself a talent, as the next extinction rule illustrates.

KNOWING HOW TO IGNORE
AGGRESSIVE BEHAVIORS

Carr (1981) has suggested three useful guidelines for ignoring low-level aggressive behaviors:

1. Do not comment to the child that you are ignoring him or her. Long (or even short) explanations provided to youngsters about why teacher, peers, or others are going to avoid attending to given behaviors provide precisely the type of social reinforcement which extinction is designed to withdraw. Such explanations are to be avoided. Ignoring behavior should simply occur with no forewarning, introduction, or prior explanation.
2. Do not look away suddenly when the child behaves aggressively. Jerking one's head away suddenly so as not to see the continuation of the aggressive behavior, or other abrupt behaviors by the teacher which may also communicate the message "I really noticed and was impelled to action by your behavior," communicate by its attending the exact opposite of an extinction message. As Carr (1981) recommends, "It is best to ignore the behavior by reacting to it in a matter of fact way by continuing natural ongoing activities" (p. 38).
3. Do protect the victims of aggression. If one youngster actually strikes another, the teacher must intervene to protect the victim. One may do so without subverting the extinction effort by providing the victim with attention, concern, and interest, and by ignoring the perpetrator of the aggression.

USING EXTINCTION CONSISTENTLY

As was true for the provision of reinforcement, its removal must be consistent for its intended effects to be forthcoming. Within a given classroom this rule of consistency means both that the teacher and classmates must act in concert, and that the teacher must be consistent with herself or himself across time. Within a given school, consistency means that to the degree possible all teachers having significant commerce with a given youngster must strive to ignore the same inappropriate behaviors. In addition, to avoid a type of "I can't act up here, but I can out there." discrimination being made by the youngster, parent conferences should be held to bring parents, siblings, and other significant real-world figures in the youngster's life into the extinction effort. As Karoly (1980) notes, when consistency of nonattending is not reached, the aggressive behavior will be intermittently or partially reinforced, a circumstance that we noted earlier would lead to its becoming highly resistant to extinction.

USING EXTINCTION FOR A LONG ENOUGH
PERIOD OF TIME

Aggressive behaviors often have a long history of positive reinforcement and, especially if much of that history is one of intermittent reinforcement, efforts to undo it have to be sustained. Teacher persistence in this regard will, however, usually succeed. Carr (1981) suggests that within a week clear reductions in aggressive behavior should be observable. There are, however, two types of events to keep in mind when judging the effectiveness of extinction efforts. The first is what is known as the *extinction burst*. When extinction is first introduced, it is not uncommon for the rate or intensity of the aggressive behavior to first *increase* sharply before it begins its more gradual decline toward a zero level. It is important that the teacher not get discouraged during this short detour in direction. Its meaning, in fact, is that the extinction is beginning to work. On occasion, inappropriate behaviors which have been successfully extinguished will reappear, for reasons that are difficult to determine. Like the extinction burst, this spontaneous recovery phenomenon is transitory, and will disappear if the teacher persists in the extinction effort.

The effectiveness of extinction in modifying inappropriate or undesirable behaviors in a classroom context has been demonstrated by many investigators, including Brown and Elliott (1965), Jones and Miller (1974), Madsen, Becker, and Thomas (1968), Wahler, Winkel, Peterson, and Morrison (1965) and Ward and Baker (1968).

Time Out. Time out is a removal from positive reinforcement procedures such that a youngster who engages in aggressive or other inappropriate behaviors is physically removed from all sources of reinforcement for a specified time period. As with extinction, the purpose of time out is to reduce the (undesirable) behavior which immediately precedes it and on which its use is contingent. It differs from extinction in that extinction involves removing reinforcement from the person, whereas time out usually involves removing the person from the reinforcing situation. In classroom practice, time out has typically taken three forms. Isolation time out, the most common form, requires that the youngster be physically removed from the classroom to a time-out room following specific procedures described later in this section. Exclusion time out is somewhat less restrictive, but also involves physically removing the youngster from sources of reinforcement. Here the youngster is required to go to a corner of the classroom, and perhaps to sit in a "quiet chair" (Firestone, 1976), sometimes also behind a screen. The youngster is not removed from the classroom, but is excluded from classroom activities for a specified time period. Nonexclusion time out (also called contingent observation), the least restrictive time out variant, requires the youngster to "sit and watch" on the periphery of classroom activities, to observe the appropriate behaviors of other youngsters. It is a varient which, in a sense, combines time out with modeling opportunities (see page 68). Its essence is to exclude the youngster from a participant role for a specified time period, while leaving intact the opportunity to function as an observer. The implementation of time out in any of its forms optimally employs the steps we now describe.

KNOWING WHEN TO USE TIME OUT

Extinction, it will be recalled, was the recommended procedure for those aggressive or otherwise undesirable behaviors which could be *safely* ignored. Behaviors potentially injurious to other youngsters require a more active teacher response, possibly time out. Yet, for many youngsters at the upper junior high-school and senior high-school levels, physical removal of the student by the teacher is often neither wise, appropriate, nor even possible. For such youngsters, procedures other than extinction or time out, which are discussed later in this chapter, have to be employed. Thus, to reflect both the potential injuriousness of the youngster's behavior and the youngster's age and associated physical status, time out is recommended as the technique of choice for youngsters aged 2 to 12 who are displaying high rates of severely aggressive behavior of potential danger to other individuals. It is also the procedure to utilize for less severe forms of aggression when the combination of extinction and positive reinforcement for milder levels of aggression has been attempted and has failed.

PROVIDING POSITIVE REINFORCEMENT
FOR APPROPRIATE BEHAVIORS

What we said in our earlier discussion of the implementation of this step as part of the extinction process (see page 54) also applies with regard to time out. Both procedures, providing positive reinforcement and time out, should be used in tandem. When possible, the behaviors positively reinforced should be opposite to, or at least incompatible with, those for which the time out procedure is instituted. Furthermore, there is an additional basis for recommending the combined use of these two techniques. As Carr (1981) observes:

> Although one important reason for using positive reinforcement is to strengthen nonaggressive behaviors to the point where they replace aggressive behaviors, there is a second reason for using reinforcement procedures. If extensive use of positive reinforcement is made, then time out will become all the more aversive since it would involve the temporary termination of a rich diversity of positive reinforcers. In this sense, then, the use of positive reinforcement helps to enhance the effectiveness of the time out procedure. (pp. 41–42)

ARRANGING AN EFFECTIVE
TIME OUT SETTING

We focus our description of the characteristics of an effective time-out setting on an *isolation* time-out arrangement, because its general principles readily carry over to both exclusion and nonexclusion time-out environments. Essentially, two general principles are involved. The first concerns the youngster's health and safety. The physical characteristics of the time-out setting should be a small, well-lit, and well-ventilated room which provides a place for the youngster to sit. The second principle reflects the fact that the central quality of this procedure is time out from positive reinforcement. It must be a boring environment, with all reinforcers removed. There should be no attractive or distracting objects or opportunities. No toys, television, radio, books, posters, people, windows to look out, sound sources to overhear, or other obvious or not-so-obvious potential reinforcers. A barren, isolation area is the optimal time-out environment.

PLACING A YOUNGSTER
IN TIME OUT

A number of actions may be taken by the teacher when initiating time out for a given youngster that serve to increase the likelihood of its effectiveness. As with the rapid presentation of positive reinforcement contingent upon appropriate behaviors, time out is optimally instituted immediately following the aggressive or other behaviors you are seeking to modify. Having earlier explained to the class as a whole the nature of time out, as well as when and why it would be used, its initiation should be implemented in a more or less "automatic" manner following undesirable behavior—that is, in a manner which minimizes the social reinforcement of the aggression. Concretely, this means placing the youngster in time out without a lengthy explanation, but with a brief, matter-of-fact description of his or her precipitating behaviors. This placement process is best conducted without anger by the teacher, and without (when possible) having to use physical means for moving the youngster from the classroom to the time-out room. Consistent with seeking to minimize reinforcement of aggression during this process, it is also best if the physical distance between classroom and time-out room is small—the less the distance, the shorter the "transportation" time, the less opportunity for inadvertent social reinforcement by the teacher. In addition to these considerations, the effectiveness of time out is further enhanced by its consistent application when appropriate, by the same teacher on other occasions as well as by other teachers. Immediacy, consistency, and the various actions aimed at minimizing teacher presentation of reinforcement following inappropriate behavior each function to augment the behavior-change effectiveness of time out.

MAINTAINING A YOUNGSTER
IN TIME OUT

The skilled contingency manager must deal with two questions during a youngster's period in time out: "What is he or she doing?" and "For how long should time out last?" Answering the first question by teacher monitoring makes certain that the time-out experience is not in fact functioning as a pleasant, positively reinforcing one for a given youngster. For example, rather than serve as a removal from positive reinforcement, time out may in reality be a removal from an aversive situation (negative reinforcement) if the teacher institutes it at a time when a youngster is in an unpleasant situation from which he or she would prefer to escape, or if time out helps him or her avoid such a situation. Similarly, if monitoring reveals that the youngster is singing or playing enjoyable games, the effectiveness of time out will be lessened. Unless the situation can be made essentially nonreinforcing, a different behavioral intervention may have to be used.

With regard to the duration of time out, most of its successful implementations have been from 5 to 20 minutes long, with some clear preference for the shorter levels of this range. When experimenting to find the optimal duration for any given youngster it is best, as White, Nielsen, and Johnson (1972) have shown, to begin with a short duration (e.g., 3 to 5 minutes) and lengthen the time out until an effective span is identified, rather than to successively shorten an initially lengthier span. This latter approach would, again, risk the danger of introducing an event experienced as positive reinforcement by the youngster when the intention was quite the opposite.

RELEASING A YOUNGSTER
FROM TIME OUT

We noted earlier in connection with extinction that the implementation of a withdrawal of positive reinforcement not infrequently leads to initial instances of an extinction burst in which more intense or more frequent aggressiveness appears before it begins to subside. This same pattern is evident with withdrawal *from* positive reinforcement—that is, time out. The first few times a youngster is placed in time out there may occur what might be termed a *time-out burst* of heightened aggressiveness. These outbursts will usually subside, especially if the teacher adds to the duration of the time-out span the same number of minutes that the outburst lasted.

Whether the release of the youngster from time out is on schedule or is delayed for reasons just specified, the release should be conducted in a matter-of-fact manner and the youngster should be quickly returned to regular classroom activities. Lengthy teacher explanations or apologies at this point in time are, once again, tactically erroneous provisions of positive reinforcement which communicate to the youngster that acting out in the classroom will bring him or her a short period of removal from reinforcement and then a (probably lengthier) period of undivided teacher attention.

The effectiveness of time out in substantially reducing or eliminating aggressive or disruptive behaviors has been shown by Allison and Allison (1971), Bostow and Bailey (1969), Calhoun and Matherne (1975), Drabman and Spitalnik (1973), Patterson, Cobb, and Ray (1973), Patterson and Reid (1973), Vukelich and Hake (1971), Webster (1976), and White et al. (1972).

Response Cost. Response cost refers to the removal of previously acquired reinforcers contingent upon, and in order to reduce future instances of, the occurrence of inappropriate behaviors. The reinforcers previously acquired and herein contingently removed may have been earned, as when the use of response-cost procedures is a component of a token-reinforcement system, or they may have been simply provided, as is the case with a "free-standing" no-token economy response-cost system. In either instance, reinforcers are removed (the cost) whenever previously targeted undesirable behaviors occur (the response). The two other means we have examined for the systematic removal of positive reinforcement, extinction and time out, have not infrequently proven insufficient for delinquent or severely aggressive mid- and late adolescents, even when combined with teacher praise or other reinforcement for appropriate behaviors. In a number of these instances, responses-cost procedures—especially when combined with the provision of positive reinforcement (via a token-economy system) for desirable behaviors—have proven effective. Thus, not only must a teacher's selection of approach be a prescriptive function of target youngster characteristics, but the teacher must also continue in implementing this approach to combine its usage with tandem procedures for providing positive reinforcement of appropriate behaviors.

We do not detail here the rules for the effective implementation of a token-economy system, as they overlap considerably with rules delineated earlier for the provision of nontoken positive reinforcers (pages 46 to 50), and may be found in Christopherson et al. (1972), Ayllon and Azrin (1968), Kazdin (1975), Morris (1976), and Walker et al. (1976). What we do wish to specify, however, are those rules for token- or nontoken-reinforcement removal which constitute the essence of the response-cost procedure.

DEFINING INAPPROPRIATE BEHAVIORS
IN SPECIFIC TERMS

As with every other contingency-management procedure, it is requisite that the teacher think, plan, and act *behaviorally.* When specifying the inappropriate target behaviors whose occurrence will cost tokens, points, privileges, or other commodities or events, specific overt acts must be delineated, not broader behavioral characterological categories. Thus, "is aggressive" (a characterological observation) or "acts aggressively" (a broad behavioral observation) are too vague, but "swears, makes threats, raises voice, raises hands, pushes classmate" are all more useful specifications.

DETERMINING THE COST OF SPECIFIC
INAPPROPRIATE RESPONSES

Just as is the case for the amount, level, or rate of positive reinforcement to be provided contingent upon desirable behaviors, the specific cost to be lost contingent upon undesirable behaviors must be determined—whether such cost is a finite number of tokens or points, a finite amount of time the television will be kept off, or otherwise. Cost setting is a crucial determinant of the success or failure of implementing this approach. For example, Carr (1981) notes:

> The magnitude of response cost must be carefully controlled. If fines are too large, bankruptcy will ensue and the child will be unable to purchase any back-up reinforcers. Further, if the child develops too large a deficit, he may adapt an attitude of "what do I have to lose?" and engage in considerable misbehavior. On the other hand, if the fines are too small, the child will be able to negate his loss easily by performing any of a variety of appropriate behaviors. (p. 52)

Yet other aspects of response-cost implementation will make demands on the teacher's skills as a creative economist. The relation of points or other reinforcers available to earn to those which can be lost, the relationship of cost to the severity of the inappropriate behavior for which that cost is levied, and a host of similar marketing, pricing, and, ultimately, motivational considerations may come into play and thus require a substantial level of contingency-management expertise on the part of the teacher. This is especially true if the teacher is not only the implementer of the response-cost system, but also its originator, planner, and monitor.

COMMUNICATING CONTINGENCIES

Once the teacher has decided upon the specific token, point, or privilege value of the appropriate and inappropriate behaviors relevant to the effective management of his or her classroom, it is necessary to communicate these values to the class. A readily visible reinforcer value list indicating earnings and losses should be drawn up and posted. Table 3.2 is a composite example of such a list, designed to be appropriate at the junior high-school level.

REMOVING REINFORCEMENT

Class members must not only be able to know in advance what earnings and losses are contingent upon what desirable and undesirable behaviors, but each must also have ongoing access to his or her own earnings status. A good example of how this may be accomplished is provided by Walker (1979) who has developed a simple, easily used delivery/feedback system which gives each youngster ongoing cumulative information indicating (1) when response cost (or earnings) has been applied; (2) to which specific behaviors it was applied; and (3) how many points have been lost (or earned) as a result. In implementing the response-cost component of this system, each youngster was given a 4 X 6 inch card once each week. The card, whose content appears in Figure 3.1., was taped to the corner of each youngster's desk. As the first step in implementing the delivery and feedback of response cost, both the use of the cards and the specific behaviors involved in their use were ex-

TABLE 3.2. Behaviors that Earn and Lose Points

BEHAVIORS THAT EARN POINTS	POINTS
1. Reading books	5 per page
2. Greeting people appropriately	100 per instance
3. Remaining in seat	100 per 15 minutes
4. Taking notes	250 per 15 minutes
5. Being on time for school	250 per day
6. Being quiet in lunch line	300 per instance
7. Being quiet in cafeteria	300 per instance
8. Displaying appropriate playground behavior	500 per 15 minutes
9. Doing completed homework	1000 per day
10. Getting an A/B/C/D grade	2000/1000/500/250 per grade
11. Talking out disagreements	1000 per instance

BEHAVIORS THAT LOSE POINTS	POINTS
1. Greeting people inappropriately	100 per instance
2. Being out of seat inappropriately	150 per instance
3. Being late for school	10 per minute
4. Being noisy in classroom	300 per instance
5. Being noisy in lunch line	300 per instance
6. Being noisy in cafeteria	300 per instance
7. Swearing	500 per instance
8. Cheating	1000 per instance
9. Having incomplete homework	1000 per instance
10. Getting an F grade	1000 per grade
11. Showing physical aggression	1000 per instance
12. Stealing	2500 per instance

FIGURE 3.1. Response–Cost Delivery/Feedback System* (from Walker, 1979, p. 127)

*The youngster whose appropriate behaviors are recorded here lost 11 points on Monday and 12 points on Tuesday.

BEHAVIORS	POINT VALUES	M	T	W	TH	F
Out of Seat	2	• •				
Talks Out	2	•	• •			
Nonattending	1	• • •	•			
Noncompliance	3		•			
Disturbing Others	2	•				
Foul Language	4		•			
Fighting	5					

plained and illustrated for the class. During the week, whenever a given youngster engaged in one of the inappropriate behaviors, the teacher walked to the youngster's desk and, with a special marking pen, placed a dot in the box corresponding to the day of the week and to the particular inappropriate behavior to which the cost was being applied. Consistent with the effort to avoid providing social reinforcement while implementing this removal-of-positive-reinforcement procedure, teachers concurrently told the youngster which behavior(s) were involved and the number of points lost, but engaged in no other dialogue with the youngster at that time.

A delivery/feedback card such as the one in Figure 3.1 may be used as part of a response-cost system in which the youngster (1) is simply given a fixed number of points initially and noncontingently; (2) keeps or loses points as a function of his or her behavior during a fixed time period; and (3) is given the opportunity to exchange points remaining for backup material or activity reinforcers at the end of that time period. Alternatively, such means for keeping a youngster posted on his or her point status may also be part of a token-economy system in which points must be earned (e.g., Table 3.2) contingent on appropriate behaviors, not awarded initially on a noncontingent basis. When this earning requirement is in effect, a second delivery/feedback card (or the reverse side of the response-cost card) may be used to keep an ongoing record of points earned by each youngster in each (appropriate) behavior category each day.

As was true for the other major procedures for the removal of positive reinforcement, extinction and time out, optimal implementation of response cost requires that the teacher be (1) *consistent* in his or her application of it across students and across time for each student; (2) *immediate* in delivering contingent costs as soon as possible after the occurrence of inappropriate behavior; and (3) *impartial* and *inevitable,* in that an instance of such behavior leads to an instance of response cost almost automatically, with an absolute minimum of special circumstances, special students, or special exceptions.

A number of investigations have independently demonstrated the behavior-modification effectiveness of response-cost procedures—for example, Burchard and Barrera (1972), Christopherson et al. (1972), Kaufman and O'Leary (1972), O'Leary and Becker (1967), and O'Leary, Becker, Evans, and Saudargas (1969).

Aversive Stimuli—Presentation and Removal

The two contingency-management approaches examined in this section—namely, the presentation of aversive stimuli (i.e., punishment) and the removal of aversive stimuli (i.e., negative reinforcement)—are in our view generally less recommendable than the positive-reinforcement presentation and removal procedures discussed in earlier sections. Our bases for this disinclination to recommend and utilize these procedures are explained in the following discussion.

Punishment

Punishment is the presentation of an aversive stimulus contingent upon the performance of a given behavior, and is usually intended to decrease the likelihood of future occurrences of that behavior. Two of the major forms that punishment has taken in American classrooms are verbal punishment—that is, reprimands—and physical punishment—that is, paddling, spanking, slapping, or other forms of corporal punishment. The effectiveness of these and other forms of punishment in altering targeted inappropriate behaviors such as aggression has been shown to be a function of several factors:

1. Likelihood of punishment.
2. Consistency of punishment.
3. Immediacy of punishment.
4. Duration of punishment.
5. Severity of punishment.
6. Possibility for escape or avoidance of punishment.
7. Availability of alternative routes to goal.
8. Level of instigation to aggression.
9. Level of reward for aggression.
10. Characteristics of the prohibiting agents.

Punishment is more likely to lead to behavior-change consequences the more certain its application, the more consistently and rapidly it is applied, the longer and more intense its quality, the less likely it can be avoided, the more available are alternative means to goal satisfaction, the lower the level of instigation to aggression or reward for aggression, and the more potent as a contingency manager is the prohibiting agent. Thus, there are clearly several determinants of the impact of an aversive stimulus on a youngster's behavior. But let us assume an instance of these determinants' combining to yield a substantial impact. What, ideally, may we hope that the effect of punishment on aggression or other undesirable behavior will be? A reprimand or a paddling will not teach new behaviors. If the youngster is literally deficient in the ability to ask rather than take, request rather than command, negotiate rather than strike out, all the teacher scolding, scowling, spanking possible will not teach the youngster the desirable alternative behaviors. Thus punishment, if used at all, must be combined with teacher efforts which instruct the youngster in those behaviors he or she knows not at all (e.g., by modeling [see page 68] or related procedures). When the youngster does possess alternative desirable behaviors, but in only approximate form, punishment may best be combined with shaping (see page 52) procedures. And, when high-quality appropriate behaviors are possessed by the youngster, but he or she is not displaying them, teacher use of punishment is optimally combined with any of the other procedures described earlier for the systematic presentation of positive reinforcement. In short, the application of punishment techniques should always be combined with a companion procedure for strengthening appropriate alternative behaviors—whether these behaviors are absent, weak, or merely unused in the youngster's behavioral repertoire.

Our urging this tandem focus on teaching desirable alternative behaviors grows in particular from the fact that most investigators report the main effect of punishment to be a *temporary* suppression of inappropriate behaviors. Although we appreciate the potential value of such a temporary suppression to the harried classroom teacher seeking a more manageable classroom environment in which teaching time can exceed discipline time, it is not uncommon—because of this temporariness—for the teacher to have to institute and reinstitute punishment over and over again to the same youngsters for the same inappropriate behaviors. To recapitulate, we have urged thus far in this section that if punishment is used, its use be combined with one or another means for simultaneously teaching desirable behaviors—a recommendation underscored by the common finding that when punishment does succeed in altering behavior, such effects are often temporary.

In part because of this temporariness of effect, but more so for a series of even more consequential reasons, a number of contingency-management researchers have assumed essentially an antipunishment stance, seeing rather little place for it, especially in the contemporary classroom. This view responds to punishment research demonstrating such undesirable side effects of punishment as withdrawal from social contact, counteraggression toward the punisher, modeling of punishing behavior, disruption of social relationships, failure of effects to generalize, selective avoidance (refraining from inappropriate behaviors only when under surveillance), and stigmatizing labeling effects (Azrin & Holz, 1966; Bandura, 1973). An alternative, propunishment view does exist. It is less widespread and more controversial but, as with the view of the investigators just cited, it seeks to make its case based upon empirical evidence. Thus, it is held that there are numerous favorable effects of punishment: rapid and dependable reduction of inappropriate behaviors, the consequent opening up of new sources of positive reinforcement, the possibility of complete suppression of inappropriate behaviors, increased social and emotional behavior, imitation and discrimination learning, and other potential positive side effects (Axelrod & Apsche, 1982; Newsom, Favell, & Rincover, 1982; Van Houten, 1982).

The evidence is clearly not all in. Complete data on which punishers should appropriately be used with which youngsters under which circumstances are only partially available. At the present time, decisions regarding the classroom utilization of aversive stimuli to alter inappropriate behaviors must derive from partial data and each teacher's carefully considered ethical beliefs regarding the relative costs and benefits of employing punishment procedures. Our own weighing of relevant data and ethical considerations leads to our differential stance favoring the selective utilization in classrooms of verbal-punishment techniques, and our rejecting under all circumstances the use of corporal punishment or similar physical-punishment techniques.

Verbal Reprimands. Though results are not wholly unmixed, the preponderance of research demonstrates that punishment in the form of teacher verbal reprimands is an effective means for reducing disruptive classroom behavior (Jones & Miller, 1974), littering (Risley, 1977), object throwing (Sajwaj, Culver, Hall, & Lehr, 1972), physical aggression (Hall, Axelrod, Foundopoulos, Shellman, Campbell, & Cranston, 1971), and other acting-out behaviors (O'Leary, Kaufman, Kass, & Drabman, 1970). These and other relevant studies also indicate, beyond overall effectiveness, that reprimands are most potent when the teacher is physically close to the target youngster, clearly specifies in behavioral terms the inappropriate behavior being reprimanded, maintains eye contact with the youngster, uses a firm voice, and firmly grasps the youngster while delivering the reprimand. Finally, White et al. (1972) and Forehand, Roberts, Dolays, Hobbs, and Resick (1976) each compared reprimands to other commonly employed forms of punishment and found reprimands to be superior in effectiveness.

Our position favoring the selective use of teacher reprimands rests jointly on our understanding of the foregoing research findings combined with our cost/benefit belief that such procedures not only have a high likelihood of being effective, but also a low likelihood of being injurious—especially when combined, as we and others have repeatedly urged, with one or another means for presenting positive reinforcement for appropriate behaviors. In this latter regard, both White (1975) and Thomas, Presland, Grant, and Glynn (1978) have independently shown that teachers deliver an average of .5 reprimands *per minute* in both elementary and junior high schools, a rate which substantially exceeds, in all grade levels beyond grade two, their rate of offering praise to students for appropriate behaviors. Stated otherwise, in contemporary educational settings, teachers now reprimand students at rates which are absolutely very high, and far too infrequently do they accompany such reprimands by social reinforcement for desirable behaviors. We are clearly urging a change in this latter regard.

Corporal Punishment. Though we do not know of empirical evidence bearing upon Newsom et al.'s (1982) speculation that physically painful punishment that succeeds in altering inappropriate behaviors may be less injurious and more helpful in toto to the target youngster than nonphysically painful but perhaps less effective alternatives, and are given pause by their speculation, we nevertheless herein take a stance opposed to corporal punishment in school (or any other) settings. As Axelrod and Apsche (1982) urge, our guiding ethical principle is to urge "the implementation of the least drastic alternative which has a reasonable probability of success" (p. 16). Given the substantial number of demonstrations of effectiveness of procedures involving the presentation of positive reinforcers, the similarly strong results bearing on techniques for removing such reinforcement, the just-cited evidence vis-à-vis verbal punishment, and the major paucity of research evaluating the effectiveness of corporal punishment, we see no place for it in the domain of effective classroom management.

Yet forty-seven of America's fifty states permit corporal punishment, and its school-house and community advocates seem to be loud, numerous, and growing. Is it, as Hagebak (1979) darkly suggests, that physically punitive teachers should ask themselves "whether they tend to interpret classroom problems as a personal threat, whether they inflict punishment to protect their self-esteem, whether they retaliate rather than consider the causes of disruptive behavior objectively, and whether they derive sexual satisfaction from inflicting physical punishment" (p. 112)? Or, more parsimoniously, recalling our definition of negative reinforcement on page 41, is teacher use and reuse of corporal punishment a simple function of the fact that it intermittently succeeds in reducing or eliminating the student disruptiveness, aggression, or other behavior experienced as aversive by the teacher?

Whatever are the motivations and reinforcements which have sustained its use, corporal punishment—as all means of punishment—fails to yield *sustained* suppression of inappropriate behaviors, *increases* the likelihood that the youngster will behave aggressively in other settings (Hyman, 1978; Maurer, 1974; Welsh, 1968), and makes no contribution at all to the development of new, appropriate behaviors. We feel quite strongly that one's behavior as a classroom teacher must ethically be responsive to such accumulated empirical evidence. Ample research exists to firmly conclude that the science of behavior modification must replace the folklore of procorporal punishment beliefs.

Negative Reinforcement

Negative reinforcement is the final contingency-management procedure we wish to consider, and our consideration of it is brief. Recall that negative reinforcement is the removal of aversive stimuli contingent upon the occurrence of desirable behaviors. Negative reinforcement has seldom been utilized as a behavior-modification approach in a classroom context. The major exception to this is the manner in which youngsters may be contingently released from time out (an aversive environment), depending upon such desirable behaviors as quietness and calmness, because such release serves as negative reinforcement for these behaviors. Unfortunately, negative reinforcement often proves important in a classroom context in a less constructive way. Consider a teacher-student interaction in which the student behaves disruptively (shouts, swears, fights), the teacher responds with anger and physical punishment toward the youngster, and the punishment brings about a (temporary) suppression of the youngster's disruptiveness. The decrease in student disruptiveness may also be viewed as a decrease in aversive stimulation experienced by the teacher, which functions to negatively reinforce the immediately preceding teacher behaviors—for example, corporal punishment. The net effect of this sequence is to increase the future likelihood of teacher use of corporal punishment. Analogous sequences may occur and function to increase the likelihood of other ineffective, inappropriate, or intemperate teacher behaviors.

OTHER BEHAVIOR-MODIFICATION
PROCEDURES

In addition to the various procedures we have examined for the presentation or removal of positive reinforcement or aversive stimuli, there are a number of behavior-modification procedures available for classroom use which do not rely upon the management of contingencies for their apparent effectiveness. In this section we briefly consider these procedures.

Overcorrection

Overcorrection is a behavior-modification approach developed by Foxx and Azrin (1973) for that circumstance when extinction, time out, and response cost have either failed or cannot be utilized, and there are few alternative appropriate behaviors available to reinforce. Overcorrection is a two-part procedure, having both restitutional and positive practice components. The restitutional aspect requires that the target individual return the behavioral setting (e.g., the classroom) to its predisruption status or better. Thus, the objects broken by an angry youngster must be repaired, the classmates struck in anger apologized to, the papers scattered across the room picked up. Further, the positive practice component of overcorrection requires that the disruptive youngster then, in the examples just cited, be made to repair objects broken by others, or apologize to classmates who witnessed the classmate being struck, or clean up the rest of the classroom including areas not messed up by the target youngster. It is clear that the restitution-positive practice requirements may jointly serve both a punitive and an instructional function.

Modeling

Modeling, also known as imitation learning, vicarious learning, and observational learning, is an especially powerful behavior-modification procedure. Modeling may teach new behaviors or strengthen or weaken previously learned behaviors. Its effects have been demonstrated across a particularly wide array of target behaviors—including student aggression (Bandura, 1969; Goldstein, Sprafkin, Gershaw, & Klein, 1979; Perry & Furukawa, 1980; Sarason, 1968). Modeling procedures, facilitators, and consequences are examined in depth in Chapter 6, a discussion of means for the direct teaching of prosocial behaviors.

Behavioral Rehearsal

With deep roots both in psychodrama and more contemporaneous role-play activities, behavioral rehearsal has become an important behavior-modification procedure. In it, appropriate alternative behaviors are enacted by the target individual in a safe, quasiprotected training environment prior to its utilization in real-world contexts. Behavioral rehearsal, which is also described in detail in Chapter 6, is often used in conjunction with modeling (which instructs *what* to rehearse) and feedback (regarding how well the behavior as rehearsed matches the model's). With both individuals and groups, behavioral rehearsal has been used effectively to teach such alternatives to aggression as assertiveness (Galassi & Galassi, 1977), negotiation (Goldstein & Rosenbaum, 1982), self-control (Novaco, 1975), and a host of other prosocial behaviors (Goldstein et al., 1979).

Contingency Contracting

A contingency contract is a written agreement between a teacher and student. It is a document each signs which specifies, in detailed behavioral terms, desirable student behaviors and their positive, teacher-provided consequences as well as undesirable student behaviors and their contingent undesirable consequences. As Homme, Csanyi, Gonzales, and Rech (1969) specified in their initial description of this procedure, such contracts will more reliably lead to desirable student behaviors when the contract payoff is immediate; approximations to the desirable are rewarded; the contract rewards accomplishment rather than obedience; accomplishment precedes reward; the contract is fair, clear, honest, positive, and systematically implemented.

Procedural Combinations

It is increasingly the accepted view in both education and psychology that interventions designed to modify overt behavior in personal, interpersonal, or academic realms are optimally designed and implemented prescriptively (Cronbach & Snow, 1969; Goldstein, 1978; Goldstein & Stein, 1976; Hunt & Sullivan, 1974). This differential or tailored intervention strategy proposes that the modification of behavior will proceed most effectively and efficiently when change methods used prescriptively fit the type or intensity of the behaviors to which they are applied. For the most part, the state of prescriptive guidelines in education and psychology is still largely rudimentary, and only approximate prescriptions are currently possible. Such prescriptions, however, are clearly superior to either trial-and-error applications of interventions, which view all interventions as more or less equivalent, or to one-true-light prescriptions, in which one's favored approach is applied to all types and intensities of undesirable behavior. Thus, beginning steps though they may be, certain rudimentary prescriptive guidelines are available in helping the teacher to determine which procedure to use with which youngster. Because their research support is as yet only modest, the reader should view these prescriptions as suggestive.

1. For youngsters who are only mildly disruptive—those who only occasionally display inappropriate behaviors—extinction will often prove to be the necessary and sufficient intervention.
2. For youngsters who are mildly to moderately disruptive—those who engage in appropriate behavior more than half of the time—procedures for the presentation of positive reinforcement of appropriate behaviors alone will often prove to be the necessary and sufficient intervention.
3. For youngsters who are moderately to severely disruptive—those who engage in appropriate behaviors less than half the time—combined procedures for both the presentation of positive reinforcement of appropriate behaviors and for the removal of positive reinforcement of inappropriate behaviors will often prove to be the necessary and sufficient intervention.

It is this third, moderate-to-severe, level of youngster disruptiveness which is most germaine to the target concerns of the present book. Drawing upon relevant empirical research, Walker (1979) has proposed the following prescriptive hierarchy of interventions of increasing potency for such particularly disruptive, acting-out, or aggressive youngsters. Note that each intervention combines means for both the presentation and removal of positive reinforcement.

1. Teacher praise for appropriate behavior and brief time out for inappropriate behavior (Wasik, Senn, Welch, & Cooper, 1968).
2. Teacher praise and token reinforcement for appropriate behavior and time out for inappropriate behavior (Walker, Mattson, & Buckley, 1971).
3. Teacher praise for appropriate behavior and response cost for inappropriate behavior (Walker et al., 1976).
4. Teacher praise and positive nonsocial reinforcement for appropriate behavior and response cost for inappropriate behavior (Walker, Street, Garrett, & Crossen, 1977).

Beyond these recommendations, we have three approximate prescriptions to offer. The first are our earlier semiprescriptions regarding the optimal utilization of extinction (p. 54), time out (p. 56), and response cost (p. 60). The second is the view also sketched in part earlier that modeling, behavioral rehearsal, and similar instructional measures are prescriptively most useful in literally teaching appropriate behaviors not yet in the individual's repertoire; shaping is especially useful when the person is capable of approximations to appropriate behavior, but no more; and presentations of positive reinforcement fit best when appropriate behaviors have been learned, but for one reason or another are not being performed. Finally, it is appropriate in terms of current knowledge to generally prescribe employment of the least restrictive, least costly, and simplest to implement a procedure or procedures which seem to hold reasonable possibility of effective outcome.

TRANSFER AND MAINTENANCE

We have completed our presentation of behavior-modification procedures currently available for the effective classroom management of aggression and other undesirable behaviors. As we stated at the outset of this chapter, and have reiterated throughout, substantial research evidence exists indicating that singly and especially in combination these procedures yield high rates of effective behavior modification. But questions of transfer and maintenance, however, must be answered less optimistically. Youngsters may indeed change in constructive directions in the classroom in which the given behavior-modification procedures were used, but the likelihood that the changes will generalize to other settings (i.e., transfer) or persist over time (i.e., maintenance) are considerably smaller. This frequent failure of gains to either generalize or endure is far from unique to behavioral interventions but, as far as we can discern, applies to almost all educational, psychoeducational, psychological, and psychotherapeutic approaches. For example, in a review of 192 outcome studies which examined the effectiveness of diverse psychotherapies, we commented:

> Though the number of studies . . . reporting positive therapeutic outcomes at the termination of treatment is high (85%), only 14% of the studies conducted report maintenance or transfer of therapeutic gains. The total sample of studies, furthermore, was selected on criteria reflecting high levels of methodological soundness, thus adding further to the tenability of the conclusion that transfer is a relatively uncommon psychotherapeutic outcome . . . . Keeley, Shemberg, and Carbonell (1976) examined an essentially different series of therapy outcome studies and came to the same conclusion as we have. They focused on the 146 investigations of operant interventions reported in a series of behaviorally oriented journals during 1972–1973. Even moderately long-term concern with transfer was rare. They comment: . . . Only 8 of the 146 studies analyzed present hard data collected at least 6 months past termination, and short term generalization data are conspicuously absent. (Goldstein, Lopez, & Greenleaf, 1979, p. 4)

Successful transfer and maintenance of intervention effects are relatively rare, we would propose, for two reasons. The first is that, as a massive amount of evidence demonstrates, behavior tends to be situation specific. That is, behavior tends to be a substantial function of the stimuli and contingencies of the environment in which it occurs. Change the environment and there is an excellent chance behavior will change accordingly. Thus, interventions, including behavior-modification interventions, tend to be effective when they are applied and not later (a nonmaintenance effect), and where they are applied and not elsewhere (a nontransfer effect).

But the effects of situational specificity of behavior on transfer and maintenance are not immutable. There exists a technology of transfer and maintenance enhancement, a series of tested techniques which may deliberately be incorporated into intervention efforts and which demonstrably function to enhance both the generalization and persistence of intervention effects. Our typical failure in most past intervention efforts to draw upon this technology markedly contributes to nontransfer and nonmaintenance. Our ability to do so now and in the future, however, can and should substantially increase our success in these transfer and maintenance regards. In the remainder of this section we describe the nature of these several potent transfer- and maintenance-enhancing techniques.

Transfer-Enhancing Procedures

Programmed Generalization. Transfer may most directly be enhanced by efforts which take the intervention which was effective in one setting—for example, the classroom—and implement it in one or more other settings in which the inappropriate behavior also occurs—for example, the cafeteria, school playground, home, and so on. Such an attempt, of course, requires not only additional teacher effort, but possibly also the involvement of other teachers, teacher aides, peers, and/or the youngster's parents as additional intervenors.

Identical Elements. A youngster will often discriminate between the setting in which the intervention is applied and another in which it is not, because the two settings are markedly dissimilar. He or she may display appropriate behaviors in the former, but not in the latter. Transfer in this context will be enhanced to the degree that the two settings can be made similar. If the intervention cannot be applied in the cafeteria (programmed generalization), temporarily create a cafeterialike corner in your classroom from where you apply your interventions to the youngster along with the interventions of his or her peers with whom he or she associates in the cafeteria. More generally, the greater the number of between-settings identical elements you can mobilize, the greater the likely transfer.

Overlearning. Transfer is facilitated the more the youngster has practiced correct or effective use of appropriate behaviors. Behavior modifiers sometimes make the error of using their interventions until a youngster responds correctly, and then they go on to work on other desirable behaviors. Research on overlearning, or overpractice, shows that transfer will be aided if, once a youngster responds in an appropriate manner, he or she is encouraged to practice the *same* response several more times. In a sense, we are urging here a strategy of "practice of perfect" to replace the more common "practice makes perfect."

Variety Learning. Transfer is enhanced not only by considerable practice of the given appropriate behaviors, but also when the behavior-change intervention is mediated by several intervenors and in a variety of settings. Consistent with our earlier observation about inappropriate discriminations, it sometimes happens that transfer fails to occur because aspects of the intervention were defined too narrowly. If one intervenor applies a given procedure in one setting, the youngster may learn to utilize appropriate behaviors only in that setting and only in response to that intervenor. Transfer, therefore, will be enhanced by the utilization of several intervenors applying the intervention across several settings.

General Principles. Although our emphasis throughout this chapter has been on the modification of specific behaviors, and not on communicating more abstract guidelines or behavior-change principles, there are youngsters for whom transfer will be promoted by teaching them general rules of conduct. General rules and principles will help these somewhat more conceptually abstract youngsters decide both when and how to utilize specific appropriate behaviors when they find themselves in settings or situations which depart somewhat from the particular settings or situations in which the behavior-modification procedure was originally applied.

Maintenance-Enhancing Procedures

Intermittent Reinforcement. It is a well-established principle of behavior modification that behaviors reinforced intermittently are much more resistant to extinction than are behaviors which are reinforced continuously. In terms of enhancing the maintenance of newly learned appropriate behaviors, the strategy should be: (1) rich, continuous levels of reinforcement initially to establish the behavior in the youngster's repertoire; (2) a shift as soon as possible to reinforcing the behavior every second or third time it occurs; and (3) a subsequent gradual shift to providing reinforcement for the behavior on only an occasional, highly intermittent basis.

Teaching Reinforceable Behaviors. The maintenance of behavior change will be enhanced if teacher decisions about which appropriate behaviors to be developed in the classroom reflect awareness of which appropriate behaviors are likely to be reinforced in other settings. Emphasize those appropriate behaviors which are likely to be relevant to and rewarded elsewhere in the school setting as well as at home, play, or other out-of-school contexts.

Create New Reinforcements. Maintenance may be facilitated by exposing the youngster to potential reinforcers not earlier chosen by him or her, but nevertheless of possible value or attractiveness. One common example of this reinforcer-creation possibility concerns youngsters who are initially minimally responsive to social reinforcement but who develop such responsiveness to praise, approval, and its other manifestations when the presentation of social reinforcement is consistently paired with presentations of material, activity, or token reinforcement.

Reprogram the Environment. Combining several of the features of the transfer-enhancing techniques of programmed generalization and variety learning, reprogramming the environment consists of having the main figures in the youngster's out-of-class environment collaborate in implementing the intervention in as many settings as possible. Other teachers, the youngster's parents, peers, and others may all profitably join in this maintenance-enhancing effort.

Self-Reinforcement. A youngster will often correctly utilize a newly learned appropriate behavior in an out-of-class setting and not be reinforced for the effort. A different teacher may ignore the behavior, peers may prefer the antisocial to the prosocial, parents may feel that the behavior is simply expected and deserves no special recognition. Whatever the sources of potential extinction, appropriate behaviors are more likely to be maintained under these circumstances when the youngster has been taught to give himself or herself what have been termed "self-messages" to the effect that he or she "did a good job" or "handled the situation well" or some similar self-reinforcing message. Developers of this technique have, furthermore, suggested that following the use of particularly difficult appropriate behaviors, the youngster might well not only say reinforcing things to himself or herself, but may also provide himself or herself with a desired material or activity reinforcer.

Transfer and maintenance enhancement are a crucial component of any behavior-modification effort, and thus we strongly urge their inclusion in classroom attempts to deal effectively with aggressive and disruptive youngsters. Further information regarding these transfer- and maintenance-enhancing techniques, as well as others, are provided at length in Goldstein and Kanfer (1979) and Karoly and Steffen (1980).

ETHICAL ISSUES

Earlier in this chapter we briefly alluded to a series of objections that have been raised, on ethical grounds, to the utilization of behavior-modification procedures in school settings. At this point, having both described these procedures in detail and underscored their behavior-change potency, we wish to readdress these ethical concerns in greater depth. The substantial, often dramatic effectiveness of behavior-modification procedures by no means inexorably dictates that such procedures must be used. There are criteria of acceptability which transcend effectiveness, criteria which—in addition to effectiveness—must unequivocally be met prior to the utilization of any behavioral or nonbehavioral procedure. Let us examine whether behavior-modification procedures meet such criteria.

Manipulation

Webster's Encyclopedic Dictionary (1973) defines manipulation as "the act of operating upon skillfully, for the purpose of giving a false appearance to" (p. 515). Unfortunately, what we perceive to be the all-too-frequent naive use of behavior-modification techniques has provided evidence for this negative view of behavioral technology as the clever (some would say Machiavellian) but not very thorough or long-lasting manipulation of surface behavior. In fact, we would agree that when behavior modification is used (as it sometimes is) by uninformed adults in a cursory and not very thoughtful way to control the behavior of other adults or of children, then Webster's definition may indeed apply. There is, however, another perspective on manipulation. With a small but significant change in its dictionary definition, we would grant that behavior modification is indeed manipulative. Were one to replace "false" in this definition with "changed," we would clearly label behavior modification as manipulation. Furthermore, in this altered definition, the term *manipulation* is in our view very far from a term of disapproval. In our sense of the term, *all* educational, psychological, and psychoeducational interventions are and optimally should be manipulative—the behavioral, the psychodynamic, the humanistic, and all others. Where approaches differ is in how effective their efforts are, and how open intervenors are—to both others and especially to themselves—to the notion that they are indeed "operating upon skillfully, for the purpose of giving a changed appearance to." Referring to therapeutic applications of behavior modification, O'Leary and Wilson (1975) have reflected this viewpoint well in their observation:

> Behavior modification is often indicted for supposedly denying individual freedom and for being a mechanistic, manipulative, and impersonal approach which deliberately sets out to control behavior. On the other hand, purportedly more humanistic forms of therapy are applauded because they claim to promote individual "growth" or "self-actualization" without imposing any external control. What such a comparison overlooks is the now widely accepted truism that all forms of therapy involve control or social influence. Truax (1966), for example, has shown how even Carl Rogers' "nondirective" therapy results in the therapist unwittingly reinforcing particular types of client verbalizations which the therapist believes to be therapeutic. The issue is not whether clients' behavior should or should not be controlled; it unquestionably is. The important question then becomes whether the therapist is aware of this control and the behaviors it is used to develop. (pp. 28–29)

Precisely the same point may be made about the everyday behavior of the typical classroom teacher. By dint of his or her presentation or withholding of approval, smiles, stares, touching, scolding, praise, permission to engage in pleasurable activities, denial of opportunity for such activities, and literally dozens of other reinforcement-relevant teacher behaviors, the teacher functions as a highly active, highly influential, highly manipulative (in our revised definitional sense) modifier of his or her students' behavior. Manipulation is present. Its effective and efficient utilization often are not. Hopefully, the presentation of behavior-modification procedures in the present chapter will serve as a small contribution to enhancing the effectiveness of their utilization.

Freedom of Choice

The technology of behavior modification has been criticized by some as resulting in a diminution of the target person's freedom of choice. Other people (the intervenor), it is held, act upon the person and, by the effective use of behavior-modification procedures, choose for that person the behaviors he or she comes to utilize. In our view, this is the least cogent argument that has been brought to bear in criticizing the ethics of behavior modification. In fact, on the contrary, we would agree with those who have held that *enhanced,* not diminished, freedom of choice is the net consequence of behavioral interventions for target youngsters. What intervenors do choose, should choose, are the *procedures* for reaching goal behaviors— that is, the "how" of behavior modification. The goals themselves, or the "what" of this intervention, as well as the "why" and "when" are at least in some instances selected not only by the teacher, and the teacher's school, and larger community but, when done properly, by the youngster himself or herself. Participation by the target youngster in goal-behavior selection is not always possible and is sometimes inappropriate. But in a great many interventions, though probably not the majority, what behaviors are pinpointed for modification will be a decision to which the youngster contributes substantially.

There is a second, equally significant way in which successful behavior modification produces enhanced freedom of choice. It does so by enlarging the target individual's behavioral repertoire. Prior to the successful application of, let us say, positive reinforcement for negotiating differences with a fellow student and time out for physically brawling with peers, a given youngster may well be essentially choiceless when faced with a dispute. That is, his or her prepotent response—to lash out, punch, fight—may be his or her *only* potential response.

Negotiation of disputes, calling upon others, withdrawal, or other possible and less aggressive responses may never have been used by the youngster, or may have been used exceedingly rarely, and hence for all practical purposes may not be alternatives he or she might choicefully call upon. In essence, not knowing alternatives at all or very well, the youngster has no choice. He or she *must* fight. When the behavioral intervention succeeds in increasing the likelihood of negotiation as a response by arming the youngster with this new alternative, the youngster is correspondingly armed with choicefulness. Now he or she may fight *or* negotiate as *he* or *she* chooses, and as *he* or *she* perceives the potential rewards and punishments of the two (or more) alternatives. The decision to use reinforcement and time out was largely the teacher's, the decision to reward negotiation behavior was hopefully jointly the teacher's and the youngster's, but the decision to actually negotiate a given dispute with a peer is and should be wholly the youngster's. Thus, the heart of our view is that by means of collaborating when possible in decisions about target behaviors to be modified, and by unilaterally deciding about the use or nonuse of newly learned (and heretofore unavailable, thus unchoosable) appropriate behaviors, behavior modification is indeed a choice-enhancing technology.

Bribery

The accusation that those behavior-modification procedures which present reinforcement for appropriate behaviors are equivalent to the use of bribery also seems erroneous to us. Bribery is defined as a prize, gift, or other favor bestowed or promised to pervert the judgment or corrupt the conduct of a person (Webster, 1973). In behavior modification, reinforcement is used neither to pervert nor corrupt but, instead, to reward and broaden the person's repertoire of personally and socially useful behaviors. A reward for the prosocial differs greatly in an ethical sense from one presented for the antisocial.

Yet the objection is raised, even when the distinction between bribery and appropriate reward is acknowledged, that youngsters should not need an external reward for doing what society expects them to do. Instead, negotiating disputes, paying attention, remaining in one's seat, speaking conversationally, not cursing, not fighting, and other desirable classroom behaviors should be intrinsically rewarding. This view, we feel, is both hypocritical and factually incorrect. It is hypocritical because reward *is* presented for appropriate behavior at all other levels of society—

not infrequently including teachers for their appropriate teaching behaviors, and to these same youngsters by these same teachers (in albeit unsystematic form) every teaching day. We also hold that it is factually incorrect that "youngster's should not need an external reward for doing what society expects them to do," because, simply put, some literally do. This generalization applies to many types of youngsters with special needs, and most certainly includes the chronically aggressive, disruptive, acting-out youngster of special concern to this book.

Whose Needs Are Served?

A further ethical concern we wish to examine pertains to decisions about whose needs will take precedence when choices must be made about whether or not to employ behavior-modification procedures in a given classroom, and about how to use them when they are employed. Among the earliest applied uses of behavior modification were attempts to employ it in mental hospitals to alter the behavior of long-term, adult psychiatric patients. Literally hundreds of research papers attest to the success of this effort. But which behaviors were altered? How was success defined? In far too large a percentage of these investigations, the "appropriate" behaviors successfully developed were patient behaviors whose occurrence met the needs of the staff (the intervenors) at least as much and often more than the patient's. "Good patient" behaviors were rewarded—that is, those behaviors which included patient compliance, passivity, and dependency, and which led to an orderly and predictable ward, one relatively comfortable and manageable for the staff. Such a regime, which has come to be appropriately known as a "colonization effect" for its robotizing influence upon patients, ill-prepared such patients for the demands of community living when the deinstitutionalization movement led to 400,000 of them (between 1965 and 1980) being discharged from America's public mental hospitals.

This apparent digression into the adult mental-health realm seems most relevant to our ethical classroom-relevant question, "Whose needs will be served?" Will it be the school's at large? The teacher's? The youngster's? Although it would be naive to argue that schools have not utilized behavior modification as a powerful tool to teach "good student" behaviors (the analog of "good patient" behaviors including compliance, passivity, and dependency), it would be equally foolish, in our view, to throw out the technology because some (perhaps many) schools and teachers have misused it. If our goal is to be truly helpful to youngsters and to enhance the educational and emotional potential of our students, and not only to maintain an orderly and manageable classroom, we would submit that teachers should and will make the decision to employ appropriate behavior-modification procedures with aggressive and other special-needs youngsters, and to apply them toward the development of appropriate behaviors which will contribute not only to a calm classroom climate, but which will also be functional and enhancing for the youngster and his or her needs both within school and elsewhere.

Responsiveness to Research

Behavior modification has suffered from bad press and bad public relations. Behavior modification—the specific procedures described in this chapter—has been both confused with Machiavellian fictional accounts of its substance (e.g., *Clockwork Orange*) and identified with other existing procedures which also seek to change behavior but by means having nothing whatsoever in common with behavior modification (e.g., psychosurgery, sterilization). This negative public image is all the more surprising when one recognizes the vast and almost unique level of empirical support which exists attesting to the real-world effectiveness of this approach. No other existing means for altering, influencing, or modifying human behavior in appropriate directions rests on a comparably broad and deep empirical foundation. It is our belief that one of our highest ethical responsibilities is to be responsive to objective evidence, to offer our students what research repeatedly demonstrates to be effective, to try to overcome one's own subjective biases, and to act in the welfare of others in ways which are most clearly indicated by cumulative scientific evidence. Meeting this ethical responsibility will, we feel, often mean modifying teacher behavior reflected in greater utilization of behavior-modification programs based on the thoughtful application of appropriate principles to the diverse manifestations of school violence. Finally, we must be careful in doing so that we not oversell this approach, however empirically based or utilitarian it appears to be. Although we have amply indicated that behavior-modification programs are quite often able to document their success in teaching appropriate behaviors to children and adults, much empirical work remains to be done. It is our hope that the creative researcher and thoughtful teacher will join one another in responding to this promising challenge.

REFERENCES

ADAMS, G. R. Classroom aggression: Determinants, controlling mechanisms, and guidelines for the implementation of a behavior modification program. *Psychology in the Schools*, 1973, *10*, 155–168.

ALLEN, K. E., HART, B., BUELL, J. S., HARRIS, F. R., & WORF, M. M. Effects of social reinforcement on isolate behavior of a nursery school child. *Child Development*, 1964, *35*, 511–518.

ALLEN, K. E., KENKE, L. B., HARRIS, F. R., BAER, D. M., & REYNOLDS, N. J. Control of hyperactivity by social reinforcement of attending behavior. *Journal of Educational Psychology*, 1967, *58*, 231–237.

ALLISON, T. S., & ALLISON, S. L. Time-out from reinforcement: Effect on sibling aggression. *Psychological Record*, 1971, *21*, 81–88.

AXELROD, S., & APSCHE, J. (Eds.). *The effects and side effects of punishment on human behavior*. New York: Academic Press, 1982.

AYLLON, T., & AZRIN, N. H. *The token economy: A motivational system for therapy rehabilitation*. New York: Appleton-Century-Crofts, 1968.

AYLLON, T., & MICHAEL, J. The psychiatric nurse as a behavioral engineer. *Journal of the Experimental Analysis of Behavior*, 1959, *2*, 323–334.

AZRIN, H. H., & HOLZ, W. C. Punishment. In W. K. Honig (Ed.), *Operant Behavior: Areas of research and application.* New York: Appleton-Century-Crofts, 1966.

BACHRACH, A. J., ERWIN, W. J., & MOHR, J. P. The control of eating behavior in an anorexic by operant conditioning techniques. In L. P. Ullmann & L. Krasner (Eds.), *Case studies in behavior modification.* New York: Holt, Rinehart & Winston, 1965.

BANDURA, A. *Principles of behavior modification.* New York: Holt, Rinehart & Winston, 1969.

BANDURA, A. *Aggression: A social learning analysis.* Englewood Cliffs, N.J.: Prentice-Hall, 1973.

BECKER, W. C., MADSEN, C. H., ARNOLD, C. R., & THOMAS, D. R. The contingent use of teacher attention and praise in reducing classroom behavior problems. *The Journal of Special Education,* 1967, *1,* 287–307.

BOSTOW, D. E., & BAILEY, J. S. Modification of severe disruptive and aggressive behavior using brief time out and reinforcement procedures. *Journal of Applied Behavior Analysis,* 1969, *2,* 31–37.

BROWN, P., & ELLIOTT, R. Control of aggression in a nursery school class. *Journal of Experimental Child Psychology,* 1965, *2,* 103–107.

BURCHARD, J. D., & BARRERA, F. An analysis of time out and response cost in a programmed environment. *Journal of Applied Behavior Analysis,* 1972, *5,* 271–282.

BUYS, C. J. Effects of teacher reinforcement on elementary pupils' behavior and attitudes. *Psychology in the Schools,* 1972, *9,* 278–288.

CALHOUN, K. S., & MATHERNE, P. The effects of varying schedules of time-out on aggressive behavior of a retarded girl. *Journal of Behavior Therapy and Experimental Psychiatry,* 1975, *6,* 139–143.

CARR, E. G. Contingency management. In A. P. Goldstein, E. G. Carr, W. Davidson, & P. Wehr. *In response to aggression.* New York: Pergamon Press, 1981.

CHRISTOPHERSON, E. R., ARNOLD, C. M., HILL, D. W., & QUILITCH, H. R. The home point system: Token reinforcement procedures for application by parents of children with behavior problems. *Journal of Applied Behavior Analysis,* 1972, *5,* 485–497.

CRONBACH, L. J., & SNOW, R. E. *Individual differences in learning ability as a function of instructional variables* (Office of Education Final Report). Stanford, Calif.: Stanford University, 1969.

DRABMAN, R. S., & SPITALNIK, R. Social isolation as a punishment procedure: A controlled study. *Journal of Experimental Child Psychology,* 1973, *16,* 236–249.

FERSTER, C. B., & DeMEYER, M. K. A method for the experimental analysis of the behavior of autistic children. *American Journal of Orthopsychiatry,* 1962, *32,* 89–98.

FERSTER, C. B., & SKINNER, B. F. *Schedules of reinforcement.* New York: Appleton-Century-Crofts, 1957.

FIRESTONE, P. The effects and side effects of time out on an aggressive nursery school child. *Journal of Behavior Therapy and Experimental Psychiatry,* 1976, *6,* 79–81.

FOREHAND, R., ROBERTS, M. W., DOLAYS, D. M., HOBBS, S. A., & RESICK, P. A. An examination of disciplinary procedures with children. *Journal of Experimental Child Psychology,* 1976, *21,* 109–120.

FOXX, R. M., & AZRIN, N. H. Restitution: A method of eliminating aggressive-disruptive behavior for retarded and brain damaged patients. *Behavior Research & Therapy,* 1973, *10,* 15–27.

GALASSI, M. D., & GALASSI, J. P. *Assert yourself!* New York: Human Science Press, 1977.

GAMBRILL, E. D. *Behavior modification.* San Francisco: Jossey-Bass, 1977.

GOLDSTEIN, A. P. (Ed.). *Prescriptions for child mental health and education.* New York: Pergamon Press, 1978.

GOLDSTEIN, A. P., & KANFER, F. *Maximizing treatment gains: Transfer-enhancement in psychotherapy.* New York: Academic Press, 1979.

GOLDSTEIN, A. P., LOPEZ, M., & GREENLEAF, D. M. Introduction. In A. P. Goldstein & F. H. Kanfer (Eds.), *Maximizing treatment gains.* New York: Academic Press, 1979.

GOLDSTEIN, A. P., & ROSENBAUM, A. *Aggress-less.* Englewood Cliffs, N.J.: Prentice-Hall, 1982.

GOLDSTEIN, A. P., SPRAFKIN, R. P., GERSHAW, N. J., & KLEIN, P. *Skillstreaming the adolescent.* Champaign, Ill.: Research Press, 1979.

GOLDSTEIN, A. P., & STEIN, N. *Prescriptive psychotherapies.* New York: Pergamon Press, 1976.

GREENWOOD, C. R., HOPS, H., DELQUADRI, J., & GUILD, J. Group contingencies for group consequences in classroom management: A further analysis. *Journal of Applied Behavior Analysis,* 1974, *7,* 413-425.

HAGEBAK, R. Disciplinary practices in Dallas. In D. G. Gil (Ed.), *Child abuse and violence.* New York: AMS Press, 1979.

HALL, R. V., AXELROD, S., FOUNDOPOULOS, M., SHELLMAN, J., CAMPBELL, R. A., & CRANSTON, S. S. The effective use of punishment to modify behavior in the classroom. *Educational Technology,* 1971, *11,* 24-26.

HALL, R. V., LUND, D., & JACKSON, D. Effects of teacher attention on study behavior. *Journal of Applied Behavior Analysis,* 1968, *1,* 1-12.

HALL, R. V., PANYAN, M., RABON, D., & BRODEN, M. Instructing beginning teachers in reinforcement procedures which improve classroom control. *Journal of Applied Behavior Analysis,* 1968, *1,* 315-322.

HOMME, L., CSANYI, A. P., GONZALES, M. A., & RECHS, J. R. *How to use contingency contracting in the classroom.* Champaign, Ill.: Research Press, 1969.

HUNT, D. E., & SULLIVAN, E. V. *Between psychology and education.* Hinsdale, Ill.: Dryden Press, 1974.

HYMAN, I. A. Is the hickory stick out of tune? *Today's Education,* 1978, *2,* 30-32.

JACKSON, D. A., DELLA-PIANA, G. M., & SLOANE, H. N. *How to establish a behavior observation system.* Englewood Cliffs, N.J.: Educational Technology Publications, 1975.

JONES, F. H., & MILLER, W. H. The effective use of negative attention for reducing group disruption in special elementary school classrooms. *The Psychological Record,* 1974, *24,* 435-448.

KAROLY, P. Operant methods. In F. Kanfer & A. P. Goldstein (Eds.), *Helping people change.* New York: Pergamon Press, 1980.

KAROLY, P., & STEFFEN, J. J. (Eds.). *Improving the long-term effects of psychotherapy.* New York: Gardner Press, 1980.

KAUFMAN, K. F., & O'LEARY, K. D. Reward, cost, and self-evaluation procedures for disruptive adolescents in a psychiatric hospital school. *Journal of Applied Behavior Analysis,* 1972, *5,* 293-310.

KAZDIN, A. E. *Behavior modification in applied settings.* Homewood, Ill.: Dorsey Press, 1975.

KAZDIN, A. E. *The token economy.* New York: Plenum, 1977.

KEELEY, S. M., SHEMBERG, K. M., & CARBONELL, J.   Operant clinical intervention: Behavior management or beyond? *Behavior Therapy,* 1976, *7,* 292–305.

KIRSCHNER, N. M., & LEVIN, L.   A direct school intervention program for the modification of aggressive behavior. *Psychology in the Schools,* 1975, *12,* 202–208.

LAZARUS, A. A., RACHMAN, S.   The use of systematic desensitization in psychotherapy. *South African Medical Journal,* 1967, *31,* 934–937.

LEITENBERG, H., AGRAS, W. S., THOMSON, L. E.   A sequential analysis of the effect of selective positive reinforcement in modifying anorexia nervosa. *Behaviour Research and Therapy,* 1968, *6,* 211–218.

LOVAAS, O. I., KOEGEL, R., SIMMONS, J. Q., & LONG, J. S.   Some generalization and follow-up measures on autistic children in behavior therapy. *Journal of Applied Behavior Analysis,* 1973, *6,* 131–166.

LOVAAS, O. I., SCHAEFFER, B., & SIMMONS, J.   Building social behavior in autistic children by use of electric shock. *Journal of Experimental Research in Personality,* 1965, *1,* 99–109.

MADSEN, C. J., BECKER, W. C., & THOMAS, D. R.   Rules, praise, and ignoring: Elements of elementary classroom control. *Journal of Applied Behavior Analysis,* 1968, *1,* 139–150.

MAURER, A.   Corporal punishment. *American Psychologist,* 1974, *29,* 614–626.

MORRIS, R. J.   *Behavior modification with children.* Cambridge, Mass.: Winthrop, 1976.

MOWRER, O. H., & MOWRER, W. A.   Enuresis: A method for its study and treatment. *American Journal of Orthopsychiatry,* 1938, *8,* 436–447.

NEWSOM, C., FAVELL, J. E., & RINCOVER, A.   The side effects of punishment. In S. Axelrod & J. Apsche (Eds.), *The effects and side effects of punishment on human behavior.* New York: Academic Press, 1982.

NOVACO, N. W.   *Anger control.* Lexington, Mass.: Lexington Books, 1975.

O'LEARY, K. D., & BECKER, W. C.   Behavior modification of an adjustment class: A token reinforcement program. *Exceptional Children,* 1967, *33,* 637–642.

O'LEARY, K. D., BECKER, W. C., EVANS, M. B., & SAUDARGAS, R. A.   A token reinforcement program in a public school: A replication and systematic analyses. *Journal of Applied Behavior Analysis,* 1969, *2,* 3–13.

O'LEARY, K. D., KAUFMAN, K. F., KASS, R. E., & DRABMAN, R. S.   The effects of loud and soft reprimands on the behavior of disruptive students. *Exceptional Children,* 1970, *37,* 145–155.

O'LEARY, K. D., & O'LEARY, S. G.   *Classroom management.* New York: Pergamon Press, 1980.

O'LEARY, S. G., & O'LEARY, K. D.   Behavior modification in the school. In H. Leitenberg (Ed.), *Handbook of behavior modification and behavior therapy.* Englewood Cliffs, N.J.: Prentice-Hall, 1976.

O'LEARY, K. D., & WILSON, G. T.   *Behavior therapy: Application and outcome.* Englewood Cliffs, N.J.: Prentice-Hall, 1975.

PATTERSON, G. R.   A learning theory approach to the treatment of the school phobic child. In L. P. Ullmann & L. Krasner (Eds.), *Case studies in behavior modification.* New York: Holt, Rinehart & Winston, 1965.

PATTERSON, G. R., COBB, J. A., & RAY, R. S.   A social engineering technology for retraining the families of aggressive boys. In H. E. Adams & I. P. Unikel (Eds.), *Issues and trends in behavior therapy.* Springfield, Ill.: Charles C Thomas, 1973.

PATTERSON, G. R., RAY, R., & SHAW, D.   *Direct intervention in families of deviant children.* Unpublished manuscript, University of Oregon, 1968.

PATTERSON, G. R., & REID, J. B. Reciprocity and coercion: Two facets of social systems. In C. Neurenger & J. Meichael (Eds.), *Behavior modification in clinical psychology.* New York: Appleton-Century-Crofts,

PERRY, M. A., & FURUKAWA, M. J. Modeling methods. In F. H. Kanfer & A. P. Goldstein (Eds.), *Helping people change* (2nd ed.). New York: Pergamon Press, 1980.

PINKSTON, E. M., REESE, N. M., LeBLANC, J. M., & BAER, D. M. Independent control of a preschool child's aggression and peer interaction by contingent teacher attention. *Journal of Applied Behavior Analysis,* 1973, *6,* 115-124.

RISLEY, T. R. The social context of self-control. In R. Stuart (Ed.), *Behavioral self management.* New York: Brunner/Mazel, 1977.

SAFER, D. J., & ALLEN, R. P. *Hyperactive children. Diagnosis and management.* Baltimore: University Park Press, 1976.

SAJWAJ, T., CULVER, P., HALL, C., & LEHR, L. Three simple punishment techniques for the control of classroom disruptions. In G. Semb (Ed.), *Behavior analysis and education.* Lawrence, Kansas: University of Kansas, 1972.

SARASON, I. G. Verbal learning, modeling, and juvenile delinquency. *American Psychologist,* 1968, *23,* 254-266.

SARASON, I. G., GLASER, E. M., & FARGO, G. A. *Reinforcing productive classroom behavior.* New York: Behavioral Publications, 1972.

SCHWITZGEBEL, R. *Street corner research: An experimental approach to the juvenile delinquent.* Cambridge, Mass.: Harvard University Press, 1964.

SEWELL, E., McCOY, J. F., & SEWELL, W. R. Modification of antagonistic social behavior using positive reinforcement for other behavior. *The Psychological Record,* 1973, *23,* 499-504.

SHERMAN, J. A. Use of reinforcement and imitation to reinstate verbal behavior in mute psychotics. *Journal of Abnormal Psychology,* 1965, *70,* 155-164.

SKINNER, B. F. *The behavior of organisms: An experimental analysis.* New York: Appleton-Century-Crofts, 1938.

SKINNER, B. F. *Science and human behavior.* New York: Macmillan, 1953.

STRAUGHAN, J. The application of operant conditioning to the treatment of elective mutism. In H. N. Sloane, Jr. & B. A. MacAulay (Eds.), *Operant procedures in remedial speech and language training.* Boston: Houghton Mifflin, 1968.

THARP, R. G., & WETZEL, R. J. *Behavior modification in the natural environment.* New York: Academic Press, 1969.

THOMAS, J. D., PRESLAND, I. E., GRANT, M. D., & GLYNN, T. L. Natural rates of teacher approval and disapproval in grade-7 classrooms. *Journal of Applied Behavior Analysis,* 1978, *11,* 91-94.

VAN HOUTON, R. Punishment: From the animal laboratory to the applied setting. In S. Axelrod & J. Apsche (Eds.), *The effects and side effects of punishment on human behavior.* New York: Academic Press, 1982.

VUKELICH, R., & HAKE, D. F. Reduction of dangerously aggressive behavior in a severely retarded resident through a combination of positive reinforcement procedures. *Journal of Applied Behavior Analysis,* 1971, *4,* 215-225.

WAHLER, R. G., & POLLIO, H. R. Behavior and insight: A case study in behavior therapy. *Journal of Experimental Research in Personality,* 1968, *3,* 45-56.

WAHLER, R. G., WINKEL, G. H., PETERSON, R. F., & MORRISON, D. C. Mothers as behavior therapists for their own children. *Behavior Research and Therapy,* 1965, *3,* 113-124.

WALKER, H. M. *The acting-out child: Coping with classroom disruption.* Boston: Allyn & Bacon, 1979.

WALKER, H. M., HOPS, H., & FIEGENBAUM, E.   Deviant classroom behavior as a function of combinations of social and token reinforcement and cost contingency. *Behavior Therapy,* 1976, *7,* 76–88.
WALKER, H. M., MATTSON, R. H., & BUCKLEY, N. K.   The function analysis of behavior within an experimental classroom setting. In W. C. Becker (Ed.), *An empirical basis for change in education.* Chicago: Science Research Associates, 1971.
WALKER, H. M., STREET, A., GARRETT, B., & CROSSEN, J.   Experiments with response cost in playground and classroom settings. Eugene, Oreg.: Center at Oregon for Research in the Behavioral Education of the Handicapped, University of Oregon, 1977.
WARD, M. H., & BAKER, B. L.   Reinforcement therapy in the classroom. *Journal of Applied Behavior Analysis,* 1968, *1,* 323–328.
WASIK, B., SENN, K., WELCH, R. H., & COOPER, B. R.   Behavior modification with culturally deprived school children: Two case studies. *Journal of Applied Behavior Analysis,* 1968, *2,* 171–179.
WATSON, J. B., & RAYNER, R.   Conditioned emotional reactions. *Journal of Experimental Psychology,* 1920, *3,* 1–114.
WEBSTER'S ENCYCLOPEDIC DICTIONARY OF THE ENGLISH LANGUAGE. Chicago: Consolidated Book Publishers, 1973.
WEBSTER, R. E.   A time-out procedure in a public school setting. *Psychology in the Schools,* 1976, *13,* 72–76.
WELSH, R. S.   Delinquency, corporal punishment and the schools. *Crime & Delinquency,* 1978, July, 336–354.
WHITE, G. D., NIELSON, G., & JOHNSON, S. M.   Time out duration and the suppression of deviant behavior in children. *Journal of Applied Behavior Analysis,* 1972, *5,* 111–120.
WHITE, M. A.   Natural rates of teacher approval and disapproval in the classroom. *Journal of Applied Behavior Analysis,* 1975, *8,* 367–372.
WOLF, M., RISLEY, T., & MEES, H.   Application of operant conditioning procedures to the behavior problems of an autistic child. *Behavior Research & Therapy,* 1964, *1,* 305–312.

4

Psychodynamic
And
Humanistic
Interventions

It has taken a long time for many child therapists and authorities in the field of early childhood education to discover that a child can derive pleasure not only by satisfying the primitive impulses of the id but by developing an ego that can control these impulses and that can function autonomously and effectively within the realm of reality. It is becoming quite evident that most disturbed children not only can find satisfaction by assuming responsibilities, following directions, completing difficult tasks, and mastering new skills—but that they grow and thrive in the process . . . .

We have found that working with seriously disturbed children the differentiation often made between education and therapy becomes largely a semantic one. A teacher who fosters self-discipline, emotional growth and more effective functioning is doing something therapeutic. Any educational process that helps to correct or reduce a child's distorted perceptions, disturbed behavior and disordered thinking, and that results in greater mastery of self and one's surroundings is certainly a therapeutic process. (Fenichel, 1966, p. 17)

In their review of research on crime in schools, McPartland and McDill (1977) identified five major themes in theories of youth crime:

1. The theme of *restricted opportunity* emphasizes the barriers many young people must hurdle to achieve the good jobs, material possessions, and status that symbolize the American dream. In this view, criminal acts are representative of youngsters' frustration directed at the system which holds them back. Schools are easily identifiable targets.

2. The theme of *subcultural differences in values and attitudes* posits that, for whatever reason, subcultures exist in which middle-class values and aspirations are rejected and crime and violence are a fact of life. In neighborhoods and communities in which the deviant subculture takes hold, residents are continually exposed to violent behaviors and the supports needed to combat such actions can deteriorate rapidly.

   Interestingly, McPartland and McDill (1977) point out that the deviant subculture may be neither deviant nor a subculture if America is indeed the "violent society" many now claim it to be.

3. The third theme, *prolonged adolescent dependence,* is based on the contradictory experience of most teenagers in America today. Even though most
adolescents have the ability to take on adult responsibilities and the desire to
be autonomous, society seems to provide no place for their contributions.
The frustrations engendered by adolescents as the result of this state of affairs
may often find an outlet in delinquent behaviors designed to demonstrate
independence.

4. The fourth theme states that *seriously damaged personalities,* more than
environmental and societal conditions, are the basis for the most serious
criminal behaviors among youth. Delinquency, in this view, is the expression
of the individual's inability to control his or her own aggressive and antisocial impulses. Youngsters who commit violent criminal acts are probably
seriously emotionally disturbed.

5. According to the theme of *labeling and stereotyping,* a youngster may come
to view himself or herself as criminal or delinquent or "bad" because others
in authority continually communicate that image to him or her. Such a
process may be viewed as an example of a self-fulfilling prophecy in which
the imposition of a label sets in motion a chain of events that validates the
label or stereotype. (pp. 86–87)

Although McPartland and McDill note that the first three themes just listed
(restricted opportunity, subcultural differences, and prolonged adolescent dependence) are primarily sociological in nature, and the last two themes (seriously damaged personalities, and labeling and stereotyping) more psychologically based, each
of the five themes may be viewed in relation to a psychodynamic perspective. Such
a viewpoint seeks to understand human nature through analysis of the internal
processes and forces which are assumed to be the basis for behavior.

In this view, deviant behavior is a symptom of unresolved (and usually unconscious) underlying disturbances and often occurs when the individual's control
system is unable to control his or her impulses. Thus, the youngster who commits a
violent or criminal act may have failed to successfully "work through" the intra-
psychic conflicts that he or she faced in the process of psychological and physical
development.

Consequently, whether it is restricted opportunity that heightens frustration
and aggressive impulses, or a deviant subculture that weakens internal controls, or
prolonged adolescent dependence that places extra strains on an already overloaded
developmental period, a psychodynamic position can be useful in understanding
motivations and in developing interventions. Such a perspective can be equally
helpful in our efforts to understand seriously damaged personalities and the effects
of labeling and stereotyping on youngsters' self-concepts.

In this chapter, we examine the psychodynamic point of view as originally
conceptualized by Freud and others. In addition, we focus on one of the major
outgrowths of psychodynamic theory: humanistic psychology. Finally, we review
pertinent research in these areas, describe programs and interventions for youngsters
who display violent and aggressive behaviors in schools that have their basis in these
theoretical positions, and try to summarize the impact of the psychodynamic perspective on the problems of violence in schools.

Although there is much to be discussed regarding the application of psychodynamic principles to the problems of aggressive and violent behavior in schools, the professional literature does not provide many examples of controlled and data-based studies that might offer valid and reliable evidence of the effectiveness of psychodynamic techniques. Nevertheless, as we shall see, the psychodynamic approach has had an enormous impact on clinical and educational efforts to serve troubled youngsters and we try to bring the most relevant aspects of this very extensive position to light in this chapter.

THE PSYCHODYNAMIC POSITION

According to Chess and Hassibi (1978):

> The central concepts of psychoanalytic theory can be described as follows: all behavior, thoughts, feelings, acts, dreams, and fantasies—whether normal or pathological, rational or accidental—are motivated and meaningful, even though the motivation may be obscure and the meaning not easily discerned. The ultimate motivating forces in all behavioral phenomena are the instinctual drives. Because the immediate and direct gratification of these drives is incompatible with the social existence of man, the individual must develop indirect means and compromises to adapt to external reality and find acceptable ways of gratification. Conflict is therefore the inevitable component of the intrapsychic life of the individual.
>
> The most important instinctual drive in psychoanalytic theory is sexuality (libido). Aggression is postulated as another basic instinct.
>
> . . . Instinctual drives are viewed as possessing energy. Although nonquantifiable, this energy is like an electrical charge that propels every aspect of behavior. (p. 46)

We can see in the preceding quotation that the core of the psychodynamic position is the continual conflict between inner impulses and the individual's efforts to control or at least assure the socially acceptable gratification of his or her instinctual drives. As each infant grows and develops, reality demands increase and immediate gratification becomes more difficult to attain. A conscious self begins to develop to control the infant's unconscious wishes and demands.

In order to fully understand psychodynamic thought, then, one must be aware of the three major personality systems: the id, ego, and superego—three hypothetical constructs that form the basis of psychological development in this view. The id represents instinctual energy (it is the only system present at birth) and its power is used in the service of the "pleasure principle" (the constant effort to achieve gratification and to avoid pain). The superego represents societal values and often conflicts directly with the id. The ego serves as the mediating system, walking through the conflicts between id and superego by the use of logic and rationality (the "reality principle"), in an effort to control or neutralize the impulses of the id.

When the three systems work together productively, the person is able to meet his or her needs without trespassing on others' rights or society's rules and he or she is said to be well-adjusted. When the systems are in conflict—if, for example, the id's impulses are too strong to control—then the child is said to be maladjusted and deviant behavior may result.

It is also necessary to understand the role of anxiety in the psychodynamic position. When instinctual drives, in their efforts to find immediate gratification, threaten to overwhelm the ego, the arousal of anxiety is the likely result. When this occurs, the ego must redouble its control efforts, using one or more of the defense mechanisms (repression, regression, rationalization, sublimation, etc.) to reassert control over the id. When the efforts of the ego fail and the impulses of the id are allowed to proceed unchecked, personality disorganization, deviant behavior, and other symptoms of emotional disturbance frequently appear.

Reinert (1976) summarizes it this way:

> From a psychodynamic point of view the child in conflict has not negotiated, at a successful level, the various intrapsychic and external conflicts that he faced in the process of psychological and/or physiological maturity. (p. 93)

In addition to the three major personality systems, psychoanalytic thought is also based on a sequence of five psychosexual developmental stages. Beginning from birth, the stages are: oral, anal, phallic, latency, and genital. Each child passes relatively systematically through the developmental stages, though some overlapping of stages does occur. Though it is not uncommon for problems to occur even in the development of typical children, disturbed youngsters often fail to resolve the dilemmas presented by one or another of the psychosexual stages.

From a psychodynamic perspective, the first three stages are critical, because by the time the youngster has completed the phallic stage the basic personality components have been established. If problems have been resolved successfully in those early years, later difficulties are less likely. Problem behaviors might develop because a child invests too much psychic energy in one stage and has insufficient resources to meet the next, or a youngster has difficulty at later stages and may regress to behavior characteristics of earlier times.

In their classic follow-up study of juvenile delinquents, Glueck and Glueck (1940) noted that many of the offenders whom they studied could be viewed as fixated at earlier levels of development:

> In fact, from many angles the conduct of not a few offenders, when passed in review over the years, may be regarded as infantile: witness their impulsiveness, their lack of planfulness, their failure to postpone immediate desires for more distant ones, their incapacity or unwillingness to profit by numerous experiences of punishment or correction, the excessive attachment of many of them to their mothers, their inability to assume marital, family, and other responsibilities appropriate to their chronological age. (p. 268)

In addition to the psychosexual stages proposed by Freud and just described, Erikson (1950) developed a sequence of eight psychosocial stages based on the developing individual's changing social relationships. In Erikson's view, psychological health and pathology are determined as much by the individual's relation to society as they are by his or her inner conflicts. Again, in order from birth, those stages are: basic trust versus mistrust, autonomy versus shame and doubt, initiative versus guilt, industry versus inferiority, identity versus identity diffusion, intimacy versus isolation, generativity versus stagnation, and ego integration versus despair. Because progress through the psychosocial developmental stages is so individualized, dependent as it is on our unconscious internal impulses and the idiosyncratic events of our external environments, each person develops a unique personal history that is critical to an understanding of behavior.

According to Morse, Smith, and Acker (1977), the assumptions made by the psychodynamic viewpoint—that unconscious internal impulses and forces motivate human behavior, that personality is dynamic and develops in terms of psychosexual and psychosocial stages, and that each person develops a unique psychological history—have important implications for work with children who commit deviant acts:

> These assumptions have important implications for educators. First, we expect that children of the same chronological age will be at different developmental levels, and that they may regress at times to earlier stages. Second, children have different degrees of knowledge and control over their internal motivating forces. Third, behaviors which appear to be abnormal may actually be normal for a child at a particular developmental stage. Fourth, a child's behavior in any setting is indicative of strong underlying needs and impulses. (pp. 12–13)

One basic premise of the psychodynamic model is that disturbed behavior is determined by psychological processes. Psychopathology is determined by the way in which the individual's psychological makeup—thoughts, feelings, perceptions, needs, and so on—responds to the events of everyday life. Though everyone brings inherited potentialities to life situations, it is the specific manner in which those genetic or biological factors interact with particular aspects of the individual's own life space that results in the development of maladaptive or disturbed behavior.

Nick Long (1966) has developed a framework for understanding the interaction between biological potential and environmental influences previously described. According to Long's cycle, each child's innate inherited potential is soon subjected to the stresses and strains of the youngster's environment with anxiety the likely result. The youngster's efforts to ward off the anxiety by employing one or another of the defense mechanisms usually results in increased conflicts, especially in school settings. Consequently, that conflict produces more anxiety and the cycle is repeated continuously.

In summary, the following characteristics are important aspects of the psychodynamic viewpoint:

1. All behavior—thoughts, feelings, acts, dreams, and so on—is meaningful though the meaning is not always clear to the behaver or to an observer. The meaning must be understood in order to develop effective behavior-change interventions.

2. All children have some basic needs that must be met in order to develop healthy personalities. These include the need for food and shelter, love, security, belonging, success, and so on.

3. The quality of the emotional relationship a child has with his or her family and other significant people in his or her life is of crucial significance.

4. Each child goes through several stages of emotional growth. Traumatic experiences and deprivations may interfere with this growth and result in lasting personality disturbances.

5. Anxiety over unmet needs and inner conflicts is an important determinant in behavior disorders. The individual's ability to cope with anxiety is critical.

6. Behaviors that reflect a state of emotional disturbance are caused primarily by internal psychic pathology—conflicts between impulses and controls.

7. Both biological forces and early environmental influences contribute to the pathological condition.

PSYCHODYNAMIC INTERVENTIONS

Although it is difficult to find in the professional literature a body of work in which psychodynamic formulations are used as the basis of intervention efforts aimed specifically at the problem of school violence, the psychodynamic viewpoint, nonetheless, has had a significant impact on efforts to control aggressive behavior in schools. When youngsters commit violent or aggressive acts in school in sufficient numbers or in sufficient intensity to require intervention by school authorities, it is quite likely that those youngsters will be viewed (and probably labeled) as emotionally disturbed. When we examine the history of interventions with youngsters labeled emotionally disturbed, it is easy to see the wide-ranging impact of the psychodynamic point of view.

For many years, at the beginning of the short history of educating disturbed children, the psychodynamic model represented the only point of view in the field. Juul (1977) noted that the exclusive usage of the model in that early time created the following lasting impact:

1. With its revelations of the rich and complex inner life of children, it has created in parents and teachers a new sensitivity to children's feelings and needs.

2. The discoveries of the devastating effects that emotional deprivation in early childhood has on personality development led to major reforms in child care institutions and agencies.

3. Teachers have become conscious about their importance to their pupils as models and as objects of identification. They also realize that through their relations with their children they can alleviate many emotional problems and create security and confidence. (pp. 13–14)

Psychodynamic theory has had a very significant influence on work with troubled children. Some applications include: milieu therapy, life-space interviewing, play therapy, art, music, and dance therapy, classrooms in psychiatric clinics, and many more. According to Newcomer (1980), the psychodynamic model has made several important contributions to educational programming for disturbed children. First, it has emphasized the premise that personality characteristics are determined by early childhood events. For disturbed youngsters, this implies that emotional distress is caused in early family relationships and that school problems are simply repeat manifestations of those early disturbances. As a result, psychodynamic thinking has focused considerably on child- and family- —not school— intervention strategies.

Second, psychodynamic models are based on the notion "that abnormal behaviors are symptoms of unconscious conflict" (Newcomer, 1980, p. 38). Consequently, educators must realize that troubled children are frequently not conscious of the rationale or motivation for their inappropriate behavior, nor are they able to consciously control that behavior. From this view, then, an additional implication is that treatment of symptoms (overt behavior) may simply result in the substitution of other more problematic symptoms and should thus be avoided. Instead, youngsters should be encouraged to express their feelings and educators should be trained to provide environments that do not repress youngsters' symptomatology and their opportunities to express the underlying conflicts.

Newcomer (1980) summarizes the positive contributions of the psychodynamic model as follows:

1. Children do not always consciously plan and cannot always consciously control disruptive behaviors, therefore when they misbehave they should not be treated punitively;
2. Hostility directed to the teacher should not be viewed as a personal insult since it might stem from a variety of motivations and does not necessarily mean that the child dislikes the teacher;
3. Children respond to internal conflicts, therefore, inconsistencies in behavior should be expected. (p. 38)

As we have seen, the psychodynamic viewpoint considers deviant behavior as the product of conflict between a child's impulse system and his or her control system. When impulses overwhelm controls, the child's behavior may be aggressive and unpredictable. When the control system is overdeveloped and impulses (even positive ones) are constantly quashed, the child may be inhibited and withdrawn. Consequently, depending on the nature of the youngster's difficulty, interventions may attempt either to help the child learn to express positive impulses appropriately and/or to develop appropriate and effective controls.

It must be emphasized that from this perspective, deviant behavior is symptomatic of underlying disturbance caused by failures to resolve developmental conflicts and/or fixation at earlier stages of development. Such underlying disturbances can manifest themselves in a variety of ways and settings; conflicts produced in the home may surely have an influence on the child's behavior at school.

According to Morse et al. (1977), the goals of psychodynamic interventions with troubled children may be internal, behavioral, or environmental. Internal goals focus on changes in the youngster's feelings about himself or herself and others. Behavioral goals may center on efforts to help children control negative impulses and to express feelings in socially acceptable ways. Environmental goals include attempts to provide children with surroundings that offer the emotional supports needed for positive growth and development.

In all cases, psychodynamic interventions assume that:

1. The youngster is usually not consciously aware of the source of his or her problem.
2. Changing surface behavior is less important than dealing with underlying conflicts.
3. Change requires the development of insight into past and present conflicts and the development of new and more productive patterns of behavior.
4. Treatment for pathological behaviors is typically long and difficult.

To a great extent, the application of psychodynamic principles to the remediation of aggressive behavior in school-age children and youth may be traced to the work of Fritz Redl and his colleagues. Redl's work with delinquent youngsters in the 1940s and 1950s served as the impetus for the creation of a variety of techniques for the control of violent actions; these are still utilized successfully by many teachers at the present time. Redl (1969) has also reaffirmed the psychodynamic emphasis on understanding underlying motivations as a necessary beginning to the planning of interventions. Such an emphasis can be clearly read in Redl's discussion of the differences between three kinds of aggression which youngsters may display in school and which teachers must confront:

> *First,* it is an input from the home or from the community. A teenager gets hopping mad at his old man, but he doesn't dare let off steam until he gets to school. Now, the teacher didn't produce the aggression, but he's there and he's got to handle it.
>
> *Second,* is the discharge from within. Some youngsters sit there daydreaming, and all of a sudden during a wild fantasy, he thinks of something that upsets him and he conks his neighbors on the head. None of them have done anything to him, and the teacher hasn't either. Something just burst out from within. (If youngsters are seriously disturbed, most of the aggression comes from way within, and neither they nor anyone else knows why.)
>
> *Third,* the aggression is engendered right there in the classroom. It may be triggered either by what the teacher does that's right but that doesn't happen to fit the kid, or by God knows what—the kid's reaction to the group or to other kids, or to something that maybe the teacher wouldn't have done if he had stopped to think. But anyway, it's reactive to something in the environment at the moment.
>
> Now, if I were a classroom teacher, I would like to know how much of which of those three packages is exploding before me, because it makes a difference in terms of long-range planning. It also makes some difference in terms of what to do at the moment.
>
> . . . The way Joe or Jane expresses aggression, while not the end of what we're looking for, certainly should be the starting point. Unless you know what lies behind their behavior, you will have trouble knowing how to handle it. (pp. 30–31)

Redl's psychodynamic view of aggressive behavior is based on the premise that aggressive youngsters have failed to develop appropriate ego skills. As a result of such disturbances in their "control systems," aggressive youngsters, in Redl's view, tend to make more than their share of faulty decisions. Frequently, such children are overwhelmed by inner impulses and find themselves unable to suppress or divert the inappropriate expression of feelings. The actions that result are often antisocial and unacceptable and have the net effect of causing further problems for the youngster in question. In turn, the youngster's likely reaction to these predicaments is even more inappropriate behavior, because his or her control system is simply unable to deal effectively with the anxiety aroused by the worsening conflict.

Interventions for such youngsters, according to Redl, fall into two major categories: assisting youngsters in the control of their aggressive impulses (manipulations of surface behavior) and helping youngsters develop better understanding of their own motivations and the options available to them for more appropriate expressions of feelings (clinical exploitation of life events). We discuss each of these intervention categories in turn, but it is important first to point out that both kinds of interventions are based on two essential principles:

1. Interpersonal relationships are essential to positive psychological growth and development. Youngsters with deficient ego skills are particularly unlikely to have developed rewarding relationships and adults who intend to intervene effectively with such children should focus on the development of a relationship right from the start.

    This is essential because the adult must often "lend" his or her own ego skills to the youngster and provide the controls which the youngster has yet to develop. Without concomitant efforts to develop a trusting and supporting relationship, such efforts are likely to be misunderstood. In addition, the development of a positive adult-child relationship can make the adult's messages more "receivable" by the youngster (If I can see that you care about me, maybe it's worth considering what you have to say or modeling some of your actions.).

2. Program planning is critical in efforts with troubled youngsters. What kinds of activities to plan, and for what particular purposes, and for which children are questions adults must continually ask themselves.

    Redl and others who espouse a psychodynamic viewpoint are most concerned with the mental-hygiene goals of programming—that is, the ability of planned activities to help youngsters drain off excessive impulsive energy, avoid frustration, reduce the threat of new situations, accept gradually increasing levels of organization, and so on. Thus, programs must be planned for the dual purpose of supporting egos, deficient though they may be, while at the same time working to increase a wide range of important ego skills and strengths.

We turn now to a more extensive discussion of Redl's techniques for assisting youngsters in the control of their aggressive impulses. Redl points out that these ideas are neither magic nor even necessarily new. All the techniques listed will not "work" for all children at all times, nor should we expect them to be so universally effective. The key to the effective usage of these intervention strategies is for adults to "know" and understand something about the youngsters who confront them.

ANTISEPTIC MANIPULATIONS
OF SURFACE BEHAVIOR

Redl and Wineman (1957) note that whereas clinicians have often been concerned with long-term change of strongly rooted problems through the slow dissolution of causal chains, educators and others who spend their days with aggressive children are more concerned with learning how to stop youngsters' inappropriate behavior immediately. From their perspective, Redl and Wineman (1957) note three major reasons for the amalgamation of clinical and educational practices:

1. Regardless of the long-term therapeutic goal, reality demands interference into a variety of child behaviors. Obviously, youngsters about to hurt themselves or others, regardless of the underlying motivation impelling them to do so, must be stopped.
2. Behaviors that call for immediate intervention also require *antiseptic* manipulation; in addition to being effective, the techniques utilized must not do *harm* to the overall clinical goals.
3. Planned interference can be a clinical tool itself, not just an unavoidable compromise of valid therapeutic technique. Total permissiveness is not the wisest clinical policy for such youngsters and the right kind of intervention applied at the proper place and time may be just what is needed.

On the basis of the rationale just outlined, Redl and Wineman described seventeen ways in which inappropriate surface behaviors can be antiseptically manipulated.

Planned Ignoring

Because much of the children's behavior that may be bothersome to adults is often abandoned when the youngsters lose interest, adults can help decrease the intensity and/or frequency of such behavior by not attending to it—that is, by planned ignoring of the behavior. Interestingly, although this is a principle of behavioral intervention developed in a psychodynamic perspective, note that planned ignoring is also an essential element of the behavioral position described elsewhere in this book (see extinction, p. 54). Redl and Wineman point out that even though it is easy to think of examples of behavior that can profitably be ignored, the deceptively simple skill of knowing which behaviors to ignore is an extremely important asset for those who work with aggressive children.

Signal Interference

A great deal of aggressive behavior may actually occur because a youngster's control system has not been alerted to rapidly developing seduction in the environment. In such cases, an adult can arrest the behavior by signaling its unacceptability in a friendly and nonthreatening way. The adult's signal reactivates the youngster's control system and the inappropriate behavior is not expressed.

Proximity and Touch Control

Under certain conditions, physical proximity lends support to the youngster's ego and consequently to the maintenance of appropriate behavior even in the fact of temptation. This may be seen as a continuum with some youngsters who respond to more active expressions of closeness (i.e., touch control) and some who need only minimal evidence of adult nearness (simply the presence of the adult in the general area) in order to control their behavior.

Involvement in Interest Relationship

Youngsters with ego disturbances, according to Redl and Wineman (1957), "seem to need a more constant revival of the vitality of their interest fields by direct adult participation" (p. 410). Adults can divert inappropriate behaviors by demonstrating interest in more socially acceptable uses of a new toy or otherwise showing interest in those things that interest the child.

Hypodermic Affection

Sometimes youngsters need a burst of affection or love to help their egos retain control of their impulses. For example, if a youngster's aggressiveness increases because of the fear that he or she is not liked, a "shot of love" is likely to be a more effective intervention than a more typical adult reaction to the aggressive act itself.

Tension Decontamination through Humor

Sometimes, despite the intensity of a youngster's ego impairment, he or she can be "kidded out of" performing aggressive or violent acts. Redl and Wineman posit that humor is probably effective because: it demonstrates the invulnerability of the adult to the child's destructive impulses, it saves the child from the retaliation and/or guilt that might have followed the inappropriate behavior, it enables the youngster to "save face," and so on. Whatever the reason, humor can be an effective way to stop the behavior *and* the production of secondary complications (i.e., contagion to other members of the group).

Hurdle Help

Aggressive outbursts may result from the inability of the control system to withstand the impulses generated by certain frustration-producing events. When goal-directed behavior is blocked, torrents of inappropriate behavior may be a troubled child's only available response. In such cases, adults can prevent the occurrence of aggression by timely efforts to help youngsters hurdle the obstacles in their paths. This is a particularly useful intervention in school programs, as the sensitive educator realizes, for example, that a child's inability to complete the first problem in a math test might result in the expression of considerable aggressive behavior.

Interpretation as Interference

Simply stated, this technique involves the use of interpretation to help a youngster understand a particular situation and his or her own contribution to it. Ultimately, of course, the purpose is to stop inappropriate behavior by interpreting it to the child. Redl and Wineman point out that this technique is effective only when there is a possibility that a youngster might act differently if he or she understood the situation differently.

Regrouping

Because problem behavior may stem from the psychological makeup of the group, changing the composition of that group may reduce the incidence of aggressive and violent episodes. This may be done on at least three different levels: total regrouping in which a particular youngster must be placed in a different setting because of the failure to match him or her to an appropriate group in the first setting; partial regrouping that involves a shift in the composition of a group within the setting; and "distributional" changes that simply alter the responsibilities and interactions within a group without necessitating a change in membership.

Restructuring

Sometimes even the most carefully planned programs do not work out as intended. In these cases, even "normal" children are known to respond by "acting out" and sensitive adults realize the need to restructure the activity. For example, if youngsters become restless because they have had to sit still for a prolonged period, a wise teacher or group leader will change to a more active format.

Direct Appeal

Perhaps because we view youngsters with ego disturbances as lacking in inner understanding, the tendency is to underutilize the technique of direct appeal. Redl and Wineman point out, however, that once relationships between children and adults begin to develop, direct appeal may be more effective than many adults realize. Depending on the youngster and his or her relationship to the adult, appeals might be made on a variety of bases, including: personal relationships, physical reality, outsiders' sensitivities, values, the group code, narcissistic pride, personal considerations, and others.

Limitation of Space and Tools

This technique may be thought of on two levels. First, problem behavior can often be prevented by the strategic limitation of space and tools. For example, it is clearly seductive to leave cash or potentially dangerous implements where youngsters with inadequate control mechanisms have easy access to them (and to the problems that will likely occur when impulses overwhelm controls).

Second, when inappropriate behavior occurs as the result of inappropriate use of space or tools, intervention of this sort (taking the tool away, refusing entrance to the space, etc.) may be necessary.

Antiseptic Bouncing

Under certain circumstances, the removal of a child from the scene of conflict may be the only way to intervene. Redl and Wineman caution that this technique ought to be used in situations of an "emergency" nature, as well as to prevent emergencies from occurring, and must be done without anger and hostility on the adult's part. For example, antiseptic bouncing may be called for when clear physical dangers exist, when the youngster's very presence stirs up unending contagion to other group members or makes it impossible for the youngster himself or herself to calm down, or when the issue is so critical that a clear demonstration of limits by the adult is mandated.

Physical Restraint

Some youngsters are prone to violent fits of rage characterized by hitting, kicking, biting, screaming, swearing, lashing out, and so on. This total loss of control may occur spontaneously and it is often difficult for adults to understand the precipitating factors. Redl and Wineman point out that the major concern with such episodes is that the child's loss of control makes it impossible to communicate with his or her ego and renders adults powerless. Whatever relationship may have developed between adult and child vanishes temporarily in the rage of the moment.

At such times, the only useful adult intervention may be physical restraint. This is to be done reasonably but firmly and should not be viewed as in any way related to physical punishment. The adult must use no more force than is absolutely necessary to restrain the youngster's inappropriate behavior. In Redl and Wineman's (1957) words, the attitude to be conveyed refuses to take the child's wild behavior seriously:

> Listen, kid, this is nuts. There is not the slightest reality reason for you to act that way. We like you. There is nothing to fear, but there is also nothing to gain by such behavior. You didn't get us mad by it, for we know you can't help it right now. But we sure hope this will reduce as time goes on. We aren't holding it against you, either. We want only one thing: get it over with, snap back into your more reasonable self, so we can communicate with you again. (p. 454)

Clearly, though Redl and Wineman would not use these words with the youngster in need of restraint, they emphasize the importance of applying physical restraint antiseptically. This is done by demonstrating a valuing of the person and a refusal to acknowledge the wild and aggressive behavior as characteristic of the child's true personality.

Permission and "Authoritative Verbot"

The use of permission falls into three categories: to begin a piece of appropriate behavior that might otherwise have been blocked, to reduce the occurrence of behavior that was meant to irritate or antagonize, or to keep an activity at a manageable level and within tolerable limits.

Authoritative verbot is simply a flowery term for the clear, firm, and unequivocal "No" which behavior sometimes mandates but adults may be hesitant to express. Again, this must be expressed antiseptically, without adult anger or anxiety, and in a friendly—not challenging—tone.

Promises and Rewards

From a psychodynamic point of view, the pleasure principle indicates that youngsters, even those with severe ego disturbances, will be inclined to engage in behavior that brings them pleasure (or the promise of pleasure). Redl and Wineman point out, however, that the effective use of promises and rewards depends on a number of factors: the youngster's ability to relate to the future and delay gratification, the youngster's ability to live up to a contract and "deserve" rewards, the youngster's ability to accept the implications of individual differences (different rewards and different expectations for different children), and so on. All of these abilities are not usually well developed in the aggressive children described by Redl and Wineman.*

Punishments and Threats

This technique also relies on the assumption that youngsters will seek both pleasure and the avoidance of pain. Punishment is very complex, however, and may raise as many problems as it seems to remediate. For the youngsters with impaired ego functioning whom they served, Redl and Wineman did not view punishment as a very viable control technique until later stages of the relationship, if at all.**

Threats may be used profitably if expressed in neutral terms as signals of the consequences of behavior ("If you do this, then that will probably happen."). As warnings of punishment about to occur, however, threats are as complex and difficult to implement as the punishments themselves.

The strategies just described above are meant to handle surface behaviors but they may also be used as part of the effort to "clinically exploit life events." In the next section we focus on the clinical exploitation of life events, paying special attention to one particularly useful tool in that domain, the Life-Space interview.

*The behavior-modification perspective on the use of rewards is presented on pages 50 to 53.

**The behavior-modification perspective on the use of punishment is presented on pages 63 to 67.

LIFE-SPACE INTERVIEWS

The concept of Life-Space stems from the work of Kurt Lewin who noted that Behavior (B) was a joint function of personal factors (P) and the perceived environment (E): ($B = f[P, E]$). A person's Life-Space then represents the continual interaction between inner and outer forces and equals the individual's psychological world at any given moment.

A Life-Space must be viewed through the eyes of its "owner." The realities of the situation are less important than the individual's interpretation or perception of the surrounding environment, because perceptions serve as guides to behavior.

From the psychodynamic view, all behavior is meaningful. The Life-Space interview tries to discover the meaning of specific behaviors by examining the reasoning that led up to them. The operating assumption here is that if the reasoning process can be understood, then new and more appropriate concluding behaviors can be developed and incorporated into the child's repertoire. The child can learn new ego skills.

Interviewing by appointment, the traditional clinical format, was not viewed by Redl and Wineman as a powerful enough tool. Alternatively, Life-Space interviewing is an attempt to help an aggressive youngster focus on feelings and actions and life events as close in time as possible to their actual occurrence. Redl and Wineman have described a number of types of interviews (the "rub-in" of outside realities, the "guilt squeeze," the "expressive" interview, etc.) that might be profitably utilized in a Life-Space interview process. Here, we can review the two major subdivisions of Life-Space interviewing: *emotional first aid* and *clinical exploitation of life events.*

Emotional first aid is the name for the quick action by adults that is necessary to prevent physical or emotional damage to the youngster. It is sometimes necessary to set the stage by using emotional first aid to help the child regain control of his or her impulses *before* meaningful talk can occur. Specific components might include:

1. *Draining off frustration acidity* by saying something such as, "It's OK to be mad." or "Let's get a drink of water before we talk about it."
2. *Support for management of panic, fury, and guilt.* "I can see you feel bad about what happened. Try to calm down and then you can tell me about it."
3. *Communication maintenance,* which includes a variety of efforts to erase blocks to communication. It includes setting limits ("You have to stay here with me right now."), changing pace (using nonthreatening "ice-breakers" to keep the talk flowing), and reflecting the child's behavior.
4. *Traffic-cop regulation of behavioral and social traffic.* Assistance in helping children remember and follow through on relevant rules and agreements ("Remember we said we'd have to talk about any fights that occurred?").
5. *Umpire services.* Adults may sometimes have to serve as judge, issuing rulings and explaining the rationale for their conclusions.

Clinical exploitation of life events is simply an elaborate title for the process of extracting every possible therapeutic and educational benefit from a given situation. Contrary to the techniques for the antiseptic manipulation of surface behavior, which aimed to stop inappropriate actions in their tracks, the notion of clinical exploitation demands a much deeper effort to turn such behaviors into viable learning situations for the youngster(s) who expressed them. Components include:

1. *Reality rub.* Often, youngsters do not "know" why they commit aggressive acts nor do they seem to understand the consequences of their behavior. Adults can help youngsters understand their own motivations and contributions to unhappy episodes by "rubbing in" the world's realities (If you swear at Mrs. K., you're going to be in trouble.).

2. *Symptom estrangement.* Feelings and behavior are connected, though the child may not see their relation. Adults must help youngsters understand the meaning of their behavior and the notion that their behavior is purposeful, not random.

3. *Massaging numb value areas.* Sometimes youngsters may demonstrate good values but find inappropriate ways to express them. It is appropriate to say "hello," but a good way to do that is *not* by hitting people whenever you see them.

4. *New-tool salesmanship.* This is an extension of the previous component, massaging numb value areas. Here, the adult's purpose is to help the youngster adopt new and more appropriate methods to express good values or valid feelings. "What's another way you might have said it?" "It's OK to be angry, but the way you showed your anger made things worse for you. What could you do instead?"

5. *Manipulation of self.* At times, a youngster's aggressive behavior may not have been intended, but was manipulated by the seduction of the group or the environment. Here the adult attempts to help youngsters maintain control of their own behavior, even in the face of future temptations.

We can see, then, that Life-Space interviewing deals with both feelings and actions. When well executed, such an interview can legitimize a troubled youngster's feeling ("You were right to feel angry."), help him or her understand the inappropriateness of the action that followed the feeling ("But it's not OK to try to stab him with your pencil."), and finally, move to the consideration of new behaviors ("What else do you think you could do when you're feeling angry?"). This focus on both feelings and actions should follow real-life events as soon as possible so that youngsters can get assistance when they most need it and when it is likely to be most meaningful.

Life-Space interviewing represents a way in which adults can assist youngsters to understand the effects of their unconscious thoughts, feelings, and actions on others. It also serves as a model for the application of psychodynamic thinking to the real-life situations encountered by educators.

Finally, before ending our discussion of Redl's work with aggressive children and youth, it is important to note two related psychological intervention formats: milieu therapy and psychoeducation. In both cases, the work of Redl and his colleagues made significant contributions to the creation and development of these two now well-known strategies.

MILIEU THERAPY

Redl defined the "children who hate" in part as the children nobody wanted. They were also the children who seemed most unlikely to profit from the standard clinical treatment at the time: psychotherapy by prearranged appointment. Such children, Redl noted, were far too destructive, had insufficient verbal abilities, and were too here-and-now focused to find much sense in dredging up incidents from the past to be viewed as viable candidates for psychotherapy.

Instead, Redl believed that such youngsters would be much more likely to profit from a total therapeutic environment in which continual efforts were made to maximize each child's psychological growth and development 24 hours a day. Following his work at Pioneer House, which was essentially an experiment in the creation and maintenance of a therapeutic milieu for a particularly difficult population of youngsters, Redl published some of his own thoughts on the concept of therapeutic environments (1959). In that paper, Redl discussed what he believed to be twelve critical variables in the success of a therapeutic milieu, including: social structure, value system, routines and rituals, impact of the group, programmed activities, staff, and others.

We can see how the Life-Space interview discussed earlier would be such an integral part of a therapeutic environment. According to Newcomer (1980), the Life-Space technique is the critical element of Redl's therapeutic milieu, and it serves to highlight the lessons of the environment:

> Although occasionally the impact of the environment is enough therapy for a given child, more often it takes a trained adult to serve as mediator between the environment and the child. The child's experiences in the therapeutic milieu may go unnoticed if there is not interpretation of those events. Even in an ordinary school environment, an adult's well-thought-out reaction to an event can clarify it for a child and prevent misinterpretation. (p. 326)

PSYCHOEDUCATION

When the principles of a therapeutic milieu are applied to a school setting, the resultant program reflects a psychoeducational model. Here, the educational program is the milieu and it is organized to provide continuous therapeutic benefits to each student. For example, Morse (1974) makes note of the following important dimensions:

1. Environments must be arranged to reflect the values and attitudes inherent in each child's Life-Space.
2. The teacher is a model for psychosocial identification as well as the more traditional imparter of knowledge.
3. The curriculum is constructed to provide opportunities to incorporate affective learning into the regular school program.
4. The group or peer culture is a focus of educational planning efforts. Helping children learn from their peer groups is of critical importance.

5. The availability of therapeutic resources is arranged and ensured. Adults who work in therapeutic environments (including teachers in the psychoeducational model) need assistance and support from colleagues.

A good example of the development of a psychoeducational program is provided by Fenichel (1965) in his description of the creation of the League School:

> In 1953 the League School started a new kind of treatment facility—one that attempted to keep severely disturbed children within the community by substituting the day treatment school and the home for the mental hospital.
> We began with the hypothesis that behavioral changes could be achieved by the use of special educational techniques in a therapeutic setting without individual psychotherapy. This hypothesis was based on the assumption that a properly planned and highly individualized educational program with interdisciplinary clinical participation could result in social and emotional growth as well as in educational achievements. (p. 6)

Fenichel noted that youngsters at the League School needed individualized learning prescriptions based on comprehensive assessments of learning strengths and weaknesses. The role of staff members was to gather the necessary information and use it to build an appropriate educational program for each youngster.

Fenichel also addressed the issue of whether psychoeducational programs are primarily psychological (therapeutic) or educational. In his remarks, Fenichel (1965) highlights the need for psychoeducational programs for aggressive youngsters:

> We have found that working with seriously disturbed children the differentiation often made between education and therapy becomes largely a semantic one. A teacher who fosters self-discipline, emotional growth and more effective functioning is doing something therapeutic. Any educational process that helps to correct or reduce a child's distorted perceptions, disturbed behavior and disordered thinking, and that results in greater mastery of self and one's surroundings is certainly a therapeutic process. (p. 17)

HUMANISTIC INTERVENTIONS

Contrary to early psychodynamic thinking, which was primarily focused on the importance of negative impulses and drives, humanistic psychology represents a recent and more positive model of dynamic thought. Theorists such as Erik Erikson, Erich Fromm, and Abraham Maslow emphasized positive human motivational impulses and the ability of men and women to control negative impulses and increase their prosocial behavior. Thus, humanistic interventions are focused on the enhancement and facilitation of individual growth, self-awareness, social interaction, love, empathy, and so on.

Maslow's theory of needs is perhaps most representative of humanistic psychology and we describe it briefly here. According to Maslow, all human behavior is aimed at the fulfillment of certain basic human needs. Further, needs may be stretched out along a continuum from basic survival needs (food and shelter) to more social needs (love and acceptance) to the ultimate life goal, self-actualization. As the individual matures, higher-level needs usually take on primary importance. Self-actualization cannot occur if needs from lower levels in the hierarchy are not fulfilled, a condition that can cause despondency and alienation.

Interventions based on Maslow's theory, then, must focus on helping people recognize their unsatisfied needs and facilitating their fulfillment. Ultimately, successful interventions should have the effect of moving people closer to the realization of their own potential, nearer to the goal of self-actualization.

More generally, humanistic interventions can be characterized by their emphasis on self-discovery and the enhancement of human potential. The client-centered therapy of Carl Rogers, the gestalt therapy of Fritz Perls, the group-dynamics movement (including the early laboratory or training (*T*) groups, sensitivity groups, encounter groups, and many, many others) are all examples of applications of humanistic psychology ideas.

Although it is not possible nor relevant to explore each of these interventions here, we briefly examine a small number of particularly interesting applications to the problems of aggressive youth. For example, Gold (1978) has argued that alternative educational programs may be a useful way to both reduce and prevent delinquent behavior. Gold subscribes to the theory that delinquent acts represent an ego defense against external threats to self-esteem.

There are two important aspects to the Gold position:

1. The threat to self-esteem is not necessarily brought from the outside world into school nor is it based on an internal impulse. Instead, the threat to self may stem directly from the realities of school itself. Indeed, Gold points to "failure in the role of student" as the source of much delinquent behavior in schools today.

2. Because it is threats to self-esteem stemming from the demands of the role of student that give rise to much delinquent behavior, Gold suggests that alternative programs with built-in capacities to increase a youngster's success experiences and provide warm and accepting relationships with adults may be the most viable remedy.

We can see, then, that according to Gold, the negative effects of threats to self-esteem can be dissipated by successful efforts to build self-concept. Although the schools and their usual programs must bear some responsibility for instigating aggressive and delinquent behavior, a more humanistic approach to educational programs could effect the necessary changes in students' self-images.

Similarly, Beatty (1977) has reported success in the use of a program called "The New Model Me" in helping adolescents curb aggressive behavior. This curriculum, which includes a variety of values-clarification exercises (see Chapter 5), situations for discussion, and lessons on decision making, has been useful even with students identified as having very serious adjustment problems. Based in part on Maslow's theory of needs described earlier, the New Model Me curriculum has eight major goals:

The curriculum developers worked out eight goals for New Model Me students: understand the human motivations underlying behavior; realize how resources and physical and social environments influence a person's behavior; study the nature and sources of frustrations and seek constructive methods for resolving them; discern that there are many ways to respond to a given situation; determine how constructive their own behavior is; make decisions based on what effects various courses of action will have on themselves and others; understand that aggressive behavior can be constructive or destructive; and use what has been learned about behavior and problem solving in everyday life. (p. 26)

Rudolf Dreikurs and his colleagues have also developed a humanistic psychodynamic approach to the remediation of children's disturbing behavior. According to Dreikurs, Grunwald, and Pepper (1971), all disturbed behavior is goal directed; they identify four major needs that such behavior may seek to gratify:

The child may try to get attention, to put others in his service, since he believes that otherwise he would be lost and worthless. Or he may attempt to prove his power in the belief that only if he can do what he wants and defy adult pressure can he be somebody. Or he may seek revenge, the only means by which he feels significant is to hurt others as he feels hurt by them. Or he may display actual or imagined deficiencies in order to be left alone: as long as nothing is demanded of him, his deficiency, stupidity or inability may not become obvious; that would mean his utter worthlessness.
Whichever of these four goals he adopts, his behavior is based on the conviction that only in this way can he be significant. His goal may occasionally vary with circumstances; he may act to attract attention at one moment, and assert his power or seek revenge at another. He can also use a great variety of techniques to obtain his goal; and, conversely, the same behavior can serve different purposes. (p. 17)

Dreikurs et al. point out that the teaching of discipline ought to be a continuing process instead of an activity to be engaged in only at times of stress. The goal should be to help children develop self-control, not blind obedience to authority. Dreikurs is positive about the ability of children to develop appropriate inner controls and he believes that a problem-solving approach can help youngsters see alternative perspectives, consider a variety of options, and make intelligent decisions. Said another way: "Children will respond in a positive way to those who are kind, but firm, fair, and consistent in maintaining discipline and order" (Dreikurs et al., 1971, p. 26).
In order to concretize their approach, Dreikurs et al. offer a number of do's and don'ts of discipline. For example:

DON'T:

1. Become preoccupied with your own authority.
2. Nag and scold children.
3. Ask a child to promise anything.
4. Give rewards for good behavior.

5. Find fault with the child.
6. Use different standards for adults and for children.
7. Use threats or intimidation.
8. Be vindictive.

DO:

1. Try to understand the goals of misbehavior.
2. Give clear directions for action.
3. Be future (not past) oriented.
4. Give misbehaving youngsters a choice between stopping their disturbance or leaving the room.
5. Build on the positive and minimize the negative.
6. Try to establish relationships built on trust and respect.
7. Discuss a child's problems at times when both of you are prepared to do so.
8. Use natural consequences instead of punishment.
9. Be consistent.
10. Be honest.

Dreikurs et al. make a number of additional concrete suggestions for improving the disturbing behavior of children. Like Gold (1978) mentioned earlier, Dreikurs et al. call for teachers to provide more opportunities for success experiences if youngsters' antisocial behavior is to be reduced.

The key elements in the Dreikurs et al. (1971) system, however, are two: natural and logical consequences:

> *Natural consequences* represent the pressure of reality or the natural flow of events without interference of the teacher or parent. The child who refuses to eat will go hungry. The natural consequence of not eating is hunger. The parent stands aside and does not become involved.
>   *Logical consequences* are arranged or applied. If the child spills his milk, he must clean it up. In this situation, the consequence is tied to the act. A power-drunk child will only respond to natural consequences; he will respond to logical consequences with rebellion. (p. 80)

Thus, Dreikurs and his colleagues suggest that we have the necessary resources available to us in order to stop antisocial behavior. If we simply let nature take its course (natural consequences) or help it along on occasion (logical consequences), inappropriate behavior will reduce itself as a result of the distasteful reactions it energizes.

Dreikurs et al. note the special problems of adolescents and believe that their approach can help effect a truce of sorts between the "warring" generations. Unfortunately, for our purposes here, no documentation of the use of natural and logical consequences toward the remediation of aggressive and violent behavior is described.

William Glasser's Reality Therapy is another alternative approach that is, however, not easily categorized. Even though some view it as behavioral because of its focus on overt behavior, it also bears considerable resemblance to the Rational-Emotive Therapy of Albert Ellis. It is also dynamic in its emphasis on the development of feelings of responsibility for one's actions and commitment to one's reference group as the goals of intervention. It is humanistic by virtue of its assumption that the failure to gratify the need for love and self-esteem may be the cause of inappropriate behavior.

In order to function effectively in the world, according to Glasser, youngsters need to learn to behave in a realistic, responsible, and morally right manner. Failure to act in accordance with these principles makes it impossible to satisfy even basic human needs and causes people to feel frustrated and distressed.

Again, like Gold and like Dreikurs, Glasser advocates the provision of more success experiences as the way to modify students' antisocial behaviors in school. Reality Therapy and the classroom-meeting techniques are strategies to be used for helping students avoid failure (one of Glasser's books is entitled *Schools Without Failure*; see Glasser, 1969), learn responsible behavior, and develop "stakes" in their situations.

Glasser sees schools' adoption of a curriculum that deemphasizes problem solving and thinking as part of the cause of emotional disturbance. He believes that group meetings with their focus on cooperative decision making and social responsibility would make failure less likely and antisocial behavior less frequent in the schools.

Though he has done considerable work with adolescents and has provided much descriptive and anecdotal documentation of the effectiveness of his approach, little in the way of comprehensive analysis of the impact of Glasser's techniques to the problem of aggression and violence in the schools is currently available. Nevertheless, like the other approaches described in this chapter, there is much to reflect on here as we consider the application of psychodynamic and humanistic perspectives to antisocial school behavior.

SUMMARY AND CONCLUSIONS

We have reviewed much of the available literature pertaining to the application of psychodynamic principles and perspectives to the problems of aggressive and violent behavior in schools. Though aspects of psychodynamic theory have clearly provided a basis for the development of the productive techniques and strategies described in this chapter, such a viewpoint has also come in for its share of criticisms. For example, the psychodynamic point of view has been criticized because:

1. It presents an extremely pessimistic view of human beings (Newcomer, 1980).
2. Its description of human behavior is based on hypothetical constructs and operations (Newcomer, 1980). Many practitioners have abandoned this hypothetical system in favor of more observable answers (Reinert, 1976).
3. It emphasizes the examination of the unconscious as the way to mental health despite the lack of evidence for such a position (Newcomer, 1980).

4. Follow-up studies of children who had received psychodynamic treatment have shown a very low success rate (Juul, 1977).
5. Teachers may have been encouraged to allow the same freedom in the classroom that was practiced in the therapeutic hours. In turn, such practices created so much aggression and destructiveness that chaos was the result (Juul, 1977).
6. In therapeutic practice, there was a preoccupation with a child's pathology and limitations and a lack of appreciation for his or her capabilities and strengths (Juul, 1977).
7. There was a tendency to ignore the powerful impact of the environment on a child's behavior. Thus, not enough efforts were made to elicit the support of the significant people in the child's daily life (Juul, 1977).

Although some of the criticisms detailed here are certainly pointed specifically at the dynamic model, others (preoccupation with deficits and little focus on strengths) may be equally valid when applied to other models. Perhaps the most critical problem with the psychodynamic perspective, however, has already been mentioned: the lack of valid and reliable documentation of its effectiveness.

Despite the lack of appropriate statistical evidence, however, there are indications that psychodynamic interventions can work. Gnagey (1968) provides us with the following criteria for judging the effectiveness of control techniques:

Does the deviant behavior cease?
Is contagion of the behavior inhibited?
Are human relations maintained?
Does learning become more desirable and efficient? (p. 134)

By these, or any other reasonable standards one might choose, it is clear that at least for individual cases, psychodynamic perspectives have demonstrated some effectiveness. Whether they work because they reduce frustration, or activate children's controls, or help youngsters develop stakes in the settings, or build ego skills, or simply impose external authority is less clear.

What is clear is that the problems of aggression and violence in schools are extensive and still growing. The failure to pursue any line of intervention that shows the promise of some of the methods described in this chapter would be unconscionable. There is room in the area of the control of aggressive and violent behavior for much research and much improvement in our strategies and techniques. The psychodynamic perspective will undoubtedly continue to play a major part in that endeavor.

REFERENCES

BEATTY, F. The new model me. *American Education*, 1977, *13*(1), 23–36.
CHESS, S., & HASSIBI, M. *Principles and practice of child psychiatry.* New York: Plenum Press, 1978.

DREIKURS, R., GRUNWALD, B. B., & PEPPER, F. C. *Maintaining sanity in the classroom: Illustrated teaching techniques.* New York: Harper & Row, 1971.
ERIKSON, E. H. *Childhood and society.* New York: Norton, 1950.
FENICHEL, C. Psycho-educational approaches for seriously disturbed children in the classroom. In P. Knoblock (Ed.), *Intervention approaches in educating emotionally disturbed children.* Syracuse, N.Y.: Division of Special Education and Rehabilitation, Syracuse University, 1966.
GLASSER, W. *Schools without failure.* New York: Harper & Row, 1969.
GLUECK, S., & GLUECK, E. *Juvenile delinquents grown up.* New York: The Commonwealth Fund, 1940.
GNAGEY, W. J. *The psychology of discipline in the classroom.* New York: Macmillan, 1968.
GOLD, M. Scholastic experiences, self-esteem, and delinquent behavior: A theory for alternative schools. *Crime and Delinquency,* 1978, 290–309.
JUUL, K. D. *Educational and psychological interactions: Models of remediation for behavior disordered children* (Bulletin No. 62). Malmo, Sweden: Department of Education and Psychological Research, School of Education, July 1977.
LONG, N. *Direct help to the classroom teacher.* Washington, D.C.: Washington School of Psychiatry, 1966.
McPARTLAND, J. M., & McDILL, E. L. *Violence in schools: Perspectives, programs, and positions.* Lexington, Mass.: Lexington Books, 1977. © D.C. Heath & Co.
MORSE, W. C. Personal perspective. In J. M. Kauffman & C. D. Lewis (Eds.), *Teaching children with behavior disorders.* Columbus, Ohio: Merrill, 1974.
MORSE, W. C., SMITH, J. M., & ACKER, N. *The psychodynamic approach: A self-instructional module* (mimeo videotape training packages in child variance). Ann Arbor: University of Michigan, School of Education, 1977.
NEWCOMER, P. L. *Understanding and teaching emotionally disturbed children.* Boston: Allyn & Bacon, 1980.
REDL, F. The concept of the life-space interview. *American Journal of Orthopsychiatry,* 1959, *29,* 1–18.
REDL, F. Aggression in the classroom. *Today's Education,* September 1969, 30–32.
REDL, F., & WINEMAN, D. *The aggressive child.* New York: The Free Press, 1957.
REINERT, H. R. *Children in conflict: Educational strategies for the emotionally disturbed and behavior disordered.* St. Louis: Mosby, 1976.

5
Teaching
Prosocial
Values*

Today, the way that our society develops the character of its young people is grossly inadequate. In recent decades (the last 70 to 100 years) there has been a steady decline in efforts to teach character in our public schools. This is a basic reason for the explosive increase in crime, violence, alcoholism, drug addiction and other disturbing manifestations of moral decay in our society. Thus, one of the most effective and economical ways to reduce these problems is to quickly improve the quantity and quality of moral instruction in all of our institutions particularly our public schools. (Goble, 1973, p. 29)

Our central goal throughout this book is the reduction of school violence and vandalism. The multilevel perspective we have adopted holds that because such violence and vandalism have multiple determinants, efforts aimed at their reduction must correspondingly be multifaceted. One major expression of such a potentially powerful, multifaceted effort is interventions concurrently applied across levels—that is, at the student, teacher, school, and community levels *simultaneously.* A second type of multifaceted intervention, one possibly and perhaps optimally combined with that just described, would be constituted of several complimentary, aggression-reducing procedures instituted at one of these four possible levels of intervention. In Chapters 3 and 4, we presented in detail two sets of effective approaches at the student level: behavior modification and humanistic interventions.

*The authors wish to extend their appreciation to Eric Edelman for his substantial assistance in the development of this chapter.

In both this and the following chapter, we offer two additional student-level sets of interventions. The first two are oriented toward the enhancement of prosocial values; the second two focus upon the direct teaching of prosocial behaviors. Although all four of these types of interventions can be and have been utilized separately, our viewpoint strongly champions their conjoint implementation.

VALUES AND BEHAVIOR

The enhancement of prosocial values in youngsters displaying aggressive behavior is relevant to the behavior-change focus of this book only if, and to the extent that, holding such values actually influences the likelihood of overt, prosocial behavior. Stated otherwise, does the degree to which a youngster believes in justice, fairness, nonviolence, and other prosocial values contribute to any appreciable extent to the frequency of his or her actually behaving in an altruistic, cooperative, nonviolent, or similarly prosocial manner or, correspondingly, to a reduction in his or her level of violence or vandalism? Early research on the antecedents of prosocial behavior pointed not so much to values or other characteristics of the individual as much as to characteristics of the individual's situation as significant in influencing the occurrence of prosocial behavior. The oft-cited research series by Hartshorne, May, and their coworkers, reported in their *Studies in the Nature of Character* (Hartshorne & May, 1928; Hartshorne, May, & Maller, 1929; Hartshorne, May, & Shuttleworth, 1930) demonstrated that the occurrence of such classroom behaviors as cheating, lying, and stealing were determined to a considerable degree by such situational factors as expediency, group approval, example of others, and the level of reinforcement involved. This early research helped give impetus to the "situationist" view of prosocial behavior. Several more recent studies similarly underscore the effect of the person's context on the likelihood that he or she will behave altruistically, cooperatively, and in other prosocial ways (Bar-Tal, 1976; Krebs, 1978; Staub, 1978). Such behaviors are more likely to occur:

1. The less the ambiguity that help in fact is needed.
2. The greater the need for help.
3. The more clearly the responsibility for helping is focused on a particular person.
4. The greater the impact of instigating stimuli—for example, the closer in space, time, and exposure the expression of need is to the potential helper.
5. The less decision making or initiative the potential helper must assume.
6. The lower the cost of helping—in time, effort, material goods, and risk to oneself.
7. The greater the social desirability of helping.
8. The existence of a relationship with the person in need.
9. When positive experiences, and hence a favorable mood state, have occurred just prior to the opportunity to help.

10. When the individual has been exposed to models displaying, and being rewarded for, the given prosocial behavior.
11. When the individual has been in the past, and expects on this occasion to be,
rewarded for engaging in the prosocial behavior.

   Opposing the situationist view is the "trait" position, which holds that it is
characteristics of the individual, especially personality traits, which are the primary
antecedents of prosocial behavior. Champions of this view point to research showing a positive association between prosocial behavior and such person dimensions as
stage of moral development, internal control, extroversion, affiliativeness, and
dependency; and a negative association with dominance, competitiveness, and hostility (Bryan, 1972; Kaufman, 1970; Krebs, 1978).
   The "trait" versus "situationist" controversy has been an active one in psychology for many years, with both sides pointing to the types of supportive evidence
just alluded to. A major consequence of this controversy has been the growing emer-
gence of a third viewpoint, one merging the supportive research of both earlier
views. This third, "interactionist" position generally holds that a person's internal
dispositions interact with his or her learning experiences in particular situations to
determine his or her behavior in these situations (Endler & Magnusson, 1976;
Mischel, 1973). Translated to the content of this multilevel-oriented book, the interactionist view holds that the likelihood that a given youngster will behave in a prosocial manner is a *joint* function of characteristics of his or her situation (e.g., the
teacher, his or her classmates, the school climate), and characteristics of the youngster himself or herself. Among these trait-characteristic determinants of prosocial
behavior is prosocial values; hence, our justification in this book of the present
chapter. This decision is convincingly supported by research demonstrating a substantial positive relationship between stage of moral development and such prosocial behaviors as altruism (Rubin & Schneider, 1973), honesty (Harris, Mussen, &
Rutherford, 1976), helping others in distress (McNamee, 1977), generosity (Ugurel-
Semin, 1951), and nonviolence (Kohlberg & Turiel, 1971). In addition, Kohlberg,
Sharf, and Hickey (1972) have shown that delinquent youngsters markedly tend to
be reasoning at low or immature levels of moral development. With the impetus of
these directional and correlational trait findings, we examine in depth in this chapter
means for effectively teaching prosocial values to youngsters in school settings.
   Three major approaches to enhancing prosocial values will be our particular
focus—namely: (1) character education; (2) values clarification; and (3) Kohlberg's
moral education. Each has had a major impact in this domain, each has developed
comprehensive values-training procedures and materials, and each has been the target
of substantial amounts of formal and informal evaluation. We are thus enabled, in
the remainder of this chapter, to examine the rationale, principles, methods, and
evaluation of each of these three approaches in depth and, thereby, make informed
decisions regarding the likely utility of each in our larger effort to identify effective
means for dealing with school violence and vandalism. Though we do not deal with
them in this book, it should be noted that a number of other, less fully developed

approaches to teaching prosocial values exist. The interested reader is referred to the following for additional approaches: Beck's Ultimate Life Goal approach (Beck, 1971; Beck, Hersh, & Sullivan, 1976; Beck & Sullivan, 1976); McPhail's Learning to Care program (McPhail, Ungoed-Thomas, & Chapman, 1975); Newmann, Oliver, and Shaver's Public Issues program (Newmann & Oliver, 1970; Oliver & Shaver, 1966); Wilson's Moral Components approach (Wilson, 1971, 1972, 1973a, 1973b); Mosher and Sprinthall's Psychological Education (Mosher & Sprinthall, 1970, 1972); Glasser's Classroom Meeting approach (Glasser, 1969); and Weinstein and Fantini's Identify Education (Weinstein & Fantini, 1970).

CHARACTER EDUCATION

The Character-Education Movement
of the 1920s

In the 1920s, values training was very much an institutionalized concern of the American public schools. Most of the approaches to moral instruction during this period comprised a major educational movement called *character education*. Although the goals and methods of these various approaches to character education were not entirely uniform, the common denominator of this movement was an emphasis on developing the "moral character" of the young. Moral character was typically defined in terms of certain personality traits, virtues, or values generally believed important to the welfare of the individual as well as of society. These desirable character traits included such values as honesty, altruism, self-control, patriotism, responsibility, friendliness, and moral courage. Unfortunately, character educators of this period were more explicit about theoretical aims than they were about concrete procedures for developing such traits in school children. Teaching methods relied heavily on discussion of the importance of such traits or values and on exhortation to use these values as guides to virtuous conduct. This period of character education culminated in the important research of Hartshorne, May, and their coworkers described earlier. Hartshorne et al. investigated the social behavior of thousands of children in various experimental situations, in and out of school, with respect to the character traits of honesty (defined as resistance to cheating and stealing), service (giving up objects for the welfare of others), and self-control (persistence in assigned tasks). Their results, it will be recalled, strongly supported the situationist view of the antecedents of prosocial behavior. As such, they constituted an impact which was nothing less than shattering to the character-education movement of the 1920s. As Hartshorne and May (1928) concluded:

> The mere urging of honest behavior by teachers or the discussion of standards and ideals of honesty, no matter how much such general ideas may be "emotional," has no necessary relation to the control of conduct. . . . This does not imply that the teaching of general ideas, standards and ideals is not desirable and necessary, but only that the prevailing ways of inculcating ideals probably do little good and may do some harm. (p. 413)

Hartshorne and May's documentation of the ineffectiveness of character education as commonly taught in the schools dealt a blow from which the character-education movement as it was practiced in the 1920s never recovered; character education as a formal, educational movement had largely disappeared by the mid-1930s.

Contemporary Character Education

Some thirty-five to forty years after Hartshorne and May's work, character education is again alive and well in new and revised forms. The goals of these contemporary forms of character education are similar to those of the 1920s: the teaching of values, character traits, and standards of ethical conduct that are considered important for constructive living in a democratic society. Indeed, character educators today lay some of the blame for the alarming increases in crime and delinquency on the public schools' abnegation of responsibility for teaching such traditional values as honesty, altruism, tolerance, justice, kindness, politeness, and convictions. Character educators maintain that the successful inculcation of such values in the schools, especially when accomplished in the formative years of elementary school, will lead to a reduction in the violence and aggression currently occurring at high levels in American society.

Although character educators today agree with the basic aims of the 1920s movement, they recognize the importance of developing more explicit, systematic, and effective methods for teaching prosocial values. The 1960s witnessed development of programs designed to bring character education back into the public schools. American Viewpoint, Inc., an organization concerned with preventing crime and delinquency, developed a teacher's manual, called "The Good American Program," for teaching citizenship values in the elementary grades (Mayer, 1964). This program was based on the premise that direct teaching of specific values at the appropriate time in the development of elementary-school children was necessary in order for such values to influence behavior. The program combined opportunities for experience and practice, along with reading and discussion (without "moralizing") in the context of social-studies class. "The Good American Program" was tried in elementary schools in Ossining, New York, and Goble (1973) reports impressionistic evidence that the program produced positive results in student behavior.

In Colton, California, a high-school teacher, Virginia Trevitt, developed a program called "As I Am, So Is My Nation" (Trevitt, 1964). Trevitt's aim was to help students view both their education and personal behavior as relevant to the needs and practices of American society, and to develop in students the moral qualities necessary for constructive contributions to society. Her methods included studying the ideals of America's founders, discussing moral concepts, and testing these concepts in daily living. Trevitt taught her course to incoming students at Colton High School for several years. She reported striking changes in student behavior in and out of school, ranging from decreases in classroom cheating to return of stolen articles to students' becoming more responsive and cooperative at home.

Russel Hill (1965) developed Freedom's Code, a statement of character traits or ideals proposed by the author as comprising (1) the historic American standards of ethical conduct and citizen responsibility, as well as (2) the standards of virtuous conduct that are necessary for the maintenance of all free and democratic societies. These traits include honesty, generosity, justice, kindness, helping others in need, courage, tolerance, and understanding and fulfilling citizenship obligations. Bain and Clark (1966) developed a teacher's handbook for developing the character traits of Freedom's Code in elementary-school children. This handbook contains various instructional strategies as well as suggested resource materials such as films, records, and books. Teaching methods include discussion of the general meaning as well as specific examples of each trait, classroom debates, role play, study of historical and contemporary American figures as exemplars of particular traits, written exercises, art and music projects, reinforcement of desired behavior, and various assignments for practicing these values in real-life situations in and out of school. Unfortunately, there is an absence of empirical research regarding the effectiveness of Bain and Clark's methods.

The Character Education Curriculum

Presently, the most comprehensive and sophisticated approach to character education in the public schools is the Character Education Curriculum (CEC) developed by the American Institute for Character Education (AICE) in San Antonio, Texas. The AICE is an organization whose avowed purpose is to help teachers develop the moral character of the young, especially elementary-school children. The rationale of the CEC is that children who are taught to consider the consequences of their behavior in terms of certain traditional values (such as those presented in Freedom's Code) will choose to behave in ways beneficial to themselves and society. Rather than simply indoctrinating students with certain standards of conduct, the CEC seeks to teach particular values in such a way that the students come to understand their reasonableness and worth as a basis for decision making in interpersonal situations.

The CEC materials for kindergarten through fifth grade are briefly described as follows:

The Kindergarten Kit. This kit contains a series of teaching units, in English and Spanish, divided into two semesters: "The Happy Life Series" (first semester) and "You and Me" (second semester). "The Happy Life Series" includes six books of animal stories, with accompanying filmstrips and songs, containing lessons on honesty, generosity, helpfulness, kindness, and fairness. "You and Me" contains lessons designed to help children transfer the values developed in "The Happy Life Series" to their interactions with family members and others in their community.

CEC Kits for Grades One through Five. A separate CEC kit for each grade level contains a teacher's guide, posters, activity sheets, a teacher's handbook, and evaluation instruments. The teacher's guide for each grade level details a sequence of step-by-step lessons, with explicit objectives, divided into two areas: "Living With Me and Others" and "Our Rights and Responsibilities." "Living With Me and Others" involves lessons on such individual virtues as honesty, truthfulness, kindness, helpfulness, generosity, politeness, justice, tolerance, courage, convictions, honor, and constructive use of time and talents. "Our Rights and Responsibilities" contains lessons on values considered important to effective citizenship in American society—for example, freedom of speech, freedom of choice, citizenship, the right to be an individual, the right to equal opportunity, and economic security. The teacher's guide for each grade level also contains a listing of relevant books, films, and other audiovisual materials. In addition, there are large posters which can be used to reiterate the lessons in the teacher's guide, activity sheets to be used with the children during the lessons, a teacher's handbook with suggestions for implementing the lessons, and evaluation forms to be used by teachers to assess the children's level of understanding of the values taught.

Teaching Methods. The CEC lessons make use of a wide variety of methods such as class discussion, role playing, written exercises, art projects, and multimedia presentations, games, and activities and projects offering opportunities to experience and practice the value being taught in a variety of group situations. For example, different lessons include such activities as role playing good manners in particular situations, discussing behaviors that show tolerance, drawing pictures of honest and dishonest behavior, and interviewing classmates about their convictions.

Regarding the implementation of the CEC, the AICE recommends the following (Mukley, 1977):

1. CEC lessons should be scheduled on a regular basis: daily for 15–20 minutes with the lower primary grades, two to three times a week for 30–50 minutes with the upper primary grades.
2. CEC lessons can be taught as a separate subject, or can be integrated with regular school subjects, preferably in the areas of social studies or language arts.
3. A child's work resulting from CEC lessons should not be graded or marked for handwriting, grammar, and so on, as such evaluation would inhibit the freedom of expression necessary for effective character education.
4. The way a teacher conducts class discussions is critical to the success of CEC lessons. The teacher should not lecture, moralize, or scrutinize. The teacher's role is that of a "facilitator" whose goal is to help the children in the class learn to think for themselves. The teacher should use discussion as a means for improving children's problem-solving and decision-making skills.
5. Role playing is an especially important instructional method and should be used as often as possible. Discussion is necessary immediately after role playing in order to provide feedback to the participants.

Examples of CEC Lessons.

TEACHING KINDNESS, HELPFULNESS,
GENEROSITY, AND POLITENESS
IN THE FIRST GRADE

The following is the third lesson in a sequence of three lessons, taken from the teacher's guide for the first grade (Anon., 1974). The explicit objective of this sequence is for students to be able to describe their feelings when someone is nice to them.

Step I.   Introduce a new game to the children called "Tell Me." Explain that it is played in this way:
1. A particular topic or idea is chosen for a lesson.
2. In relation to the topic, the children tell about something that really happened to them or someone they know. (No names shall be used.)
3. When the person telling the story gets to the end, instead of finishing it, he or she says to the group, "How would you feel? Tell Me!"
4. Class members make up different endings and share their feelings as if they were the characters themselves.

Step II. Explain that today the topics and stories will be about one of the following ideas: Politeness, helpfulness, generosity, or kindness. List these words on a chalkboard.

Step III. Go over the rules in Step I again.

Step IV. Give the following examples as you, the teacher, start off by telling the first two or three stories:
1. It's your birthday today. Your friends brought you a present, and you really liked it. How would you feel? Tell Me!
2. You're playing out on the playground. You fall down and really scare yourself. You want to cry, but some of the other children come to see what they can do for you. How would you feel? Tell Me!
3. You have been at home sick for several days and now that you're back in school you can't run outside with the other children. You go over to sit down by yourself. In a little while, two or three classmates come over and sit down with you and begin to talk to you. How would you feel? Tell Me!

Step V.   Seek volunteers to relate stories from their own experience when someone showed them kindness, politeness, helpfulness, or generosity.

Step VI. After each story ask these questions:
1. Which of the four qualities was shown? Check on the board.
2. How was it shown?
3. Why did you feel the way you did? (p. 19)

TEACHING TOLERANCE IN THE FIFTH GRADE

The following lesson is taken from the teacher's guide for the fifth grade (Anon., 1974). The objective is for students to be able to describe ways in which people can work to become more tolerant.

Step I.   Have each student select from magazines two pictures—one which she or he thinks is ugly and the other, beautiful. Have the class write their descriptions (ugly or beautiful) on the back of the pictures and pin them on the bulletin board.

Step II. Number each picture.

Step III. Ask each student to select five pictures from those displayed on the bulletin board which she or he thinks are ugly and five, beautiful. Have them write their choices on paper.

Step IV. Allow two or three students at a time to check to see how the person who put the picture up considered it.

Step V.   Tally the marks for each picture on the chalkboard using the following form:

PICTURE	UGLY	BEAUTIFUL
1.		
2.		
3.		

Step VI. Discuss with the class whether or not they can accept what other people think is beautiful and what they think is ugly. If they can, why? If they cannot, why not? What are the consequences of each? (p. 26)

Evaluation of Critique
of Character Education

Thousands of teachers have used the CEC materials in their classrooms. Questionnaire surveys conducted by the AICE, they report, reveal widespread approval by teachers and favorable student interest and involvement. The AICE has received numerous reports and testimonials from various teachers and educators claiming that use of the CEC has led to a reduction in violence, vandalism, cheating, and stealing in the schools. There is, however, an absence of carefully controlled empirical research examining the effectiveness of the CEC. This void is also a major problem with other character-education programs briefly described earlier. Beyond the CEC in particular, a number of criticisms have been leveled against the character-education approach in general. Objections have been raised on empirical, philosophical, ethical, and practical grounds.

The empirical argument is that character traits such as honesty are merely labels used by other people to describe or evaluate a person's behavior in certain situations, rather than a reflection of any consistent dispositions or internal structures in the person who is labeled. This is part of the "situationist" argument, discussed earlier, against the existence of any internalized, cross-situational personality traits, moral or otherwise. We are inclined toward the "interactionist" position which, as noted previously, maintains that a person's internal dispositions interact with his or her learning experiences in particular situations to determine his or her behavior in these situations. For example, Burton (1976) reanalyzed the original intercorrelations of the Hartshorne and May (1928) data with multivariate methods. He concluded from this and other studies that a "small but consistently manifested factor" (Burton, 1976, p. 176) that differentiates individuals interacts with their differential learning experiences in specific situations to determine how honest or dishonest they are in these situations. The implications of this "interactionist" position for character education is that, while a person could develop a character "trait" of some generality such as "honesty," he or she could not learn by being taught either the meaning of "honesty" per se or how to behave honestly in general. The person would have to be taught the meaning of honest behavior in certain situations and then to generalize this behavior to a class of situations perceived as similar.

The philosophical objection to CEC is related to the empirical argument just discussed; it holds that character traits are vague constructions open to differing interpretations as to their meaning, depending on one's perspective. Kohlberg and Turiel (1971) observe:

> What is one man's integrity is another man's stubbornness; what is one man's honesty in expressing his true feelings is another man's insensitivity to the feelings of others. . . . Those sympathetic with a social movement, such as that of student protesters, view their behavior as reflecting the virtues of altruism, idealism, awareness, and courage. Those in opposition to the movement regard the same behavior as reflecting the vices of irresponsibility and disrespect for law and order. (p. 431)

Even if one were to arrive at clear definitions of different character traits through consensual agreement regarding their behavioral referents, there is the further objection that it is simply not plausible to assume that in a pluralistic and democratic culture there exists or can ever exist a societal consensus regarding which traits are "desirable" and should be taught. We would agree that certain traits are subject to much divergence of opinion concerning their moral worth. We wonder, however, if there are not some traits or values that can be both operationally defined and subject to general societal agreement on their desirability. Thinking rationally (e.g., taking alternatives into consideration and weighing the consequences of alternatives) self-awareness (e.g., an ability to identify and label one's feelings), getting along with others (e.g., empathy and considering the needs of others) are just three that come to mind.

Perhaps the most serious criticism of character education is an ethical criticism—mainly that the teaching of certain values, such as those taught in the CEC, constitutes indoctrination. Indoctrination refers to the teaching of certain values, attitudes, or beliefs without due regard to thoughtful reflection and direct, open inquiry and discussion concerning their reasonableness and worth in light of other, alternative values or beliefs. Because we believe that the teaching of certain values in the schools is both desirable and possible by means of nonindoctrinative procedures—a number of which are part of the CEC approach—we are certain that the blanket condemnation of character-education programs as indoctrination is unfair. Whether or not character education or any other approach to teaching values involves indoctrination depends on the *manner* in which certain values are taught. If CEC lessons could be taught in a nonindoctrinative way, and subsequent empirical research should provide evidence that they indeed lead to reductions in violence and vandalism in the schools, then we would maintain that it would be unethical not to teach them.*

Finally, an objection has been raised that the teaching of individual values, as in the CEC, does not realistically prepare the student to deal effectively with the difficult choices and decisions he or she must make in many problematic situations that involve a conflict of values. How does a student who has been taught the desirability of honesty, tolerance, and kindness, for example, decide what to do in a situation in which these three values might be in conflict? How does this student solve the dilemma presented by a particular situation in which being honest would involve being unkind or intolerant? The argument here is that character-education programs do not give sufficient attention to the explicit teaching of these cognitive processes involved in rational problem solving and decision making. We feel that this objection has some merit, and believe that this approach to prosocial value enhancement would thus benefit from the inclusion of the teaching and development of the cognitive skills necessary for effective problem solving and decision making in value-conflict situations. In this regard we wonder whether character education might be more prescriptively appropriate for younger than for older children. We see the nonindoctrinative teaching of individual values such as kindness, honesty, helpfulness, justice, or tolerance as especially beneficial to children in the early primary grades. Older children, however, from the upper primary grades through high school, are more likely to understand the inherent conflict among individual values in many situations, and are likely to be faced with increasingly complex choices and decisions in such conflictual situations. Other approaches with a greater emphasis on cognitive processes and development might be more appropriate for these children.

VALUES CLARIFICATION

Rationale

In 1966, Raths, Harmin, and Simon wrote a book, *Values and Teaching,* which was to exert a profound influence on values education in the schools. In it, the authors strongly oppose any approach to enhancing prosocial values whose ob-

---

*Although indoctrination of values via explicit teacher behaviors may be minimized with comparative ease, a second source of in-school value indoctrination is somewhat less readily dealt with. We refer to the indirect and implicit value transmission which accompanies the so-called "hidden curriculum" of classroom behavior management, automatized rules and regulations, evaluation and grading procedures, seating arrangements, and teacher-student interactions and role relationships. The "hidden curriculum," with its implicit value-transmitting function, has been rightfully criticized by many writers (Beck et al., 1976; Fenton, 1975; Hersh & Mutterer, 1975; Kohlberg, 1970b; Ringness, 1975). Values taught covertly and indirectly through the "hidden curriculum" constitute, by definition, a subtle form of indoctrination. Furthermore, a careful examination of the values often indoctrinated through the "hidden curriculum" of many classrooms reveals that some of these values, such as unquestioning conformity to rules and obedience to authority, are antithetical to other values consciously desired and taught in a democratic society. The best antidote to such indoctrination is, in our view, to make the implicit values of the hidden curriculum explicit and to subject them to direct scrutiny and reasoned debate regarding their desirability.

jective is the direct teaching of certain "desirable" values. In raising these objections, Raths et al. delineated a set of assumptions and guiding principles for a different approach to value enhancement; they called their approach *values clarification*.

Values are relative to subgroups within societies, and to individuals within subgroups. It is impossible for a pluralistic society such as ours to reach a general consensus as to which "desirable" values ought to be taught. Youngsters of today find themselves increasingly exposed to a bewildering array of divergent values from parents, peers, television, newspapers, teachers, and other sources. Those values considered "desirable" by one source may be "undesirable" to another. There are no universally "correct" values.

Values are relative to time, place, and circumstances in a rapidly changing world. In a rapidly changing technological society, the values that one finds useful and satisfying one year may become obsolete and unsatisfying the next. Desirable values in one situation may not be desirable in another. Youngsters have to learn to examine, evaluate, and revise their values as necessary in light of changed circumstances.

Values often conflict with one another. Youngsters are frequently faced with complex value choices in situations in which there are no simple answers and in which values may conflict. They must learn to choose what they value in given situations from among competing alternatives.

Values are a matter of personal discovery and choice. A person's values develop from personal experience and must be freely chosen by the person if they are to become effective guides for living. A teacher cannot teach certain values to a student directly. The teacher can, however, help the student discover and develop his or her own values.

Youngsters need help in developing and clarifying their own values. Values are those beliefs, attitudes, and goals that one especially cherishes and that give meaning, direction, and purpose to one's life. They are guideposts in one's continued efforts to make sense of and adapt to one's world in a constructive and satisfying way. It is becoming increasingly difficult for the young in our society, bombarded as they are by contradictory and constantly changing values from a multitude of sources, to develop a clear and coherent set of values of their own. Many young people today suffer from a common malady: value confusion or lack of values.

Value confusion in the young leads to certain kinds of behavioral problems. Value confusion may result in such behaviors as apathy, flightiness, inconsistency, overconformity, and chronic oppositionalness.

The schools have a responsibility to help youngsters clarify and develop their own values. The consequences of widespread value confusion in the young are too deleterious for individual and societal well-being for the schools to adopt a laissez-faire position toward values education. Young people need and want help in developing, clarifying, and applying their values and the schools have a responsibility to provide this help.

The Value Process

With these guiding principles in mind, Raths et al. (1978) developed what has become perhaps the most widely used approach to teaching values in the schools: values clarification. The authors maintained that although students could not be taught certain values, they certainly could learn a *process of valuing,* how to develop and to clarify their own values. Raths et al. defined this process of valuing as consisting of seven subprocesses:

1. *Choosing freely.* If [a value] is in fact to guide one's life . . . it must be a result of free choice. If there is coercion, the [value] is not likely to stay with one long, especially when out of range of the source of that coercion.
2. *Choosing from among alternatives.* . . . [T]here can be no [free] choice if there are no alternatives from which to choose.
3. *Choosing after thoughtful consideration of the consequences of each alternative.* . . . For [a value] to intelligently and meaningfully guide one's life, it must emerge from a weighing and an understanding of alternative consequences.
4. *Prizing and cherishing.* When we value something, it has a positive tone. We prize it, cherish it, esteem it, respect it, hold it dear. We are happy with our values.
5. *Affirming.* When we have chosen [a value] freely, after consideration of the alternatives, and when we are proud of our choice . . . we are likely to affirm that choice when asked about it. We are willing to publicly affirm our values. . . .
6. *Acting upon choices.* When we have a value, it shows up in aspects of our living. . . . We budget time or energy for our values. Nothing can be a value that does not, in fact, give direction to actual living. The person who talks about something but never does anything about it is dealing with something other than a value.
7. *Repeating.* Where something reaches the stage of a value, it is very likely to reappear on a number of occasions in the life of the person who holds it. It shows up in several different situations, at several different times. . . . Values tend to have a persistency, tend to make a pattern in a life. (pp. 28–29)

To simplify, these seven subprocesses can be grouped into three categories of choosing, prizing, and acting; and, in turn, these three categories involve cognitive, affective, and behavioral components, respectively. Thus, the goal of values clarification is to help students develop, clarify, and apply their own values by learning to use these seven subprocesses of valuing in their own lives. To accomplish this, Raths, Simon, and their associates have provided teachers with a variety of suggested methods, materials, activities, and exercises that help students learn, practice, and apply the seven subprocesses of valuing. It is in part this provision of numerous and easy-to-implement classroom activities or value-clarifying exercises that has made values clarification such a popular and widely used approach. The creative teacher can choose from these many activities or develop his or her own, always with the goal of providing students with opportunities for practicing one or more of the seven subprocesses of valuing.

Teaching Methods:
The Value-Clarifying Response

Fundamental to the success of all the values-clarification activities is a certain method of discussing value-related issues and problems with students. This method is the *value-clarifying response,* and more than any other technique, it captures the spirit of the values-clarification approach. Although originally designed as a way for the teacher to respond extemporaneously to value-related comments made by individual students in relatively informal situations (e.g., in the hallways between classes), it is critical for conducting value-clarifying classroom discussions in general.

The clarifying response is a way of responding to a student so as to raise questions in the student's mind, to encourage the student to examine his or her beliefs and actions, and thus to stimulate the student to clarify his or her values. The clarifying response avoids moralizing, sermonizing, advice giving, or evaluating. Proponents of values clarification are passionate in their insistence that the teacher avoid any and all traces of moralizing in his or her comments. With value issues, the teacher should avoid all "why" questions, which tend to make a student feel defensive or judged, "yes-or-no" questions, which limit a students' choices, and leading questions to which the teacher already has a predetermined "correct" answer in mind. There are no "correct" answers or values in values clarification. The teacher's comments must place the responsibility on the student to think about his or her own behavior and ideas and decide for himself or herself what it is that he or she values. The teacher must genuinely be ready to accept any value decisions that the student makes as a result of their discussions, including the student's choice not to think about or clarify his or her values. It should be noted that Raths et al. believe that there is nothing wrong with the teacher's eventually sharing his or her own values on an issue, as long as he or she lets the student think about it for himself or herself first, and is careful to present his or her opinion as just another alternative that the student might want to consider.

Examples of Value-Clarifying
Responses

Raths et al. (1966) list numerous kinds of clarifying responses that teachers might use. Some of these responses are oriented toward promoting one or more of the seven valuing components; others encourage reflection more generally. The following are several examples of clarifying responses suggested for stimulating some of the seven valuing components of subprocesses noted previously:

1. CHOOSING FREELY.

a. Where do you suppose you first got that idea?
b. Are you the only one in your crowd who feels this way?
c. What do your parents want you to do?

2. PRIZING AND CHERISHING.

a. Are you glad you feel that way?
b. Should everyone do it your way?
c. In what way would life be different without it?

3. ACTING UPON CHOICES.

a. I hear what you are for. Now is there anything you can do about it? Can I help?
b. Are you willing to put some of your money behind this idea?

Teaching Methods: Value-Clarifying Classroom Strategies

Raths, Simon, and their colleagues have suggested that teachers make use of a broad array of methods, including numerous types of class and small-group discussions, written exercises, homework assignments, role playing, and interviewing, as well as other activities in and out of class. In *Values Clarification: A Handbook of Practical Strategies for Teachers and Students* (Simon, Howe, & Kirschenbaum, 1972), the authors provide seventy-nine classroom activities, each designed to promote one or more of the seven subprocesses or components of valuing.

Guidelines for Implementation. Simon and his coworkers recommend the following guidelines for implementing these value-clarifying classroom strategies (Simon et al., 1972; Simon & Harmin, 1973):

1. Most values-clarification strategies can be used with any age levels, from elementary-school through high-school and adult groups, as long as the activities are adapted to the particular age group.
2. Many activities can be used with the entire class and/or small groups in the class.
3. Values clarification can be taught as a separate subject, with teachers' setting aside 5 minutes to an hour or more each day or week depending on goals and circumstances. Some schools may offer elective courses in values clarification.
4. Alternatively, values clarification can be integrated with standard subject matter taught in many regular courses such as social studies, history, literature, science, and health education. Most courses or subject matter can be taught on a facts level, a concepts level, and a values level. For example, Simon and Harmin (1973) illustrate these three levels with respect to teaching the United States Constitution in social-studies class: *On a facts level* the teacher might want the class to know such information as (1) where and when the Consti-

tution was drawn up; and (2) how the Constitution differed from the Articles of Confederation. *On a concepts level,* the teacher might discuss with the class (1) how the Constitution was a landmark in the evolving concept of a democracy; or (2) the concept of amendment and how it has operated in Congress. *On a values level,* the teacher might ask the class to consider some of the following issues: (1) Many student governments are really token governments controlled by the "native country"—that is, the administration. Is this true in your school? What can you do about it? If not you, who should do it? (2) When was the last time you signed a petition? and (3) Where do you stand on wire tapping, financial aid to parochial schools, censorship of pornographic magazines, and so on.

5. Although the strategies are explicit and easy to implement, it is up to the creative teacher to decide which of them he or she wants to use, how to adapt them to the particular needs of his or her class, and how much time to spend on each activity and the discussion following the activity.

6. When using these activities, it is critical that the teacher facilitate a classroom atmosphere of openness, acceptance, respect, and trust. The teacher must model this in his or her own behavior.

7. The teacher should share his or her values (or value confusion) on a particular issue *after* the students have had a chance to think for themselves and to express their own points of view. The teacher's particular values should be presented as just another alternative point of view, holding no more weight than anyone else's.

Examples of Classroom Strategies

Forced-Choice Ladder. This activity promotes choosing from alternatives and choosing by considering the consequences of alternatives. The teacher asks students to construct a *forced-choice ladder,* with eight to sixteen steps. Then the teacher presents a series of alternatives which reflect particular values. Using a key word, the student ranks each alternative in terms of whether he or she is for or against the value. In the following example, taken from Miller (1976), the student ranks the following eight alternatives ranging from "the person I'd least like to be like" at the bottom of the ladder to "the position I'd most like to be like at the top."

```
                                                        The person I'd
                                                        most like to
                                            8           be like.
                                    7
                                6
                            5
                        4
                    3
                2
The person I'd  1
least like to
be like.
```

1. A rich person who gives very generously to charities. (Philanthropist)

2. A person whose prime concern is conserving the environment so that he becomes involved in various conservation projects. (Ecologist)
3. An individual whose main concern in life is integrating himself through self-help techniques, such as meditation and yoga. (Meditator)
4. An individual whose main focus in life is getting involved with and helping other people through the Salvation Army. (Helper)
5. An individual whose main value is serving his country through the armed forces. (Patriot)
6. A person whose primary focus in life is his small business. He devotes most of his energy toward running an efficient and profitable business. (Business person)
7. An individual whose primary concern is taking care of and spending time with his family. (Family head)
8. A person who feels that the only hope for humanity is through world organizations and who commits his life to working for the World Federalists. (Internationalist) (Miller, 1976, p. 53.)

After the students complete this exercise individually, they can be divided into small groups to compare their choices. This gives them an opportunity to clarify the reasoning behind their value choices.

Public Interview. This popular strategy gives the student the opportunity to affirm and explain his or her stand on various value issues publicly. The teacher asks for volunteers who would like to be interviewed in front of the class about some of their beliefs, feelings, and actions. The volunteer sits in front of the room, with the teacher asking questions from the back of the room.

The following are some examples of interview questions suggested by Simon et al. (1972) for secondary-school students:

1. How do you feel about grades in school?
2. What are some of the things you really believe in?
3. What do you see yourself doing five years from now? Ten years? Twenty?
4. Would you bring up your children differently from the way you are being [were] brought up?
5. Can you think of something you would like to say to the group that you think might be good for them to hear? (p. 218)

Alternative-Action Search. In this strategy students learn to consider alternatives for action in various situations and to make their everyday actions more consistent with their values. The student is presented with a specific vignette that calls for some proposed action. The teacher then asks, "Now, given all your beliefs, feelings, and values related to this vignette, ideally, what would you want to do in this situation?" The following is a sample vignette provided by Simon et al. (1972):

You are on a vacation trip and are driving to the beach with your parents. You would like to go to the amusement park, but you are concerned because you have spent most of the money you had saved for your vacation earlier.

Your father stops for gasoline and you get out and walk around. A lady is walking back to her car and you see her purse fall open and her wallet fall out. You walk over, pick up the wallet just as the lady gets into her car to drive away. The edges of several ten dollar bills are sticking out of the wallet. No one saw you pick it up. What would you do? (p. 200)

Evaluation and Critique

The popularity of values clarification is beyond dispute. The many strategies and activities developed by its proponents are interesting, highly structured, and easily applied and integrated into the school curriculum. Nevertheless, there is considerable confusion as to what this approach to values training actually accomplishes—that is, what behavioral and attitudinal changes it facilitates in students. Unfortunately, the empirical research conducted has not done much to clarify this confusion.

The original hypotheses proposed by Raths et al. (1966) were that: (1) certain kinds of behavioral problems often seen in school—for example, chronic apathy, flightiness, overconformity, overdissension—are related to a lack of values or value confusion in students; (2) by helping students develop and clarify their own values, values-clarification activities would lead to a reduction in frequency and severity of these behavior patterns; and (3) these activities would also lead to an increase in such constructive behaviors as active interest and involvement in school, more positive attitudes toward learning, persistence in school tasks, improved decision-making abilities, and greater self-esteem and confidence. Empirical research has provided some tentative and partial support for the effectiveness of values clarification in decreasing some of the inappropriate behaviors and increasing some of the constructive attitudes and behaviors mentioned previously in students ranging from primary grades to college level (Raths et al., 1966; Kirschenbaum, 1975). Much of this research, however, is methodologically weak. There have been inadequate control groups, measurement problems, and assessment of constructive behaviors and attitudes by simplistic scales of questionable reliability and validity.

There is also the theoretical and empirical problem of identifying the active ingredients in a values-clarification program. Are all seven valuing subprocesses proposed by Raths et al. (1966) necessary? Are there other operative subprocesses or components? For example, Kirschenbaum has rejected Raths et al.'s original seven components and has constructed a more elaborate framework which includes the components of feeling, thinking, and communicating (each with its own set of subprocesses), in addition to choosing and acting as critical in the valuing process (Kirschenbaum, 1973). Alternately, one might ask whether any of these proposed valuing components are necessary. Raths et al. (1966) claim that an open and trusting classroom climate facilitated by a warm, nonjudgmental teacher is a prerequisite for an effective values-clarification program. Could this classroom climate be more important than the actual learning of the valuing components in helping students become less apathetic, more actively involved in learning, more purposeful and confident, and so on? These are questions that only further, more rigorous research will answer.

The confusion in the values-clarification movement over just what kinds of changes or behavioral outcomes this approach facilitates in students is made more acute by the "value relativity" issue. Proponents of this approach maintain, as a major guiding principle, that values are relative to the individual, that no values are better or more desirable in general than others and that there are no valid, non-relativistic criteria for judging behavior as right or wrong. The teacher must accept the student's right to arrive at any values he or she chooses through the valuing process. It is our view that "value-relativity" (1) is a value position in itself; (2) is an empirically unsupported value position; and (3) has deleterious practical implications for values training in particular and social behavior in general. The "value-relativity" position is antithetical to the very premise of this book. In emphasizing the importance of learning constructive alternatives to violence and vandalism, we are assuming that these various alternatives reflect more desirable values than violence and vandalism. We believe that a general societal consensus does exist on this issue, and that the schools have a responsibility to teach students alternative values to violence and aggression in a nonindoctrinative way.

KOHLBERG'S MORAL EDUCATION

Lawrence Kohlberg believes that the direct teaching of particular values, as in character education, constitutes indoctrination. He also believes that the principle of value relativity, embodied in values clarification, is philosophically and scientifically unsound and that it leaves teachers as well as students in a morass of value confusion as to the meaning of morality and the aims of moral education. Over a span of twenty years, Kohlberg has elaborated an alternative position on moral development and education which he claims is philosophically justified, empirically supported, and which escapes the quagmires of indoctrination and value relativity. Kohlberg's position, based on cognitive-developmental principles, represents the most theoretically sophisticated contemporary approach to values training and has generated much needed debate as well as empirical research (Kohlberg, 1968, 1969, 1970a, 1971a, 1971b, 1972a, 1972b, 1973, 1975).

Rationale and Background

To understand Kohlberg's theory we must first understand the meaning and implications of a "cognitive-developmental" approach to morality. A cognitive perspective on morality emphasizes that there are qualitatively different ways in which people think about, reason, and make sense of basic moral issues (e.g., value of life, truth, or justice) in their continual attempts to relate effectively to other human beings in their world. A developmental perspective on morality emphasizes that these fundamentally different ways of reasoning about and making sense of basic moral issues change over time—that is, over the course of a person's growth. Central to a cognitive-developmental perspective is the notion of stages. Stages are structured or organized systems of thought. When we say that there are qualitatively different ways of thinking about moral issues over the course of a person's growth, we are saying that there are distinct *stages* of moral reasoning that characterize a person's development. Critical to the cognitive-developmental concept of stages are the following:

1. *The final or "highest stage" represents the theoretically "ideal" endpoint of development.* As a person develops from a young child to a mature adult, his or her ways of reasoning about moral issues progress through a series of stages toward a final or highest stage that may or may not be reached.

2. *Stages form an invariant sequence.* As a person develops, his or her ways of reasoning about moral issues progress through a series of stages (to the hypothesized final stage) in a fixed order or sequence. Although a person may progress through this sequence of stages more slowly or more rapidly than others, and although his or her development may become arrested or fixated at a particular stage (which may then become the highest stage that that person achieves), if that person does progress, it is always to the next stage up. This invariant sequence of stages is assumed to be true for all people—that is, there is according to Kohlberg a hypothesized universally invariant sequence of stages of moral development.

3. *Stages are "hierarchical integrations": Higher stages are "better" than lower stages.* Each successive stage represents an increasingly integrated and more effective mode of moral reasoning and problem solving than the previous stage.

4. *The motivation for stage transition is cognitive conflict.* During certain critical periods in a person's development, he or she experiences his or her current mode of moral reasoning (current stage) as increasingly inadequate for understanding and resolving more complex problems and dilemmas in value-conflictual situations. This induces a state of cognitive conflict, doubt, or uncertainty and dissatisfaction which in turn induces him or her to begin experimenting with modes of reasoning characteristic of the next higher stage.

According to Kohlberg, the cognitive-developmental approach to moral education is nonindoctrinative because it involves the stimulation of a natural progression of development in the direction in which a person is already heading. Furthermore, it is contrary to the premise of value relativity because the notion of a universally invariant sequence of stages or moral reasoning implies that (1) there are universal modes of reasoning about moral issues or values and, thus, for judging behavior as right or wrong; and (2) that some of these modes of reasoning are "better" or more adequate than others.

The background for this approach to moral development and education lies in the educational philosophy of John Dewey and the developmental psychology of Jean Piaget. Dewey believed that cognitive-intellectual and moral development were inseparable as educational goals. In further suggesting that (1) development, both cognitive and moral, occurs in an invariant sequence of stages; and (2) developmental progression requires the stimulation of the child's critical thinking processes through the arousal of cognitive conflict (intellectual uncertainty, confusion, doubt), Dewey laid the foundation for a cognitive-developmental approach to moral education. In so doing, Dewey looked to psychology to provide the necessary knowledge about the stages and processes of cognitive and moral development.

For some fifty years, Jean Piaget has been engaged in theorizing and research concerning the process of cognitive-intellectual development. He has also investigated the development of thinking or reasoning concerning explicitly moral situations. In his seminal work in this area, *The Moral Judgment of the Child* (Piaget, 1932), Piaget theorized that there were two major stages of moral development: (1) an earlier stage—heteronomous morality (or moral realism or morality of constraint); and (2) a later stage (beginning roughly at 10 to 11 years)—autonomous morality (or moral relativism or morality of cooperation). Discussion of these stages is beyond the scope of this chapter. We wish only to comment that in addition to certain conceptual ambiguities (Ginsberg & Opper, 1969), an extensive review of the research by Lickona (1976a) indicates that Piaget's two-stage theory is lacking empirical support as a comprehensive theory of moral development. Nevertheless, it provided the basis for Kohlberg's more elaborate and systematized six-stage perspective.

Kohlberg's Six Stages
of Moral Reasoning

Kohlberg's Hypothesis. Kohlberg's consideration of moral philosophy led him to conclude that (1) the moral domain is essentially limited to those situations wherein conflicting interests and values—the competing claims of different parties—are at stake; (2) morality involves those modes of reasoning and problem solving necessary for resolving such competing claims in value-conflictual situations; and (3) the essence of morality is the principle of justice—the primary regard for the value and equality of all human beings, and for reciprocity in human relations; that is, the principle of "justice" is philosophically the most justifiable criterion or standard for resolving conflicting claims and interests in problematic social situations. Thus, Kohlberg used moral philosophy to hypothesize that moral development proceeds through a universally invariant sequence of stages of moral reasoning based primarily on increasingly adequate conceptions of "justice" toward a postulated "ideal" endpoint (highest or final stage) of a fully differentiated, hierarchically integrated, and universalized sense of justice.

Research Methods: The Moral-Judgment Interview. To investigate his hypothesis, Kohlberg studied the development of moral reasoning through a *moral-judgment interview.* In this method, a trained interviewer presents the interviewee with a series of brief stories, each of which contains a moral dilemma involving value-conflicting alternative actions with which the protagonist is confronted. The interviewee is asked which action the protagonist *should* take and why, and a series of probe questions attempt to ascertain the nature of the interviewee's reasoning and decision-making processes vis-à-vis certain moral issues such as the value of human life, laws and rules, punishment, and justice.

Longitudinal and Cross-Cultural Research: Kohlberg's Six Stages. In 1957, Kohlberg began investigating through moral dilemmas the moral reasoning of

seventy-two lower- and middle-class urban American boys aged 10 to 16. He classified their responses on the basis of the similarity of the reasoning process used and
was able to distinguish six basic types of moral reasoning that he felt corresponded
to a developmental sequence of stages. Subsequent retesting of fifty of these same
subjects every three years (Kohlberg, 1969, 1976; Kohlberg & Kramer, 1969)
essentially confirmed his hypothesis that the development of moral reasoning pro-
gressed through an invariant sequence of six stages, although the rate of development and the highest stage achieved varied somewhat (e.g., many subjects did not
progress to the final one or two stages).

Based on his cross-cultural research, Kohlberg also concluded that (1) people
in all cultures and subcultures reason about the same basic moral concepts or values—for example, the value of life, love and affection, contract and trust, laws and
rules, authority, punishment, property, truth, liberty, and most fundamentally,
justice; and (2) each successive stage in his universally invariant sequence represents
an increasingly differentiated and hierarchically integrated mode of reasoning about
these universal moral concepts or values. It is difficult to overemphasize the significance of such conclusions. For one thing, if valid, they would put the final "nail in
the coffin" of value relativity. Needless to say, "No issue has stirred more heated
debate in the ranks of social scientists engaged in the study of values" (Lickona,
1976b, p. 9). Although we submit that there is not enough sound empirical research
at present either to support or refute Kohlberg's cross-cultural conclusions, we wish
to emphasize that they are fundamental to his theory. To summarize: Kohlberg
claims to have provided empirical support for the existence of a universally invariant
sequence of six stages of reasoning about certain fundamental, universal moral
values, the most fundamental of which is justice. The following description of these
six stages, hierarchically ordered in three levels of two stages each, is taken from
Kohlberg (1971b):

I. Preconventional Level

At this level the child is responsive to cultural rules and labels of good and
bad, right or wrong, but interprets these labels in terms of either the physical
or the hedonistic consequences of action (punishment, reward, exchange of
favours) or in terms of the physical power of those who enunciate the rules
and labels. The level comprises the following two stages:

Stage 1. Punishment and obedience orientation. The physical consequences of
action determine its goodness or badness regardless of the human meaning or
value of the consequences. Avoidance of punishment and unquestioning defer-
ence to power are valued in their own right, not in terms of respect for an
underlying moral order supported by punishment and authority (the latter
being stage 4).

Stage 2. Instrumental relativist orientation. Right action consists of that which
instrumentally satisfies one's own needs and occasionally needs of others. Human relations are viewed in terms similar to those of the market place. Elements of fairness, or reciprocity, and equal sharing are present, but they are
always interpreted in a physical pragmatic way. Reciprocity is a matter of
"you scratch my back and I'll scratch yours," not of loyalty, gratitude, or
justice.

II. Conventional Level

At this level, maintaining the expectations of the individual's family, group, or nation is perceived as valuable in its own right, regardless of immediate and obvious consequences. The attitude is one not only of *conformity* to personal expectations and social order, but of loyalty to it, of actively *maintaining,* supporting, and justifying the order and of identifying with the persons or group involved in it. This level comprises the following two stages:

Stage 3. Interpersonal concordance or "good boy-nice girl" orientation. Good behavior is that which pleases or helps others and is approved by them. There is much conformity to stereotypical images of what is majority or "natural" behavior. Behavior is frequently judged by intention: "he means well" becomes important for the first time. One earns approval by being "nice."

Stage 4. "Law and order" orientation. There is orientation toward authority, fixed rules, and the maintenance of the social order. Right behavior consists of doing one's duty, showing respect for authority, and maintaining the given social order for its own sake.

III. Post-Conventional, Autonomous, or Principled Level

At this level there is a clear effort to define moral values and principles that have validity and application apart from the authority of the groups or persons holding these principles and apart from the individual's own identification with these groups. This level again has two steps.

Stage 5. Social-contract legalistic orientation. Generally, this stage has utilitarian overtones. Right action tends to be defined in terms of general individual rights and terms of standards that have been critically examined and agreed upon by the whole society. There is a clear awareness of the relativism of personal values and opinions and a corresponding emphasis on procedural rules for reaching consensus. Aside from what is constitutionally and democratically agreed upon, the right is a matter of personal "values" and "opinion." The result is an emphasis upon the "legal point of view," but with an emphasis upon the possibility of changing law in terms of rational considerations of social utility (rather than freezing it in terms of stage 4 "law and order"). Outside the legal realm, free agreement, and contract is the binding element of obligation. This is the "official" morality of the United States government and constitution.

Stage 6. Universal ethical-principle orientation. Right is defined by the decision of conscience in accord with self-chosen *ethical principles* appealing to logical comprehensiveness, universality, and consistency. These principles are abstract and ethical (the Golden Rule, the categorical imperative); they are not concrete moral rules like the Ten Commandments. At heart, these are universal principles of justice, of the reciprocity and equality of human rights and of respect for the dignity of human beings as individual persons. (Kohlberg, 1971b, pp. 86–88)

The Relationship Between Kohlberg's
Stages and Behavior

As we noted earlier in this chapter, the major basis for our interest in this book in values training lies in the degree to which prosocial values actually enhance the likelihood that prosocial behavior will occur and/or decrease the probability of antisocial behavior. Kohlberg and his colleagues have provided evidence showing a positive relationship between (1) preconventional moral reasoning (stages 1 and 2) and certain forms of antisocial behavior; and (2) postconventional moral reasoning (stages 5 and 6) and certain kinds of principled, prosocial behaviors.

The Importance of Conventional Moral Reasoning. Research indicates that in the United States, preconventional moral reasoning is characteristic of children under age 10, some adolescents, and the *vast majority of adolescent delinquents and adult criminals* (Kohlberg, 1976).

PRECONVENTIONAL MORAL REASONING AND ANTISOCIAL BEHAVIOR

The relationship between preconventional moral reasoning and delinquency and crime is especially relevant to us. A study by Freundlich and Kohlberg (see Kohlberg, 1973) found that 83 percent of 15 to 17 year old working-class delinquents were at preconventional stages, compared with only 23 percent of working class nondelinquent adolescents. Subsequent studies have shown that adolescent delinquents or adult inmates almost invariably scored at the preconventional level (Fodor, 1972; Hudgins & Prentice, 1973; Kohlberg, Sharf, & Hickey, 1972). These studies suggest that preconventional moral reasoning may well be a critical factor in consistent delinquent and criminal behavior. This should not be surprising because the preconventional individual, by definition, has not yet developed to the point at which he or she can really understand, let alone consistently uphold, conventional societal rules, laws, and expectations. For the stage-1 individual, the reason for doing right is simply to avoid punishment from powerful authority figures; for the stage-2 individual, the reason for doing right is to "serve one's own needs or interests in a world where you have to recognize that other people have their interests, too" (Kohlberg, 1976, p. 34). Thus, for preconventional individuals, there simply are no adequate reasons for obeying and conforming to societal rules and laws in the absence of powerful authority figures or concrete payoffs.

CRITICAL PERIOD FOR THE TRANSITION TO CONVENTIONAL MORAL REASONING

Kohlberg's research suggests that in this country pre- to early adolescence (roughly ages 10 to 13) seems to be a developmentally "critical period" for the transition from preconventional (i.e., stage 2) to conventional (i.e., stage 3) moral reasoning. Those children who do not begin to evidence at least *some* stage-3 moral reasoning during this period may get "locked into" or fixated at the preconventional level. For example, compared with a 12 year old at stage 2, it is very difficult for a 17 year old at stage 2 to move to stage 3. Thus, for Kohlberg, one important goal of moral education would be to prevent preconventional-level fixation in those upper-elementary and junior high-school students whose moral development is beginning to lag behind.

The Importance of Postconventional Moral Reasoning. Research indicates that in this country conventional moral reasoning (stages 3 and 4) is characteristic of the vast majority of adolescents and adults. Stage 3 is reached as early as age 9, but usually later, whereas stage 4 is usually reached by middle or late adolescence. *Postconventional moral reasoning (stages 5 and 6) is attained by only a small minority of the adult population,* with perhaps 10 to 15 percent reaching stage 5 in their late teens, early twenties, or even later; very few people reach stage 6 at all, and those who do may be older than 30 (Fenton, 1977).

For Kohlberg, such findings have particularly important implications for moral education because he maintains that postconventional moral reasoning is critical for (1) effective citizenship in a just and democratic society; and (2) the consistent performance of certain kinds of prosocial behaviors in situations in which conventional rules and expectations are ambiguous or actually oppose such prosocial behaviors.

POSTCONVENTIONAL MORAL REASONING AND EFFECTIVE CITIZENSHIP

Even though the achievement of conventional moral reasoning may be laudable for adolescent and adult criminal offenders, it is not, according to Kohlberg, a satisfactory long-term goal for the majority of citizens in a participatory democracy such as ours. For example, the conventional individual believes in obeying and upholding societal laws as an end in itself. The postconventional individual believes that society's laws are rules of conduct designed to protect the fundamental rights (e.g., life, liberty, truth) and well-being of its members; these fundamental rights are in turn based on the universal principle of justice—that is, "of the reciprocity and equality of human rights and respect for the dignity of human beings as individual persons" (Kohlberg, 1971b, p. 88). For the conventional individual, the law is right because it is the law; there is a confusion between the legal and the moral. For the postconventional individual, the law is right if it is just; the moral is differentiated from and considered superordinate to the legal. The postconventional person believes in changing those laws that are contrary to the principle of justice and, thus, to the welfare of society's members. Thus, Kohlberg and his colleagues maintain that it is the postconventional rather than the conventional citizen who is necessary for the development and maintenance of a free and just democracy. The very structure of our government as embodied in the social contract of the Constitution is based on postconventional (specifically, stage-5) conceptions of the values of justice, life, liberty, contract and trust, laws and rules, and authority. Because only a small minority of adults in this country reach stage-5 moral reasoning, we are left with the alarming conclusion that the vast majority of adult American citizens do not fully understand the principles of justice, contract, and law on which their government is based.

POSTCONVENTIONAL MORAL REASONING
AND PRINCIPLED, PROSOCIAL BEHAVIOR

Kohlberg and his colleagues have provided empirical support for a positive relationship between postconventional moral reasoning and such principled pro-social behaviors as honesty (resistance to cheating), nonviolence (refusal to inflict pain on another person), and altruistic bystander intervention (intervening to help someone in distress) in situations in which conventional authoritative rules and social expectations are ambiguous or even opposed to such prosocial behaviors.

Concerning honesty, studies by Brown (Kohlberg & Turiel, 1971) with college students and Krebs (1967) with children found that a much greater percentage of postconventional than conventional students actually refrained from cheating in experimental situations characterized by an absence of explicit authoritative or group sanctions against cheating. Kohlberg and Turiel (1971) explain that only the postconventional student can formulate adequate reasons for cheating in the absence of *explicit* conventional rules against cheating. Such reasons, based on post-conventional conceptions of justice, contract, and trust, involve an understanding that (1) a mutual trust, agreement, or contract not to cheat is *implicit* in such a situation; (2) while it does not seem that bad if one person cheats, what holds for all must hold for one; and (3) in cheating, one is taking unfair advantage over those who do not cheat.

Concerning nonviolence, Kohlberg (Kohlberg & Turiel, 1971) gave the moral-judgment interview to subjects in Milgram's (1963) classic study. In Milgram's study, undergraduate subjects were required, in the guise of a learning experiment, to administer increasingly severe electric-shock punishment to a "stooge victim" (an experimental confederate). Kohlberg found that 75 percent of the stage-6 subjects, compared with only 13 percent of all the subjects at lower stages (including stage-5), refused to continue shocking the "victim." Kohlberg and Turiel (1971) explain that only stage-6 students could formulate a clear reason for not shocking the "victim" under orders from the experimenter—that is, the experimenter did not have the moral right to ask them to inflict pain on another person. Even stage-5 students were unable to reach a clear decision as to what to do in this situation because, according to stage-5 principles of social contract, both the "victim" and the subjects had voluntarily contracted to participate in the experiment.

Concerning altruistic bystander intervention, McNamee (1977) created the following experimental situation in which it was necessary to violate the experimenter's authority to help someone. The experimenter and subject (college student) enter a room in which the latter is to receive the moral-judgment interview. An experimental confederate arrives, presents himself or herself as the next subject, and tells the experimenter he or she cannot do the experiment because he or she has just taken drugs and is having "a bad time." In the real subject's presence, the confederate persists in asking the experimenter for help with his or her distress, with the experimenter refusing until, finally, the confederate leaves the room. Thus, the subject is faced with the choice of remaining an uninvolved bystander or intervening to help the confederate. McNamee (1977) found that 100 percent of stage-6 subjects and 68 percent of stage-5 subjects, compared with only 38 percent of stage-4 subjects and 28 percent of stage-3 subjects, actually intervened in some way (e.g., offering a referral or personal assistance) to help the confederate. Again, only stage-6 subjects could consistently formulate a clear reason for intervening, as expressed in the following representative stage-6 response: "I felt an obligation to the experimenter to finish, but in this case, helping a person in trouble took priority" (McNamee, 1977). Representative stage-based responses from those subjects who did not intervene were: (1) stage 3: "I was concerned about what the experimenter would think of me—her disapproval"; (2) stage 4: "My role was that of a subject. I'm not qualified as a psychologist. I had to trust the experimenter's judgment"; and (3) stage 5: "I wanted to help, but I had an obligation to the experimenter to finish the experiment" (McNamee, 1977, p. 30).

CRITICAL PERIOD FOR THE TRANSITION
TO POSTCONVENTIONAL MORAL REASONING

Kohlberg's research suggests that, in this country, late adolescence to early adulthood (roughly ages 16 to 20) appears to be a developmentally "critical period" for the transition from conventional to postconventional (i.e., stage-5) moral reasoning. Those people who do not begin to use *at least some* stage-5 moral reasoning during this period may fixate at the conventional level, making it increasingly difficult to develop postconventional reasoning as they get older. Thus, for Kohlberg, another major goal of moral education would be to prevent conventional-level fixation in those high-school and college students whose moral development is beginning to lag behind.

The Goal of Moral Education: A Recap. We have spent considerable time elaborating the background, rationale, and some of the theoretical principles of Kohlberg's perspective. We feel this is necessary in order to provide an understanding of the basic goal and teaching strategy of this complex approach to values training. The goal, to recapitulate, is to facilitate the development of moral reasoning through each of the stages, and the eventual attainment of postconventional reasoning (at least stage-5, although ideally stage-6). The aim is also to prevent developmental fixation or retardation at preconventional and conventional levels, especially during the critical transitional periods of pre- to early adolescence and late adolescence to early adulthood, respectively.

We now turn our attention to methods for achieving this goal. In the next

section we (1) discuss conditions that facilitate moral development; and (2) introduce a specific teaching strategy designed to provide these conditions.

FACILITATIVE CONDITIONS
FOR MORAL DEVELOPMENT
AND A TEACHING STRATEGY
FOR MORAL EDUCATION

Facilitative Conditions
for Moral Development

Kohlberg and his colleagues have explored the question of which conditions
are facilitative of the development of moral reasoning. The following represent some
pertinent generalizations from their thinking and research:

Role-Taking Opportunities through Reciprocal Social Interaction. Moral
problems arise when the differing interests, values, and perspectives of different
individuals come into conflict. It follows that moral reasoning about such problems
requires the ability to perceive and to comprehend the differing perspectives of
other people. This ability to take the role or perspective of others, to put oneself in
their shoes and see the world through their eyes has been variously referred to as
role taking, social perspective taking, or empathy (in the cognitive rather than affective sense).

Concerning moral education, the provision of role-taking opportunities—that
is, exposure to and mutual exchange among students (as well as between teacher
and student) of different ways of reasoning about moral problems—is necessary for
moral development, although it is not sufficient in itself.

Cognitive Conflict over Genuine Moral Dilemmas. As previously discussed, it
is axiomatic to Kohlberg's theory that the motivation for transition from one stage
to the next higher stage is the subjective experience of cognitive conflict. Cognitive
conflict, it will be recalled, is a state of intellectual doubt, uncertainty, and dissatisfaction arising out of the felt inability of one's current mode of moral reasoning
(one's current stage) to resolve moral problems adequately. This can only happen,
the theory holds, if during certain developmentally optimal or critical periods, the
person is repeatedly confronted with moral problems that represent genuine moral
dilemmas—that is, situations involving a conflict of fundamental human values and
interests with no clear-cut, culturally approved right or wrong answers. The resulting experience of cognitive conflict is heightened if these moral dilemmas, whether
actual or hypothetical, are (1) genuinely meaningful or relevant to the person;
(2) cognitively stimulating and challenging to him or her; and (3) presented *in a
social context that provides for role-taking opportunities*—that is, for exposure to
and exchange of conflicting opinions and different modes (stages) of reasoning

about these dilemmas. In such a social context, the cognitively conflicted person will begin experimenting with some of these different modes or stages of moral reasoning.

Exposure to the Next Higher Stage of Reasoning. If the cognitively conflicted person is exposed to a mode of moral reasoning one stage above his or her own, this will increase his or her sense of conflict still further and will induce him or her to begin experimenting with that stage of reasoning in particular. This is because it is also axiomatic to Kohlberg's theory that the cognitively conflicted person is attracted to the next higher stage of reasoning because it appears more integrated, logical, and adequate for resolving moral dilemmas. Kohlberg and his colleagues have provided empirical evidence in support of this axiom. Specifically, Rest (1973) and Rest, Turiel, and Kohlberg (1969) have demonstrated that people subjectively prefer the highest stage of reasoning about moral dilemmas that they can comprehend (paraphrase without distortion), which is typically one stage above the one they predominantly use.

A Teaching Strategy for Moral Education: Classroom Discussions of Moral Dilemmas

On the basis of these considerations concerning facilitative conditions for moral development, Kohlberg and his colleagues developed a specific teaching strategy designed to provide these conditions in the classroom. Whereas character education and values clarification use numerous instructional methods and strategies for achieving their respective objectives, Kohlberg's approach to moral education, insofar as it is limited to the confines of the classroom, relies exclusively on one basic strategy: classroom discussions of moral dilemmas (Kohlberg's approach also involves intervention strategies aimed at the structural-organizational level of the entire school as a moral-educational institution). In this strategy, meaningful and cognitively stimulating moral dilemmas are used to trigger teacher-led moral discussion and debate among student peers, especially in social-studies and English classes. Because the typical upper-elementary, junior-high, senior-high, or college class consists of students who are at two or three adjacent stages of moral reasoning, such moral discussions are likely to induce the most cognitive conflict in the relatively lower-stage students in the class and to provide them with critical role-taking opportunities, particularly in the form of exposure to modes of reasoning one stage above their own. If such moral discussions are continued over a period of time and across numerous dilemmas, the "lower-stage" students should gradually begin to make the transition to the next higher stage of reasoning. This is consistent with the goal of moral education as preventing fixation or retardation in the moral development of students who are beginning to lag behind their peers during critical transitional periods, as opposed to accelerating the development of "higher-stage" students who are progressing satisfactorily.

Recently, several experimental investigations have attempted to facilitate stage change through moral-dilemma discussion programs, ranging from upper-elementary through college levels (Blatt & Kohlberg, 1975; Boyd, 1973; Colby, Kohlberg, Fenton, Speicher-Dubin, & Lieberman, 1977; Rest, 1974). Results generally indicated that a greater percentage of students in the "experimental" classrooms (i.e., who participated in teacher-guided peer discussion of moral dilemmas) made notable progress toward the next higher stage of reasoning than did students in various types of control-group classrooms. An important investigation in this context was conducted by Blatt and Kohlberg (1975). They led moral discussions (18- to 45-minute sessions held twice weekly) with forty-four public-school students divided into four "experimental" classrooms varying systematically in age (sixth graders, ages 11 to 12, and tenth graders, ages 15 to 16) and race-related socioeconomic status (lower-class blacks and lower middle-class blacks and lower middle-class whites). Results indicated that students in these "experimental" classrooms showed significant upward change in moral reasoning (they moved an average of one-third of a stage up) compared with students in various control-group classrooms (who remained essentially unchanged); furthermore, "experimentals" maintained this upward-change advantage over "controls" at a one-year follow-up investigation. Blatt and Kohlberg (1975) also found the following: (1) almost all changes in moral reasoning occurring through moral discussions were in the direction of the next higher stage (e.g., students at stage 2 moved in the direction of stage 3, while students at stage 3 moved in the direction of stage 4); this suggested that these changes were due to genuine stimulation of the "natural" sequence of moral development rather than mere verbal learning of phrases and concepts at other stages of reasoning; and (2) about as much over-all change in moral reasoning occurred in lower-class black children as in lower middle-class white children; this suggested that moral discussions, although relying heavily on verbal exchange, were effective regardless of differences in verbal skills and social background.

Colby, Kohlberg, Fenton, Speicher-Dubin, and Lieberman (1977) essentially replicated Blatt and Kohlberg's (1975) findings, although with regular high-school teachers' leading moral discussions in their social-studies classes. Importantly, Colby et al. (1977) also found that, compared with students in the "experimental" classrooms who showed minimal change in moral reasoning, students who showed the greatest degree of upward change were more likely to have (1) initially begun the experiment at some optimal or critical period for stage transition (e.g., 13-year-old preconventional students showed more upward change than older preconventional students who "may have been at stage 2 long enough to have 'fixated' at that level" (Colby et al., 1977, p. 102); (2) been in "experimental" classrooms consisting of students who represented an initially wider range of adjacent stages (e.g., three as opposed to two) of moral reasoning; (3) had teachers who used a greater number of moral dilemmas or discussion periods; and (4) had teachers who were more skillful in eliciting moral reasoning from students at adjacent stages during discussion.

Now that we have established the rationale, principles, and research base for conducting classroom discussions of moral dilemmas, we examine the concrete implementation of this teaching strategy.

Conducting Classroom Discussions
of Moral Dilemmas:
The Teaching Process

Most of the material in this section comes from Galbraith and Jones' (1976) book, *Moral Reasoning: A Teaching Handbook for Adapting Kohlberg to the Classroom,* and Beyer's (1976) article "Conducting Moral Discussions in the Classroom." The interested reader is encouraged to consult these sources for further information as well as for variations on the basic teaching strategy. This strategy requires that the teacher help students engage in the following four-step process: (1) confront a moral dilemma; (2) state a tentative position; (3) examine the reasoning; and (4) reflect on an individual position. In discussing each of these four steps, we include recommendations for implementation as well as illustrations of the teaching process with reference to discussion of a particular moral dilemma. The following points should be kept in mind for a clearer understanding of this discussion:

1. Although the teaching process as illustrated in this section is geared to a standard 45-minute class period, a given moral-dilemma discussion can be organized in advance by the teacher to extend over a number of class periods, or alternately, can spontaneously arise within the context of teaching regular subject matter and take only 10 to 15 minutes.
2. Moral-dilemma discussions can take place at any level of education, from upper-elementary to college, and in the context of almost any regular subject-matter course. Indeed, it is recommended that such discussions, rather than being taught as "pure" moral-education lessons, be integrated within the regular school curriculum, particularly in social-studies, English-literature, history, and civic-education classes.
3. Teachers do *not* have to be able to identify the stages of reasoning their students use in order to lead moral discussions. Unless a class is extraordinarily homogeneous, it will usually contain students who reason predominantly at two or three adjacent stages. It is the mutual interaction and confrontation among students at adjacent stages which is critical.
4. The teachers' primary roles, then, are to promote such interaction and confrontation among students, as well as to keep the focus of the discussion explicitly on those moral issues involved in the particular dilemma. The teachers' skills in communication and group facilitation are more important in leading moral discussions than are their skills in stage identification and interpretation.
5. It is critical that the teachers be able to facilitate nonjudgmental classroom climates that reflect trust, informality, and tolerance. It is recommended that students sit in a large circle so that everyone can face and hear each other. By joining this circle, a teacher can assume the role of discussion leader, mediator, or facilitator, rather than of an authority figure who has established a separate "teacher space."

Confront a Moral Dilemma. Let us present the dilemma we will be using for purposes of illustration throughout this section:

> Sharon and her best friend Jill walked into a department store to shop. As they browsed, Jill saw a sweater she really liked and told Sharon she wanted to try the sweater on. While Jill went to the dressing room, Sharon continued to shop.
>
> Soon Jill came out of the dressing room wearing her coat. She caught Sharon's attention with her eyes and glanced down at the sweater under her coat. Without a word, Jill turned and walked out of the store.
>
> Moments later the store security officer, sales clerk, and the store manager approached Sharon. "That's her, that's one of the girls. Check her bags," blurted the clerk. The security officer said he had the right to check bags, and Sharon handed them over. "No sweater in here," he told the manager. "Then I know the other girl has it," the clerk said, "I saw them just as plain as anything. They were together on this." The security officer then asked the manager if he wanted to follow through on the case. "Absolutely," he insisted. "Shoplifting is getting to be a major expense in running a store like this. I can't let shoplifters off the hook and expect to run a successful business."
>
> The security officer turned to Sharon, "What's the name of the girl you were with?" he asked. Sharon looked up at him silently. "Come on now; come clean," said the security officer. "If you don't tell us, you can be charged with the crime or with aiding the person who committed the crime."
>
> *Question:* Should Sharon tell Jill's name to the security officer? Why, or why not? (Colby et al., 1977, p. 104)

A dilemma story such as the preceding one includes the following components:

1. *Central character:* Students make moral judgments about what the central character should do.
2. *Choice:* The central character should have two action alternatives which present a definite conflict. Neither action choice should represent a culturally approved "right" answer.
3. *Moral issues:* A dilemma should involve a conflict between two or more fundamental moral issues or values. In Sharon's dilemma, for example, Sharon's affectional relationship and implicit contract and trust with Jill conflict with issues of authority, property, truth, and punishment. Sharon faces the prospect of being punished herself if she fails to give Jill's name or of bringing punishment on Jill if she does tell her name. Also, Sharon faces the possibility of losing Jill's friendship if she tells or of losing the affection of her own family if she becomes a party to the shoplifting.
4. *"Should" question:* Asking what the central character *should* do keeps the ensuing discussion focused on moral judgments or reasoning, for it asks students to decide what is the "right," "correct," or "good" thing to do.

In general, dilemmas may be derived from three main sources: (1) current issues in contemporary society (e.g., Should a terminally ill patient be allowed to die or be kept alive by a life support system?); (2) the real-life experiences of students (e.g., Should a student let another student copy test answers?); (3) the specific content of a course such as social studies (e.g., Should Thoreau have gone to jail rather than pay taxes to support a war of which he disapproved?). Such dilemmas may be used as they are found or recast as hypothetical incidents involving fictional characters.

Dilemmas may be presented through written handouts, readings from novels, role playing, films, filmstrips, audiotapes, newspaper articles, or other media. While most dilemmas for secondary students are presented via written handouts or various readings, it is suggested that dilemmas for elementary students make more use of story telling, role playing, and a variety of audiovisual means of presentation.

The teacher should begin a moral discussion by presenting the dilemma to the class. It is often helpful to precede presentation of the dilemma with comments or questions designed (1) to prepare students for the kind of situation or character(s) described in the dilemma; (2) to help students see the relationship between the dilemma and what they have been studying; and (3) to build up student interest in the dilemma. (This kind of "warm-up" is especially important for younger, elementary students). For example, before presenting Sharon's dilemma to the class, the teacher might (1) point out that crimes involving property are a major type of teenage crime today; and (2) ask if students have known of someone who actually stole something from a store, or of someone who had to decide whether or not to tell on a friend.

After presenting the dilemma, the teacher should ask questions in order to help students clarify the circumstances involved, define terms, identify the characteristics of the central character, and state the exact nature of the dilemma and the action choice open to the central character.

State a Tentative Position.   Once students have understood the nature of the dilemma, the teacher should give them the opportunity to state a tentative position on what action alternative they think the central character should take. This is accomplished in the following sequence of steps:

1. Students should be given time to think quietly about where they stand.
2. Each student should then individually write down what action alternative he or she tentatively recommends for the central character, as well as his or her reasons for this position.
3. The teacher then needs to find out what action positions were taken by the students. A good dilemma usually generates a division within the class on the action that the central character should take; this division is necessary for engendering the kind of confrontation that motivates a critical evaluation of moral reasoning. Students can indicate by a show of hands how many support each position, as well as how many are initially undecided. If students divide on action on at least a 70–30 basis, discussion can begin. However, if the class fails to divide satisfactorily, the teacher should be prepared to add one or more alterations to the original dilemma to create the necessary class division. For example, concerning Sharon's dilemma, if almost the entire class agrees that Sharon *should* tell, the teacher might add this twist: Suppose that Jill has done Sharon many favors and that Sharon knows that she will lose many

of her friends if she tells on Jill; what should she do in that case? Or, alternately, if nearly the entire class agrees that Sharon should *not* tell, the teacher might add this: Suppose that instead of being a best friend, Jill was only a casual acquaintance; what should Sharon do in that case?

4. After determining that there is a satisfactory class division on action, the teacher should spend a few minutes asking different students to volunteer their reasons for their action positions. This will help prepare students for the discussion to follow as well as indicate to them that people have many different reasons for recommending a particular action position.

Examine the Reasoning. This step is the actual discussion of the moral dilemma and represents the heart of the teaching process. As previously stated, the teacher's two main tasks are (1) promoting student-to-student interaction; and (2) keeping the discussion focused on the moral issues involved in the dilemma. Student interaction can be promoted by the way student seating is arranged, by the classroom climate, and by using questions or comments to draw students into the discussion. The teacher can keep the discussion focused on the moral issues involved by (1) not permitting students to dwell on comments, arguments, or speculation about the *facts* and *circumstances* of a dilemma; the teacher can simply restate what the facts are and return to the discussion of *reasoning*; and (2) using *probe questions* to help students examine issues they had ignored or to think about reasoning at a higher stage. The following types of probe questions can be used, along with examples specific to Sharon's dilemma:

1. *Clarifying probes* call on students to define terms or explain comments that do not convey reasoning. For example, if a student says, "I think stealing is immoral," the teacher might ask "What do you mean by immoral?"
2. *Issue-specific probes* encourage students to examine their reasoning about a fundamental moral issue involved in the dilemma. For example, to get at the issue of affectional relations, the teacher might ask, "What obligations do you owe to a friend?"
3. *Interissue probes* encourage students to think about what to do when a conflict occurs between two separate yet critical moral issues or values—for example, "Which is more important, loyalty to a friend or the obligation to obey the law? Why?"
4. *Role-switch probes* encourage the students to take the perspective of another figure in the dilemma in order to help them see another side of the problem— for example, "From the point of view of Jill's parents, should Sharon tell?"
5. *Universal consequence probes* ask students to consider what might happen if such a position or such reasoning were applied to everyone—for example, "Is it ever right to tell on a friend?"

Effective use of probe questions are critical to a teacher's efforts in leading a successful moral discussion. Probe questions facilitate movement to the next higher stage of moral reasoning by helping students (1) focus increasingly on the more fundamental, universal moral issues and values implicit in a moral dilemma; (2) develop an ability to empathize with and understand other perspectives on a moral issue; and (3) reason in increasingly generalizable ways. The teacher should prepare in advance a list of specific probe questions relevant to the particular dilemma (such as the previous questions regarding Sharon's dilemma) as part of his or her teaching plan.

The recommended procedure for moral-dilemma discussions involves small-group discussions followed by a discussion involving the entire class. The small-group discussions are less critical, and serve more as "warm-ups" for the entire-class discussion. Nevertheless, small-group discussions are helpful in that they (1) maximize student-to-student interaction; (2) generate thinking about a variety of reasons for supporting a particular position; and (3) allow each individual to share his or her own reasoning with a few other class members with less fear of failure or disapproval than might otherwise be felt in an entire-class discussion. Any of several different small-group strategies may be used. The following are two of the most common: (1) *homogeneous groupings,* in which all members within a group hold the same action position—they list all the reasons they have for their position, choose the best two reasons, and then state why these reasons are the best; and (2) *heterogeneous groupings,* in which members within a group represent opposing positions ("undecided" students can be included too)—they discuss their positions and reasons and then make a list of the two best reasons for each position represented.

While students meet in small groups, the teacher should move from one group to another, helping students focus on the assigned tasks, facilitating group interaction, and asking occasional probe questions to help them clarify and examine their reasoning. Students should feel free to switch their positions as the group discussions develop. When the group tasks have been completed, students can then convene as an entire class to continue their discussion.

Reflect on an Individual Position. During the final phase of the class discussion, the teacher should help students to reflect once again on the positions considered and then to choose individually the reason(s) and/or positions they now find most persuasive. Although some students may indicate that they have changed their thinking during the discussion, the objective is *not* to form a consensus or to try to reach a conclusion regarding the "correct" action for the dilemma character. The process remains open-ended; students should be encouraged to continue thinking about positions taken and reasons heard in the discussion. The teacher might also ask students to (1) question their parents about how they would respond to the class dilemma; or (2) find dilemmas in newspapers and television shows involving moral issues similar to the class dilemma. Finally, in subsequent weeks students can discuss other dilemmas that involve similar issues and compare their reasoning across these dilemmas.

Beyond the Classroom: The Creation of the "Just Community School"

As noted earlier in this chapter, writers from nearly every contemporary approach to values training, including character education and values clarification, have discussed with great concern how their objectives in integrating values training within the formal curriculum of the classroom are often subverted through the so-called "hidden curriculum" of arbitrary rules and regulations, authoritative administration (and teacher)-student interactions, and homogenizing evaluation and grading procedures. This "hidden curriculum" is derived from, and reflects, the organizational and governance structure of the school as an institution. Thus, for example, the explicit goals of moral education in the classroom are often diametrically opposed by the implicit goals of the "hidden curriculum" of the school. Indeed, the implicit goals of the "hidden curriculum"—such as unquestioning obedience and conformity to authoritative rules and conventional expectations—are considered by many educators to be deleterious to the functioning of a free, just, and democratic society. The multilevel orientation of the present book demands our attention and concern to this central aspect of school and classroom climate as it interacts with teacher-initiated and student-oriented efforts at value enhancement.

Of the proponents of the three major values-training approaches examined in this chapter, Kohlberg and his colleagues have been especially articulate in their discussions concerning the dangers of the "hidden curriculum" and have been bold and imaginative in developing intervention strategies aimed at changing it (Fenton, 1975, 1977; Kohlberg, 1970b, 1972a; Wasserman, 1976). From their perspective, the "hidden curriculum" often hampers, rather than facilitates, moral development. Kohlberg proposes that the school as a moral-educational institution—the "moral atmosphere of the school"—should facilitate moral development by providing students with opportunities to try out and consolidate their developing moral reasoning (their developing conceptions of justice, laws and rules, authority, etc.) through exposure to and participation in real-life moral dilemmas and that discussions of moral dilemmas should be part of a "broader, more enduring involvement of students in the social and moral functioning of the school" (Kohlberg, 1972a, p. 16). These considerations led Kohlberg to develop as well as to implement the concept of a "Just Community School" (Fenton, 1975, 1977; Wasserman, 1976). Here the administration, teachers, and students work together to (1) establish a school with a governance structure based on a participatory democracy; (2) develop a school community based on principles of justice or fairness; and (3) examine the hidden curriculum and make it congruent with the explicit curriculum; for example, if the explicit curriculum stresses the importance of participatory democracy vis-à-vis the issue of school rules, then students as well as staff should be involved in the process of developing the school's rule structure. In 1974, the Kohlberg group opened the first Just Community School, called the "Cluster School," by setting up a self-governing, participatory, democratic, alternative school unit within a traditional urban public high school in Cambridge, Massachusetts (Cambridge High and Latin School). About seventy students were voluntarily recruited for this school-within-a-school; students were drawn from all four high-school classes and from the varied socioeconomic and racial groups of the wider school population. Eight staff members (representing a variety of academic backgrounds) volunteered and were accepted without screening. Early in the school year, students and staff together drew up a constitution by making a set of rules and developing a system to enforce them.

Staff and students in the Cluster School govern themselves through community meetings in which each person has one vote. During these community meetings, members constantly confront and discuss real-life moral dilemmas such as: (1) How should you punish a student who has broken the rule against stealing when you know that other students have also stolen but have not been caught? or (2) Should you suspend a member of the community who constantly disrupts classes but who has found for the first time a real home in the community? The students take their social-studies and English courses with the Cluster School, and they take the rest of their courses with other students from Cambridge High and Latin School. Both the social-studies and English courses include class discussions of moral dilemmas. In a progress report on the Cluster School, Wasserman (1976) indicates that (1) students have assumed increasing responsibility for their own behavior and that of others; (2) a genuine sense of community has emerged; (3) many students have become competent at participating in community meetings and a smaller number have learned to lead these meetings skillfully; (4) the staff reports positive changes in the behavior of students with long histories of difficulty in school; and (5) the staff believes that many students have begun to progress in moral reasoning, although actual research has only begun.

Following the lead of the Cluster School, other Just Community School programs have since been established (Felton, 1977; Wasserman, 1976). The Kohlberg group have also implemented the Just-Community approach within a woman's prison (Kohlberg et al., 1972).

Critique and Evaluation

We begin our evaluation by stating our belief that Kohlberg's classroom discussions of moral dilemmas represent a particularly useful approach for the facilitation of the development of those *cognitive* skills and abilities necessary for rational reasoning, problem solving, and decision making in value-conflictual social situations. Some writers, though, have argued that exclusive reliance on moral-dilemma discussions represents too limited a teaching strategy (Fraenkel, 1976; Miller, 1976). Specifically, they maintain that students may get bored with both hypothetical moral dilemmas that may be too narrow in scope, too simple, or too remote from their real-life experiences and problems, and constant verbal discussion of dilemmas to the exclusion of other, more varied instructional methods. We believe that these criticisms underscore the importance of using moral dilemmas that are more real-life than hypothetical in origin and that confront students with complex moral issues that are directly relevant to their day-to-day experiences, and of using instructional methods such as role playing within the context of the basic teaching strategy.

Although we feel confident that Kohlberg's classroom teaching strategy is facilitative of the development of moral reasoning and problem solving *in general,* we are less certain that this strategy stimulates moral reasoning in the specific direction that Kohlberg's theory postulates, especially vis-à-vis the final two stages. Our uncertainty is well founded; in fact, Kohlberg's theory of moral development rests on rather limited empirical grounds and has generated considerable empirical, philosophical, and theoretical criticism. A full discussion of these criticisms would take a separate book, and we can only briefly touch on some of them here. Nevertheless, in Kohlberg's defense, we wish to say that these criticisms have arisen largely because Kohlberg has been bold enough to elaborate a complex and controversial theory in great depth, and has attempted to provide empirical support for it—something that very few writers in the field of values training have done. Regardless of the ultimate outcome of Kohlberg's theory, it has provided the impetus of much-needed debate in this field; for this alone, he deserves much credit.

Much of the empirical and philosophical objections to Kohlberg's theory are directed toward his fundamental hypothesis that there exists a universally invariant sequence of six stages of moral reasoning, culminating in postconventional reasoning in general, and in the "ideal" final stage of a fully universalized and hierarchically integrated sense of justice in particular.

This fundamental hypothesis rests on longitudinal and cross-cultural research that is methodologically problematic. Kohlberg's contention that there exists an invariant sequence of six stages is based on his seventeen-year longitudinal study of the moral development of a sample of lower and middle-class urban American males. There are basic problems throughout this research regarding Kohlberg's moral-judgment interview as an instrument for assessing the predominant stage of his subjects. From 1958 to around 1972, Kohlberg's moral-judgment interview was based on a certain system for scoring subjects' responses to moral dilemmas and determining modal stage (called the aspect scoring system). Kurtines and Greif (1974) have roundly criticized this aspect scoring-based moral-judgment interview on several grounds: (1) lack of standardized administration; (2) lack of evidence of reliability and validity; and (3) lack of a published scoring manual, making independent validation of Kohlberg's theory next to impossible. Kurtines and Greif (1974) also criticized Kohlberg's omission of such basic information as the number of dilemmas used, and interrater reliability in the reporting of his longitudinal research.

Kohlberg himself found data discrepant with his "invariant-sequence" hypothesis (e.g., stage regression) in his longitudinal research using the aspect scoring system. In addition, using the same scoring system, Holstein (1973) also found such theoretically unexpected findings as skipping of stages and stage regression. As a result, Kohlberg began to develop and refine a new scoring system (issue scoring) which could account for his own as well as for Holstein's discrepant data, in effect making such data "fit" his "invariant-sequence" hypothesis. Critics have charged that Kohlberg cannot keep changing and refining his scoring system (Fraenkel, 1976), while Kohlberg supporters counter that such methodological refinement is critical to the process of validating his theory (Broughton, 1978). Perhaps the greatest objection in this regard, though, concerned Kohlberg's failure to clarify, until recently (Kohlberg, 1976), the properties and implications of his newer-issue scoring system publicly, thereby making it difficult for anyone outside his immediate circle to make sense of discrepancies between his earlier research (longitudinal or otherwise) using aspect scoring and his later research using issue scoring. The unavailability of a published scoring manual is simply inexcusable, although Fenton

(1977) reports that the Kohlberg group is currently developing a "definitive" scoring manual for publication in which they describe standardized procedures for conducting and scoring a moral-judgment interview.

Kohlberg's cross-cultural research, which led to his claim that there exists a culturally universal invariant sequence of stages of reasoning about certain universal moral values or concepts, has been criticized on the following grounds:

1. The failure to report important information such as subject characteristics or sample sizes, or to describe fully the method used to determine stages of reasoning in the various cultures (Kurtines & Greif, 1974).
2. The failure to investigate enough cultures to support claims of universality (Fraenkel, 1976; Simpson, 1974).
3. The use of an assessment instrument (the moral-judgment interview) that may be invalid in cultures in which analytical modes of thinking and language are not valued or developed (Simpson, 1974).
4. The a priori scoring of moral dilemmas vis-à-vis certain moral values or concepts (e.g., "property rights," "justice") without consideration as to whether such values or concepts were valid or relevant to the particular culture studied, and then using results of such scoring to claim that these moral values or concepts are culturally universal (Simpson, 1974). We maintain that this kind of methodological "self-fulfilling prophecy" is unjustifiable; thus, the issue of whether there are universal moral values remains an empirically open question.
5. The relative scarcity (and sometimes total absence) of postconventional moral reasoning (especially stage 6) in the various cultures studied (Simpson, 1974).

It is intrinsic to the "invariant-sequence" hypothesis that not everyone necessarily reaches the higher stages. Nevertheless, because of the general lack of postconventional reasoning in the various cultures studied, there simply does not exist at present a sufficient database to support or refute empirically Kohlberg's theorizing concerning the nature and universal existence of the final two stages. In particular, the paucity of empirical data on stage 6 has, in effect, confined discussion of this ideal stage to the level of philosophical presupposition and speculation.

In this regard, a number of writers have objected on philosophical grounds to Kohlberg's a priori definition of the highest stage of moral development in terms of a universalized sense of justice (Fraenkel, 1976; Peters, 1978; Simpson, 1974; Sullivan, 1977). Kohlberg's stage-6, "ideal" moral individual is someone who in a totally rational and impartial way, considers and reasons through the conflicting interests and values of different individuals on the basis of an abstract respect for the universal equal rights of all people. The problems several writers have with this definition of the "ideal" moral individual is best expressed in Sullivan's (1977) comment that this "ideal principled person is a moral entity without flesh or bones" (p. 21). Specifically, objections converge on the notion that this definition of the highest stage of moral development neglects or minimizes the importance of concrete moral habits and basic moral feelings (e.g., compassion, caring, guilt)—two aspects of morality which, along with moral reasoning, are necessary for actual moral behavior.

Concerning moral habits, Alston (1971) argues that in dismissing conventional character traits (e.g., cooperative, sympathetic, polite) as an irrelevant "bag of virtues," Kohlberg has thrown out the critical concept of "habits"—regularities in the way people behave or respond to certain social situations. Peters (1978) maintains that certain conventional moral habits or codes of conduct are critical for the moral behavior of the vast majority of people (e.g., the non-"postconventional" people) and essential to "the maintenance of social life under almost any conceivable conditions" (p. 155).

Concerning moral feelings, Peters (1970) maintains that people have to be passionately and emotionally devoted to their moral principles in order for these principles to influence behavior. Peters (1978) also criticizes Kohlberg for subordinating the affective-based moral principle of concern for human welfare (consideration or caring for others) to the cognitive-based moral principle of universalized justice. In a biting critique, Sullivan (1977) remarks that Kohlberg's stage-6 individual "will ultimately have to face the dilemma that thinking thoughts of universal brotherhood and sisterhood is a far cry from the passion, care, and commitment that will bring that ideal into being" (p. 31).

These philosophic objections to Kohlberg's stage-6 conception of morality have extremely important practical implications for a comprehensive program in moral education. Such a program would include yet transcend Kohlberg's approach. Its goals are development in the explicitly behavioral and affective, as well as the cognitive, aspects of morality. For example, we have reviewed research suggesting that preconventional moral reasoning is a necessary though insufficient condition for consistent and repetitive delinquent and criminal behavior; for example, even though adolescent criminal offenders almost invariably reason at preconventional levels, many preconventional adolescents do *not* engage in repetitive delinquent or antisocial behavior. This would suggest that, compared with the former group, the latter group may have learned more alternative, prosocial behaviors. Thus, a comprehensive prosocial training program for repetitively delinquent adolescents would aim to (1) teach certain alternative, prosocial behaviors directly (see Chapter 6) so that they have the necessary behavioral competence and skills; (2) facilitate the development of underlying and perhaps motivating prosocial values by means described in the present chapter.

SUMMARY

We began this chapter by justifying our interest in the training of prosocial values based on the moderate but clearly significant impact such training was likely to have on overt, prosocial behavior. School violence and vandalism, we held, are proportionately less likely to occur to the degree that youngsters are armed with such prosocial behavioral alternatives. We have now examined the three most influencial, contemporary approaches to values training: character education, values clarification, and moral education. It is our belief that these three approaches, despite theoretical and methodological differences, need not be considered as mutually exclusive in practice, and offer important possibilities toward a comprehensive program in values training.

We suggest that the direct and nonindoctrinative teaching of certain prosocial values through a character-education curriculum such as the one discussed in this chapter would be most valuable in the early primary grades. Such prosocial "character traits" as taught in character education are neither abstract principles nor general personality dispositions; rather, they reflect concrete moral habits or prosocial patterns—regularities underlying the way people can behave in certain kinds of social situations. Children should be given opportunities to practice such moral values or habits and to learn about their desirability at an early age so that they can develop a foundation of prosocial attitudes.

Unfortunately, the early primary-grade child often confronts a value-conflicted society as he or she progresses through childhood and adolescence, and the simple moral values and habits learned through character education, although they provide a necessary foundation, are not likely to suffice. With his or her expanding social awareness, the person will encounter constructive values such as nonviolence, cooperation, and generosity existing side-by-side with their respective destructive opposites: aggression, cut-throat competition, and greed. Furthermore, with his or her increasing cognitive capacity, the person will be able to understand rationales in favor of destructive values (e.g., aggression may be the easiest way to get what you want: "Do unto others before they do unto you.") as well as constructive ones. This is why Kohlberg's approach to the development of moral reasoning becomes so important, from the upper primary grades through high school and college. Unless the student can rationally arrive at "better," subjectively preferred reasons for constructive values and behaviors (e.g., conventional and postconventional moral reasons) than for destructive ones (e.g., preconventional moral reasons), the former may not prevail in situations in which they conflict with the latter.

Yet, even if the student has learned constructive moral values and habits, appreciates their desirability, and can formulate good reasons for putting them into practice in problematic social situations, he or she is still unlikely to behave accordingly unless he or she is motivated to do so. Such motivation can come from the kind of affective learning and development that results in a predominantly positive feeling toward oneself and others—in feelings of self-esteem as well as respect and caring for the needs and feelings of others. It occurs to us that it is in this area that values clarification can make an important contribution. Though we reject the premise of value relativity, we believe that learning to feel proud enough of one's beliefs and values ("prizing and cherishing") to be willing to stand up for them ("affirming") and to act on them consistently ("acting upon choices," "repeating") encourages and develops self-respect, confidence, and self-esteem.

It is our view that if we are to meet the challenge of the development of constructive alternatives to interpersonal aggression, then the schools must get involved in the values training of our young. The aim of the present chapter has been to provide some helpful considerations and practical suggestions for such involvement.

REFERENCES

ALSTON, W. P.   Comments on Kohlberg's "from is to ought." In T. Mischel (Ed.), *Cognitive development and epistemology.* New York: Academic Press, 1971.

ANON.   *Living with me and others.* San Antonio, Texas: American Institute for Character Education, 1974.

BAIN, O., & CLARK, S.   *Character education: A handbook of teaching suggestions based on freedom's code for elementary teachers.* San Antonio, Texas: The Children's Fund, 1966.

BAR-TAL, D.   *Prosocial behavior: Theory and research.* New York: Wiley, 1976.

BECK, C.   *Moral education in the schools: Some practical suggestions.* Toronto: Ontario Institute for Studies in Education, 1971.

BECK, C., HERSH, R., & SULLIVAN, E.   *The moral education project (year 4): Annual report, 1975-1976.* Toronto: Ontario Institute for Studies in Education, 1976.

BECK, C., & SULLIVAN, E.   *The reflective approach in values education: The moral education project, year 3.* Toronto: Ontario Institute for Studies in Education, 1976.

BEYER, B. K.   Conducting moral discussions in the classroom. *Social Education,* 1976, *40,* 194-202.

BLATT, M., & KOHLBERG, L.   The effects of classroom moral discussion upon children's level of moral judgment. *Journal of Moral Education,* 1975, *4,* 129-161.

BOYD, D.   *Education toward principled moral judgment: An analysis of an experimental course in undergraduate moral education applying Lawrence Kohlberg's theory of moral development.* Unpublished doctoral dissertation, Harvard University, 1973.

BROUGHTON, J.   The cognitive-developmental approach to morality. *Journal of Moral Education,* 1978, *7,* 81-96.

BRYAN, J. H.   Why children help: A review. *Journal of Social Issues,* 1972, *28,* 87-104.

BURTON, R. V.   Honesty and dishonesty. In T. Lickona (Ed.), *Moral development and behavior: Theory, research, and social issues.* New York: Holt, Rinehart & Winston, 1976.

COLBY, A., KOHLBERG, L., FENTON, E., SPEICHER-DUBIN, A., & LIEBERMAN, M.   Secondary school moral discussion programmes led by social study teachers. *Journal of Moral Education,* 1977, *6,* 90-111.

ENDLER, N. S., & MAGNUSSON, D.   Toward an interactional psychology of personality. *Psychological Bulletin,* 1976, *83,* 956-974.

FENTON, E.   A developmental approach to civic education. In J. R. Meyer, B. Burnham, & J. Cholvat (Eds.), *Values education: Theory/practice/problem/prospects.* Waterloo, Ontario: Wilfrid Laurier University Press, 1975.

FENTON, E.   The implications of Lawrence Kohlberg's research for civic education. In F. Brown (Ed.), *Education for responsible citizenship: The report of the national task force on citizenship education.* New York: McGraw-Hill, 1977.

FODOR, E.   Delinquency and susceptibility to social influence among adolescents as a function of level of moral development. *Journal of Social Psychology,* 1972, *86,* 257-260.

FRAENKEL, J. R.   The Kohlberg bandwagon: Some reservations. *Social Education,* 1976, *40,* 216-222.

GALBRAITH, R. E., & JONES, T. M.   *Moral reasoning: A teaching handbook for adapting Kohlberg to the classroom.* Anoka, Minn.: Greenhaven Press, 1976.

GINSBERG, H., & OPPER, S. *Piaget's theory of intellectual development: An introduction.* Englewood Cliffs, N.J.: Prentice-Hall, 1969.

GLASSER, W. *Schools without failure.* New York: Harper & Row, 1969.

GOBLE, F. *The case for character education.* Pasadena, Calif.: Thomas Jefferson Research Center, 1973.

HARRIS, S., MUSEEN, P., & RUTHERFORD, E. Some cognitive, behavioral and personality correlates of maturity of moral judgment. *Journal of Genetic Psychology,* 1976, *128,* 123-215.

HARTSHORNE, J., & MAY, M. A. *Studies in the nature of character. Vol. 1: Studies in deceit.* New York: Macmillan, 1928.

HARTSHORNE, J., MAY, M. A., & MALLER, J. B. *Studies in the nature of character. Vol. 2: Studies in service and self-control.* New York: Macmillan, 1929.

HARTSHORNE, J., MAY, M. A., & SHUTTLEWORTH, F. K. *Studies in the nature of character. Vol. 3: Studies in the organization of character.* New York: Macmillan, 1930.

HERSH, R. H., & MUTTERER, M. Moral education and the need for teacher preparation. In J. R. Meyer, B. Burnham, & J. Cholvat (Eds.), *Values education: Theory/practice/problems/prospects.* Waterloo, Ontario: Wilfrid Laurier University Press, 1975.

HILL, R. C. *Freedom's code: The historic American standards of character, conduct, and citizen responsibility.* San Antonio, Texas: The Children's Fund, 1965.

HOLSTEIN, C. B. *Moral judgment change in early adolescence and middle age: A longitudinal study.* Paper presented at the Society for Research in Child Development, Philadelphia, 1973.

HUDGINS, W., & PRENTICE, N. Moral judgments in delinquent and non-delinquent adolescents and their mothers. *Journal of Abnormal Psychology,* 1973, *82,* 145-152.

KAUFMAN, H. *Aggression and altruism.* New York: Holt, Rinehart & Winston, 1970.

KIRSCHENBAUM, J. Beyond values clarification. In H. Kirschenbaum & S. B. Simon (Eds.), *Readings in values clarification.* Minneapolis, Minn.: Winston Press, 1973.

KIRSCHENBAUM, J. Recent research in values education. In J. R. Meyer, B. Burnham, & J. Cholvat (Eds.), *Values education: Theory/practice/problems/ prospects.* Waterloo, Ontario: Wilfrid Laurier University Press, 1975.

KOHLBERG, L. The child as a moral philosopher. *Psychology Today,* 1968 (Sept.), *7,* 25-30.

KOHLBERG, L. Stage and sequence: The cognitive-developmental approach to socialization. In D. A. Goslin (Ed.), *Handbook of socialization theory and research.* Chicago: Rand McNally, 1969.

KOHLBERG, L. Education for justice: A modern statement of the platonic view. In N. F. Sizer, & T. R. Sizer (Eds.), *Moral education: Five lectures.* Cambridge, Mass.: Harvard University Press, 1970.

KOHLBERG, L. The moral atmosphere of the school. In N. Overley (Ed.), *The unstudied curriculum.* Washington, D.C.: Association for Supervision and Curriculum Development, National Education Association, 1970(b).

KOHLBERG, L. From is to ought: How to commit the naturalistic fallacy and get away with it in the study of moral development. In T. Mischel (Ed.), *Cognitive development and epistemology.* New York: Academic Press, 1971(a).

KOHLBERG, L.   Stages of moral development as a basis for moral education. In
  C. M. Beck, B. S. Crittenden, & E. V. Sullivan (Eds.), *Moral education: Inter-
  disciplinary approaches.* Toronto: University of Toronto Press, 1971(b).
KOHLBERG, L.   A cognitive-developmental approach to moral education. *The
  Humanist,* 1972 (Nov.-Dec.), *32,* 13-16(a).
KOHLBERG, L.   Indoctrination versus relativity in value education. *Zygon,* 1972,
  2, 285-310(b).
KOHLBERG, L.   *Collected papers on moral development and moral education.*
  Cambridge, Mass.: The Center for Moral Education, Harvard University, 1973.
KOHLBERG, L.   The relationship of moral education to the broader field of values
  education. In J. R. Meyer, B. Burnham, & J. Cholvat (Eds.), *Values edu-
  cation: Theory/practice/problems/prospects.*   Waterloo, Ontario: Wilfrid
  Laurier University Press, 1975.
KOHLBERG, L.   Moral stages and moralization: The cognitive-developmental ap-
  proach. In T. Lickona (Ed.), *Moral development and behavior: Theory, re-
  search, and social issues.* New York: Holt, Rinehart & Winston, 1976.
KOHLBERG, L., & KRAMER, R. B.   Continuities and discontinuities in childhood
  and adult moral development. *Human Development,* 1969, *12,* 93-120.
KOHLBERG, L., SHARF, P., & HICKEY, J.   The justice structure of the prison: A
  theory and an intervention. *The Prison Journal,* 1972, *51,* 3-14.
KOHLBERG, L., & TURIEL, E.   Moral development and moral education. In G. S.
  Lesser (Ed.), *Psychology and educational practice.* Chicago: Scott Foresman,
  1971.
KREBS, D.   A cognitive-developmental approach to altruism. In L. Wispé (Ed.),
  Altruism, sympathy and helping. New York: Academic Press, 1978.
KREBS, R. L.   *Some relationships between moral judgment, attention and resist-
  ance to temptation.* Unpublished doctoral dissertation, University of Chicago,
  1967.
KURTINES, W., & GREIF, E. B.   The development of moral thought: Review and
  evaluation of Kohlberg's approach. *Psychological Bulletin,* 1974, *81,* 453-
  470.
LICKONA, T.   Critical issues in the study of moral development and behavior. In
  T. Lickona (Ed.), *Moral development and behavior: Theory, research, and
  social issues.* New York: Holt, Rinehart & Winston, 1976(a).
LICKONA, T.   Introduction. In T. Lickona (Ed.), *Moral development and be-
  havior: Theory, research, and social issues.* New York: Holt, Rinehart &
  Winston, 1976(b).
MAYER, H. C.   *The good American program: A teacher's guide to the direct teach-
  ing of citizenship values in the elementary grades.* New York: American View-
  point, 1964.
McNAMEE, S.   Moral behaviour, moral development and motivation. *Journal of
  Education,* 1977, *7,* 27-31.
McPHAIL, P., UNGOED-THOMAS, J. R., & CHAPMAN, H.   *Learning to care:
  Rationale and method of the lifeline program.* Niles, Ill.: Argus Communi-
  cations, 1975.
MILGRAM, S.   Behavioral study of obedience. *Journal of Abnormal and Social
  Psychology,* 1963, *67,* 371-378.
MILLER, J. P.   *Humanizing the classroom: Models of teaching in affective edu-
  cation.* New York: Praeger, 1976.
MISCHEL, W.   Toward a cognitive social learning reconceptualization of person-
  ality. *Psychological Review,* 1973, *80,* 252-283.
MOSHER, R., & SPRINTHALL, N.   Psychological education in the secondary
  schools. *American Psychologist,* 1970, *25,* 911-916.

MOSHER, R., & SPRINTHALL, N. Psychological education: A means to promote personal development during adolescence. In R. E. Purpel & M. Belanger (Eds.), *Curriculum and the cultural revolution.* Berkeley, Calif.: McCutchan, 1972.

MULKEY, Y. J. *Character education and the teacher.* San Antonio, Texas: American Institute for Character Education, 1977.

NEWMANN, F., & OLIVER, D. *Clarifying public issues: An approach to teaching social studies.* Boston: Little, Brown, 1970.

OLIVER, D., & SHAVER, J. *Teaching public issues in the high school.* Boston: Houghton Mifflin, 1966.

PETERS, R. S. Concrete principles and the rational passions. In N. F. Sizer & T. R. Sizer (Eds.), *Moral education: Five lectures.* Cambridge, Mass.: Harvard University Press, 1970.

PETERS, R. S. The place of Kohlberg's theory in moral education. *Journal of Moral Education,* 1978, *7,* 147-157.

PIAGET, J. *The moral judgment of the child.* London: Routledge and Kegan Paul, 1932.

RATHS, L. E., HARMIN, M., & SIMON, S. B. *Values and teaching: Working with values in the classroom,* 2nd edition. Columbus, Ohio: Charles C Merrill, 1978.

REST, J. The hierarchical nature of moral judgment: A study of patterns of comprehension and preference of moral stages. *Journal of Personality,* 1973, *41,* 86-109.

REST, J. Developmental psychology as a guide to value education: A review of "Kohlbergian" programs. *Review of Educational Research,* 1974, *44,* 241-259.

REST, J., TURIEL, E., & KOHLBERG, L. Level of moral development as a determinant of preference and comprehension of moral judgments made by others. *Journal of Personality,* 1969, *37,* 225-252.

RINGNESS, T. A. *The affective domain in education.* Boston: Little, Brown, 1975.

RUBIN, K. H., & SCHNEIDER, L. The relationship between moral judgment, egocentrism, and altruistic behavior. *Child Development,* 1973, *44,* 661-665.

SIMON, S. B., & HARMIN, M. Subject matter with a focus on values. In H. Kirschenbaum & S. B. Simon (Eds.), *Readings in values clarification.* Minneapolis, Minn.: Winston Press, 1973.

SIMON, S. B., HOWE, L. W., & KIRSCHENBAUM, H. *Values clarification: A handbook of practical strategies for teachers and students.* New York: Hart, 1972.

SIMPSON, E. L. Moral development research: A case of scientific cultural bias. *Human Development,* 1974, *17,* 81-106.

STAUB, E. *Positive social behavior and morality.* New York: Academic Press, 1978.

SULLIVAN, E. V. *Kohlberg's structuralism: A critical appraisal.* Toronto: Ontario Institute for Studies in Education, 1977.

TREVITT, V. *The American heritage: Design for national character.* Santa Barbara, Calif.: McNally & Loftin, 1964.

UGUREL-SEMIN, R. Moral behavior and moral judgment of children. *Journal of Abnormal & Social Psychology,* 1951, *47,* 463-474.

WASSERMAN, E. R. Implementing Kohlberg's "just community concept" in an alternative high school. *Social Education,* 1976, *40,* 203-207.

WEINSTEIN, G., & FANTINI, M. *Toward humanistic education: A curriculum of affect.* New York: Praeger, 1970.

WILSON, J. *Education in religion and the emotions*. London: Heinemann Educational Books, 1971.
WILSON, J. *Practical methods of moral education*. London: Heinemann Educational Books, 1972.
WILSON, J. *The assessment of morality*. Windsor, Berks.: National Foundation of Educational Research, 1973(a).
WILSON, J. *A teacher's guide to moral education*. London: Geoffrey Chapman, 1973(b).

6
Teaching
Prosocial
Behaviors

Maximizing the frequency and quality of prosocial behavior used by youngsters who more characteristically act in antisocial ways is the central concern of this book. Earlier chapters examining student-level interventions were each concerned with enhancing behavior change in a somewhat indirect manner. Humanistic interventions provide a supportive, growth-promoting context; psychodynamic efforts seek to remove blocks to its expression; values training provides an attitudinal foundation from which prosocial behavior may emerge; and behavior modification, the motivational component, reinforces its occurrence when it does emerge. But none of these approaches directly confronts the absence of such behaviors by actually teaching them to youngsters. Support, removal of blocks, an attitudinal foundation, and reinforcement are all useful and important behavior-change-enhancing activities, but a central intervention, one targeted directly at instilling prosocial skills and abilities, is a vital component in building a comprehensive, multifaceted, effective program to reduce violence and vandalism in school settings.

154

Teaching prosocial behavior is, therefore, the focal concern of the present chapter. Two important approaches to this goal have emerged in the past several years, and we examine them in depth here. The first is *psychological skills training,* a group of procedures deriving from both contemporary psychology's long-term special interest in learning processes and modern education's more effective pedagogical techniques. *Interpersonal cognitive problem solving* is the second approach to direct enhancement of prosocial behavior we consider. It is an approach which places heavy reliance for its success on training youngsters to proceed systematically in their problem-solving efforts through that sequence of constituent steps which have been identified as essentially defining effective problem-solving attempts. The two approaches—psychological skills training and interpersonal cognitive problem solving—singly and in combination constitute an especially potent contribution to solving the broad problem of aggression and its consequences in American schools.*

PSYCHOLOGICAL SKILLS
TRAINING

Until the early 1970s, the student-level interventions examined in earlier chapters were the only types of psychological/psychoeducational interventions available for purposes of altering the behavior of youngsters who chronically engaged in aggressive and disruptive acts. These interventions—psychodynamic/psychoanalytic, humanistic/nondirective, and behavior modification—while differing from one another in both rationale and format, shared one highly significant assumption. Each rested on the belief that the antisocially behaving youngster had somewhere within himself or herself, as yet largely unexpressed, the prosocial, constructive, or healthy behaviors whose expression was among the intervention's major goals. Such latent potentials, in all three approaches, would find overt expression by the youngster if the intervenor were sufficiently skilled in reducing or removing obstacles to such expression. The psychodynamically oriented intervenor sought to do so by eliciting and interpreting unconscious material, analyzing motivations, and relating present behavior to past events. The nondirectivist, believing that the potential for change resided mostly within the youngster, sought to set this potential free by pro-

---

*In addition to these skill-enhancement procedures, the use of diverse types of games has in recent years begun to represent a significant and growing approach to both preventing and remediating psychological skill deficiencies and building prosocial-skill alternatives to aggression. Cooperation, in particular, has been an important target for such efforts. Although little rigorous evaluation research has been reported as yet, this use of indoor and outdoor games, simulations, and like activities to straightforwardly teach cooperative behavior has reflected considerable innovation and creativity. The interested reader is referred in particular to Deacove's (1974) *Cooperative Games Manual* and his (1978) *Sports Manual of Cooperative Recreation;* Fluegelman's (1974) *The New Games Book;* Harrison's (1975) *For the Fun of It!;* Judson's (1977) *A Manual on Nonviolence and Children;* Orlick and Botterill's (1975) *Every Kid Can Win,* Orlick's (1978) *Winning through Cooperation,* and his (1978) *The Cooperative Sports and Games Book;* and Stadsklev's (1975) *Handbook of Simulation Gaming in Social Education.*

viding a warm, empathic, maximally accepting counseling environment. And the behavior modifier, by means of one or more contingency-management procedures, attempted to see to it that when the latent desirable behaviors or approximations thereto did occur, the youngster received contingent reinforcement, thus increasing its probability of reoccurrence. Therefore, whether sought by means of therapeutic interpretation and working through, by provision of a benevolent counseling climate, or by dint of offering contingent reward, all three approaches assumed that within the individual's repertoire, somewhere, resided the desired, effective, prosocial goal behaviors.

In the early 1970s, an important new intervention approach began to emerge—psychological skills training—which rests upon rather different assumptions. Viewing youngsters more in psychoeducational terms than as patients in need of therapy, the psychological skills trainer assumed he or she was dealing with an individual lacking, deficient in, or, at best, weak in the skills necessary for effective and satisfying daily living in school and out. The task of the skills trainer became, therefore, not interpretation, reflection, or reinforcement, but, instead, active and deliberate *teaching* of desirable behaviors. Rather than psychotherapy, between a patient and a psychotherapist, or counseling, involving a counselor and a client, what emerged was training, between a trainee and a psychological skills trainer.

Not only did a change in available interventions thus occur but, in companion with it, there also occurred a change in the very definition of "aggressive youngsters." No longer, at least for the psychological skills trainer, would efforts to understand such youngsters rely so heavily and exclusively on psychodynamic notions of repressed impulses breaking through or the behavior modifier's concepts of reinforcement histories and the learning of aggression. Such descriptions focus, each in their own way, on what each youngster does. From a skills-training perspective, however, it is important to stress in particular what aggressive youngsters characteristically fail to do. Thus, the aggressive youngster, proficient as he or she is in an array of antisocial behaviors, is usefully seen as deficient in such prosocial skills as self-control, negotiation, empathy, dealing with others' anger, and many others. It is prosocial skills such as these, as we will see, which constitute the teaching curricula of the skill-training interventions we examine shortly.

The roots of the psychological skills training movement lay within both education and psychology. The notion of literally seeking to teach desirable behaviors has often been a significant goal of the American educational establishment. As noted in the previous chapter, character education, values clarification, and moral education each indirectly aspire to behavior-change consequences of their value-training efforts. Much the same can be said for American psychology, as it too laid the groundwork in its prevailing philosophy and concrete interests for the development of this new movement. The learning process has above all else been the central theoretical and investigative concern of American psychology since the late nineteenth century. In the 1950s, this focal interest also assumed major therapeutic form, as psychotherapy practitioners and researchers alike came more and more to view psychotherapeutic treatment in learning terms. The very healthy and still expanding field of behavior modification, described in Chapter 3 as it applies to aggressive youngsters, grew from this joint learning-clinical focus, and may appropriately be viewed as the immediately preceding context in which psychological skills training came to be developed. In companion with the growth of behavior modification, psychological thinking increasingly shifted from a strict emphasis on remediation to one equally concerned with prevention, and the bases for this shift included movement away from a medical-model conceptualization toward what may most aptly be called a psychoeducational-theoretical stance. Both of these thrusts—heightened concern with prevention and a psychoeducational perspective—gave strong added impetus to the viability of the psychological skills-training movement.

Psychology's final, and perhaps most direct, contribution to psychological skills training came from social-learning theory, and in particular the work conducted by and stimulated by Albert Bandura. Based upon the same broad array of modeling, behavioral rehearsal, and social-reinforcement investigation which helped stimulate and direct the development of the structured learning skill-training approach described later in this chapter, Bandura (1969) comments:

> The method that has yielded the most impressive results with diverse problems contains three major components. First, alternative modes of response are repeatedly modeled, preferably by several people who demonstrate how the new style of behavior can be used in dealing with a variety of . . . situations. Second, learners are provided with necessary guidance and ample opportunities to practice the modeled behavior under favorable conditions until they perform it skillfully and spontaneously. The latter procedures are ideally suited for developing new social skills but they are unlikely to be adopted unless they produce rewarding consequences. Arrangement of success experiences, particularly for initial efforts at behaving differently, constitute the third component in this powerful composite method. . . . Given adequate demonstration, guided practice, and success experiences, this method is almost certain to produce favorable results. (p. 253)

A Functional Definition

Hopefully the foregoing, brief overview of the historical roots of psychological skills training provides a contextual perspective on both its development and intended thrust. To offer a more concrete statement of its content and operations, we now formally define psychological skills training: *Psychological skills training is the planned, systematic teaching of the specific behaviors needed and consciously desired by the individual in order to function in an effective and satisfying manner over an extended period of time, in a broad array of positive, negative, and neutral interpersonal contexts. The specific teaching methods which constitute psychological skills training directly and jointly reflect psychology's modern social-learning theory and education's contemporary pedagogic principles and procedures.*

In this definition, we have described psychological skills training as *planned and systematic* to emphasize the organized, premeditated, and step-wise quality of such training, in contrast to the much more typically haphazard, unplanned, and unsystematic way in which most individuals are "taught" psychological skills—that is, by naturalistic reliance upon the parents, friends, religious leaders, school, and other people, institutions, and events which may or may not cross one's path and which may or may not exert positive skill-development influence on the individual.

Psychological skills training seeks to teach *specific behaviors*, and not—at least directly—values, attitudes, or insight. It is a behavioral approach, designed to enhance the overt actions of the trainee, in contrast to those psychotherapeutic and educational interventions which seek to alter the individual's beliefs about himself or herself, or self-understanding, in the (typically vain) hope that somehow behavior change will follow.

In our definition, it is important that, if at all possible, the behavior changes toward which the training is oriented be both *needed and consciously desired* by the trainee. Overt behavior change in the form of higher levels of skill competence, especially on an enduring basis, will not result, however good the psychological skills training, if the trainee's motivational level is not adequate. The training may be recommended by a parent, teacher, friend, or other interested party in the trainee's life, but a definition of successful training ideally includes a perceived skill deficiency, a felt need, a desire for improvement on the part of the trainee. For training to succeed, there must be adequate levels of what we would term trainee *competency motivation.*

The goals of psychological skills training, optimally, are *both effectiveness and satisfaction.* Effectiveness, we feel, pertains to the impact on others deriving from one's newly enhanced skill level. Effectiveness pertains to the questions "Does it work?" "Did I succeed?" "Was I competent?" Satisfaction, in our view, is where behavior and feelings meet. Satisfaction is the inner consequent of overtly effective skill behavior. We have included both effectiveness and satisfaction in this definition of psychological skills training because we are aware of skill-training programs in many settings in which trainee skill competence is the sole training-program goal. We are also aware of the many therapies and educational interventions initiated at the urging of, and for the satisfaction of, a parent, teacher, or other figure, and not the student or trainee himself or herself. We feel strongly that this is insufficient and short-sighted, and urge that the trainee's pleasure, gratification, or personal satisfaction be accepted as a regular, companion goal of equal importance to effectiveness in all such programs.

For a psychological skills-training program to be satisfactory, it must in our view energetically aspire to lead to trainee effectiveness and satisfaction *over an extended period of time and in a variety of positive, negative, and neutral contexts.* This part of our definition speaks to the issues of maintenance and transfer. Far too many psychotherapeutic and educational interventions succeed in changing trainee behaviors in the training setting, but fail to yield sustained change where it counts—in the real-world contexts in which the trainee works, plays, and exists. Thus, a satisfactory psychological skills-training program will actively seek to incorporate specific procedures which help the trainee perform the skills acquired in the training context both when he or she is in a variety of other contexts (i.e., setting generalization) and over a sustained period of time (i.e., response maintenance). The skill-training targets which constitute the actual content of a psychological skills-training program are optimally both diverse and numerous, and should include both *interpersonal and personal skills.* Interpersonal skills are the competencies that individuals must bring to bear in their interactions with other individuals or groups of individuals. Communication skills, leadership skills, relationship skills, and conflict-management skills are but a few examples. Personal skills are emotional, cognitive, observational, or related to practical aspects of daily living in school, community, or home environments. They include self-control, decision making, goal setting, preparing for stressful conversations, and setting problem priorities.

Finally, a comprehensive definition of psychological skills training must address not only matters of skill content, as we have just done, but also teaching procedure. Optimally, psychological skills training consists of *procedures derived from psychology's social-learning theory* (e.g., modeling, behavioral rehearsal, performance feedback) *and education's contemporary pedagogic principles and procedures* (e.g., instructional texts, simulation and gaming, structured discussion).

These, then, are the definitional characteristics of psychological skills training. As best we can discern, approximately fifteen programs oriented to chronically aggressive adolescents and children and reflecting most or all of these definitional characteristics currently exist. Table 6.1 provides an overview of these programs.

All of the programs represented in Table 6.1 meet most or all of the criteria we have included in our formal definition of psychological skills training. Nevertheless, considerable diversity is represented. Some programs are broadly comprehensive in the interpersonal and personal skill competencies they seek to enhance. Others focus more narrowly, on single skills or skill areas, for example. Yet others seem especially concerned with particular settings. Across programs, the range of potential trainees is especially broad, varying from early elementary-school children through all types and stages of adolescence. The trainees represented are also quite diverse in their pretraining levels of overall skill competence, varying from significantly unskilled, retarded individuals to essentially "average" individuals whose general skill-competence level is adequate, but who are seeking to enhance a few "weak spots."

Consistent with what has occurred with psychotherapists in psychotherapy and, to a lesser extent, with teachers in education, the range of persons successfully utilized as trainers in these psychological skills-training programs is not only broad and quite diverse, but also includes a substantial number of different types of paraprofessionals. That is, in addition to credentialed teachers or psychologists, we find that teachers' aides, college undergraduates, group-home parents, and others can and do serve successfully in these programs as, to use Carkhuff's (1974) apt term, "functional professionals."

Somewhat in contrast to the apparent diversity across programs in skills, trainers, and trainees, the training methods involved seem to consist largely of one or two possible procedural combinations. The first, a series of procedures derived

TABLE 6.1. Psychological Skills-Training Programs for Adolescents and Children

DEVELOPER	PROGRAM	TRAINERS	TRAINEES	TRAINING METHODS	SKILLS
Adkins (1970, 1974)	Life-skills education	Professional and paraprofessional	Disadvantaged adolescents and adults	Instruction, A/V demonstration, discussion	Developing oneself and relating to others Managing home and family responsibilities Exercising community rights
Bash & Camp (1980)	Think aloud	Teachers	Elementary-school children	Modeling, self-instruction, scripts, games, role playing	Problem solving Interpersonal skills Self-control Emotional awareness
Cox & Gunn (1980)	Interpersonal skills in the schools	Teachers	Elementary-school children	Modeling, didactic instruction, performance feedback	Interpersonal-conflict reduction skills
Elardo & Cooper (1977)	AWARE: Activities for social development	Teachers	Elementary-school children	Structured discussion, exercises, games, role playing	Getting-acquainted skills Recognizing-feelings skills Understanding individuals Social-living skills
Goldstein, Sprafkin, Gershaw, & Klein (1979)	Structured learning	Teachers	Adolescents	Modeling, role playing, feedback, transfer training	Conversational skills Expressive skills Responsive skills Dealing-with-feelings skills Dealing-with-stress skills Alternative-to-aggression skills Planning skills
Hare (1976)	Teaching conflict resolutions	Teachers	High-school students	Exercises, simulations, role play	Developing awareness of conflict-management styles Building trust Alternatives to conflict
Hawley & Hawley, (1975)	Developing human potential	Teachers	Elementary-school children	Exercises, simulations, structured discussion	Self-awareness skills Communication skills Relationship skills Creativity skills

Reference	Program	Trainer	Population	Methods	Skills
Heiman (1973)	Interpersonal communication	Teachers	High-school students	Lecture, exercises, role play	Trust building, Sharing of self, Communication, Listening
Oden (1980)	Social isolation intervention	Teachers	Elementary-school children	Coaching, games, behavioral rehearsal	Participation, Cooperation, Communication, Validation-support
Rinn & Markle (1979)	Social-skills deficit modification	Clinicians	Children, ages 8 to 11	Instruction, questioning, modeling, review, feedback	Self-expressive skills, Other-enhancing skills, Assertiveness skills
Robin (1980)	Problem-solving communication training	Family therapists	Parents and adolescents	Modeling, didactic instruction, behavioral rehearsal, performance feedback	Interpersonal-conflict reduction skills
Rotheram (1980)	Cognitive behavioral assertion	Paraprofessionals	Elementary-school children	Simulation, coaching, shaping, behavioral rehearsal	Interpersonal problem-solving skills
Stephens (1976, 1978)	Directive teaching	Teachers	Children, ages 7 to 12	Modeling, rehearsal, social reinforcement, contingency contracting	Environmental behaviors, Interpersonal behaviors, Self-related behaviors, Task-related behaviors
Terkelson (1976)	Parent-Child communication skills	Counselors	Parents, children grades 4 to 6	Exercises, role playing, review	Listening, Sending "I" messages
Wehman & Schleien (1980)	Leisure skills	Teachers	Severely disturbed children and adolescents	Games, coaching, modeling, feedback	Social, cognitive, gross/fine motor skills

from social-learning theory principles and research, typically consists of instruction, modeling, role playing, and feedback. The skills-training approach we wish to consider in detail here is of this type, and thus the nature and utilization of these procedures are elaborated in depth later. The second subgroup of programs, those growing more from strictly educational contexts, usually rely upon a combination of instructional texts, gaming and simulation exercise, structured discussion, and related didactic procedures. Perhaps most striking about both the social-learning-based and education-based procedural combinations is the degree to which they initially grew from, and are continuing to receive, careful and extensive experimental scrutiny. This reliance upon a substantial research foundation is clearly one of the strongest qualities of the psychological skills-training movement (Authier, Gustafson, Guerney, & Kasdorf, 1975; Cartledge & Milburn, 1980; Goldstein, 1973, 1981; Hersen & Eisler, 1976; L'Abate, 1980; McFall, 1976; Neitzel, Winett, McDonald, & Davidson, 1977; Rathjen & Foreyt, 1980; Twentyman & Zimering, 1979).

Having completed our introduction to psychological skills training, defined it, and provided an overview of the major, psychological skills programs currently available, we now turn to the major concern of this section, an in-depth consideration of one such program, structured learning. Our focus is on its rationale and development, its methods and materials, its utilization with aggressive adolescent- and child-trainee populations, and its supporting research.

WHAT IS STRUCTURED LEARNING*

Structured learning consists of four components—modeling, role playing, feedback, and transfer training—each of which is a well-established behavior-change procedure. *Modeling* refers to providing small groups of students with a demonstration or example of the skill behaviors one wishes the youngsters to learn. If the skill to be learned were *negotiating,* one would present students with a number of vivid, live, audiotaped, videotaped, or filmed displays (geared to maximize attention and motivation to learn) of adolescents who use the skill effectively. In the display, the skill of negotiating would be broken down into a series of behavioral steps which make up negotiation, and each example presented or modeled would illustrate the use of these behavioral steps. Thus, students would see and hear the models negotiating successfully in a variety of relevant settings: at home, at school, and with peer groups.

Once the modeling display has been presented, the next step in learning the skill is *role playing,* which is behavioral rehearsal or practice for eventual real-life use of the skill. To use our example of negotiation, individuals in the group would

---

*A further examination of the background and content of this approach appears in Goldstein et al. (1979). This source also contains a detailed presentation of the structured-learning skills taught to adolescents and the forms (checklists, grouping charts, homework reports, etc.) used in selecting and grouping trainees, as well as in recording their skill-acquisition progress.

be asked to think about times in their own lives when they would benefit from using the skill they have just seen modeled or demonstrated. In turn, each youth is given the opportunity to practice using the skill (i.e., the steps which make up the skill) as he or she might eventually use it in real life. This role playing is accomplished with the aid of other group members, as well as the group leaders, who simulate the real-life situation. The teenager who enacts a scene in which there is negotiation with a friend regarding where to go after school might role play the scene with another group member who acts out the part of the friend.

Feedback, the third component of structured learning, refers to providing the youngster with an evaluation of the role-played rehearsal. Following each role play, group members and trainers provide the role player with praise (and sometimes material rewards) as his or her behavior becomes more and more like that of the model. During this part of the group session, adolescents are given corrective instruction which enables them to continue to improve their skill use.

The fourth element in structured learning is *transfer of training.* This refers to a variety of procedures used to encourage transfer of the newly learned behaviors from the training setting to the real life situation. Homework assignments, use of real or imaginary props and procedures to make role playing realistic, and rerole playing a scene even after it is learned well (i.e., overlearning) are some of the transfer-enhancing procedures which are part of structured learning.* In a real sense, transfer of training is the most important, and often the most difficult, aspect of structured learning. If the newly learned behavior does not carry over to the real-life environment, then a lasting and meaningful change in the youngster's behavior is extremely unlikely to occur.

ORGANIZING THE STRUCTURED-LEARNING GROUP

Selecting Participants

Each structured-learning group should consist of trainees who are clearly deficient in whatever skills are going to be taught. If possible, trainees should also be grouped according to the degree of their deficiency in the given skill. Trainees can be selected who are all deficient on certain common groups of skills, as assessed by the Structured-Learning Skill Checklist. The *behavioral objectives* for the trainees in the class are to define on which skills to work. The optimal size group for effective structured-learning sessions is five to eight trainees plus two trainers.** The trainees selected for a structured-learning group need not be from the same class or even the same grade. However, since behavioral rehearsal or role playing in the group is most

---

*Several additional means of potential usefulness for increasing transfer of training are described in detail in Goldstein and Kanfer (1979).

**We recognize that most classes in school settings are much larger than is desirable for a structured-learning class. Often it is possible for two or more teachers to combine their classes for a period or two and have one teacher take the larger group while the other takes a smaller group of five to eight students to participate in structured learning. Other means for organizing structured-learning groups in regular classes are described in Goldstein et al. (1979).

beneficial when it is as realistic as possible, it is often useful to include trainees whose social worlds (family, school, peer groups) have some important elements of similarity. In this way, when a participant is asked to role play a part, he or she can role play this part in a reasonably accurate fashion.

There are times when it will not be possible to group trainees according to shared skill deficits. Instead, the trainer may want to group according to naturally occurring units, such as school classes, residential cottages, and so on. If the trainer decides to use naturally occurring units, the group members will probably reflect some range of skill strengths and weaknesses. In this case, it will be helpful to fill out a Skill Checklist for each trainee in order to obtain a class profile. Starting skills should be those in which many of the class members show a deficiency. In such a potentially divergent group it is likely that one or two class members will be proficient in the use of whatever skill might be taught on a given day. In that case, those more skillful youngsters can be used in helper roles, such as coactors or providers of useful feedback.

Number, Length, and Spacing of Sessions

The structured-learning modeling displays and associated procedures typically constitute a training program which can be broken into segments matching part or all of the semesters of the school or training setting. It is most desirable that training occur at a rate of one or two times per week. Spacing is crucial. Most trainees in skill-training or other programs learn well in the training setting. However, most fail to transfer this learning to where it counts—at home, in school, with friends, in the community. In order to provide ample opportunity for trainees to try out in real life what they have learned in the training setting, there must be ample time and opportunity for skill use between sessions.

Typically, each training session should focus on learning one skill, and it should include one sequence of modeling, several role plays, feedback, and assignment of homework. Each session should be scheduled to be 1 hour in length. Session length should be determined by a number of factors, such as attention span, impulsivity, verbal ability, and so on. If most trainees in a given group show a particularly brief attention span, the session can be as brief as 20 minutes. In such cases, more frequent sessions are advisable. Sessions longer than an hour are possible for trainees whose capacity for sustained attention is greater. Since structured learning is intensive, we recommend that sessions not last beyond 1½ hours, as learning efficiency tends to diminish beyond that length of time.

Trainer Preparation*

The role-playing and feedback activities which make up most of each structured-learning session are a series of "action-reaction" sequences in which effective

---

*Individuals serving effectively as structured-learning trainers have included special-education and regular-classroom teachers, teachers' aides, adolescent peers, cottage house parents, and several types of juvenile-detention-center staff.

skill behaviors are first rehearsed (role play) and then critiqued (feedback). Thus, the trainer must both lead and observe. We have found that one trainer is hard pressed to do both of these tasks well at the same time, and, thus, we recommend strongly that each session be led by a team of two trainers.

Two types of trainer skills seem to be necessary for successful structured-learning leadership. The first might best be described as general trainer skills—that is, those skills requisite for success in almost any training or teaching effort. These include:

1. Oral communication and listening skills.
2. Flexibility and capacity for resourcefulness.
3. Enthusiasm.
4. Ability to work under pressure.
5. Interpersonal sensitivity.
6. Broad knowledge of human behavior, adolescent development, and so on.

The second type of requisite skills are specific trainer skills—that is, those germane to structured learning in particular. These include:

1. Knowledge of structured learning: its background, procedures, and goals.
2. Ability to orient both trainees and supporting staff to structured learning.
3. Ability to initiate and sustain role playing.
4. Ability to present material in concrete, behavioral form.
5. Ability to deal with classroom-management problems effectively.
6. Sensitivity in providing corrective feedback.

For both trainer-selection and development purposes, potential trainers should first participate, in the role of trainees, in a series of structured-learning sessions. These sessions should be led by two experienced trainers. After this experience, beginning trainers can then colead a series of sessions with an experienced trainer. In this way, trainers can be given several opportunities to practice what they have seen and also to receive feedback regarding their performances. In effect, we recommend that use of the structured-learning procedures of modeling, role playing, and feedback as the method of choice for training structured-learning techniques appropriately.

THE STRUCTURED-LEARNING SESSIONS

The Setting

One major principle for encouraging transfer from the classroom and training room to the real-life setting is the rule of identical elements. This rule states that the more similar or identical the two settings—that is, the greater the number of physical and interpersonal qualities shared by them—the greater the transfer from one setting to the other. We urge that structured learning be conducted in the same general setting as the real-life environment of most participating students and that the training setting be furnished to resemble or simulate as much as possible the likely application settings. In a typical classroom one can accomplish this in part through the creative use of available furniture and supplies. Should a couch be needed for a particular role play, several chairs can be pushed together to simulate the couch. Should a television set be an important part of a role play, a box, a chair, or a drawing on the chalkboard can, in imagination, approximate the real object. If actual props are available, for example in the form of an actual TV set, store counter, living room furniture, and so on, they should certainly be used in the role-play scenes.

The horseshoe seating arrangement is one good example of how furniture might be arranged in the training room. Participating trainees can sit at desks or tables so that they are provided some writing space. Role playing could take place in the front of the room. Behind and to the side of one of the role players could be a chalkboard displaying the behavioral steps which make up the skill being worked with at that time so that the role player can glance up at the steps during the role play. If film strips or other visual modeling displays are used, the screen should be easily visible to all.

Premeeting Preparation of Trainees

Preparation of trainees individually may be helpful prior to the first meeting of the structured-learning class. This orientation or structuring should be tailored to the individual needs and maturity level of each trainee. It should be designed to provide each group member with heightened motivation to attend and participate in the group, as well as to provide the trainee with accurate expectations of what the activities of the group will be like. Methods of trainee preparation might include:

1. Mentioning what the purposes of the group will be, as they relate to the specific skill deficits of the youngsters. For example, the trainer might say, "Remember when you got into a fight with Billy, and you wound up restricted for a week? Well, in this class you'll be able to learn how to stay out of that kind of trouble so you don't get restricted."
2. Mentioning briefly and generally what procedures will be used. The trainee must have an accurate picture of what to expect so as not to feel as if he or she has been tricked. You might say something like, "In order to learn to handle (these kinds of) situations better, we're going to see and hear some examples of how different kids do it well, and then actually take turns trying some of these ways right here. Then we'll let you know how you did, and you'll have a chance to practice them on your own."
3. Mentioning the benefits to be gained from participation, stating that the group will help the trainee work on particular relevant issues such as getting along in school, at home, and with peers.
4. Mentioning the tangible or token (e.g., points, credits, etc.) rewards which trainees will receive for participation.

5. Using the trainer-trainee relationship to promote cooperation. For example, the trainer might ask the youngster to "Give it a try. I think you'll get something out of it."
6. Presenting the structured-learning class as a new part of the curriculum in which the trainee is expected to participate. As part of the message of expected participation, trainees should also understand that the group is not compulsory and that confidentiality will be respected. A verbal commitment from the youngster to "Give it a try." is useful at this point.
7. Mentioning the particular skills that the youngster is likely to identify as his or her major felt deficiency, and how progress might be made in working on such skills.

The Opening Session

The opening session is designed to create trainee interest in the group as well as to educate the group regarding the procedures of structured learning. The trainers open the session by first introducing themselves and having each trainee do likewise. A brief familiarization period or warm-up follows, with the goal of helping trainees to become comfortable interacting with the group leaders and with one another in the class. Content for this initial phase should be interesting as well as nonthreatening. Next, trainers introduce the structured-learning program by providing trainees with a brief description of what skill training is about. Typically, this introduction covers such topics as the importance of interpersonal skills for effective and satisfying living, examples of skills which will be taught, and how these skills can be useful to trainees in their everyday lives. It is often helpful to expand upon this discussion of everyday skill use, so as to emphasize the importance of the undertaking and its personal relevance to the participants. The specific training procedures (modeling, role playing, etc.) are then described at a level which the group can easily understand.

New trainers should note that although this overview is intended to acquaint trainees with structured-learning procedures, frequently trainees do not grasp the concepts described until they actually get involved in the training process. Because of this, we do not advise trainers to spend a great deal of time describing the procedures. Instead, we recommend that they describe procedures briefly, as an introduction, with the expectation that trainees will actually experience and understand the training process more fully once they have actually gotten started.

Modeling

As the first step, the trainer should describe the skill to be taught and hand out skill cards to all trainees on which the name of the skill and its behavioral steps are printed. The trainer should then enact the first live modeling display of the skill. Students are told to watch and listen closely to the way the actors in each vignette portray the behavioral steps. Following is a list of the skills taught by structured learning:

1. Listening: Does the student pay attention to someone who is talking and make an effort to understand what is being said?
2. Starting a Conversation: Does the student talk to others about light topics and then lead into more serious topics?
3. Having a Conversation: Does the student talk to others about things of interest to both of them?
4. Asking a Question: Does the student decide what information is needed and ask the right person for that information?
5. Saying Thank You: Does the student let others know that he or she is grateful for favors, and so on?
6. Introducing Yourself: Does the student become acquainted with new people on his or her own initiative?
7. Introducing Other People: Does the student help others become acquainted with one another?
8. Giving a Compliment: Does the student tell others that he or she likes something about them or their activities?
9. Asking for Help: Does the student request assistance when he or she is having difficulty?
10. Joining In: Does the student decide on the best way to become part of an on-going activity or group?
11. Giving Instructions: Does the student clearly explain to others how they are to do a specific task?
12. Following Instructions: Does the student pay attention to instructions, give his or her reactions, and carry the instructions out adequately?
13. Apologizing: Does the student tell others that he or she is sorry after doing something wrong?
14. Convincing Others: Does the student attempt to persuade others that his or her ideas are better and will be more useful than those of the other person?
15. Knowing Your Feelings: Does the student try to recognize which emotions he or she is feeling?
16. Expressing Your Feelings: Does the student let others know which emotions he or she is feeling?
17. Understanding the Feelings of Others: Does the student try to figure out what other people are feeling?
18. Dealing with Someone Else's Anger: Does the student try to understand other people's angry feelings?
19. Expressing Affection: Does the student let others know that he or she cares about them?
20. Dealing with Fear: Does the student figure out why he or she is afraid and do something to reduce the fear?
21. Rewarding Yourself: Does the student say and do nice things for himself or herself when the reward is deserved?
22. Asking Permission: Does the student figure out when permission is needed to do something, and then ask the right person for permission?
23. Sharing Something: Does the student offer to share what he or she has with others who might appreciate it?
24. Helping Others: Does the student give assistance to others who might need or want help?

25. Negotiating: Does the student arrive at a plan which satisfies both the student and others who have taken different positions?

26. Using Self-Control: Does the student control his or her temper so that things do not get out of hand?

27. Standing up for Your Rights: Does the student assert his or her rights by letting people know where he or she stands on an issue?

28. Responding to Teasing: Does the student deal with being teased by others in ways that allow the student to remain in control of himself or herself?

29. Avoiding Trouble When with Others: Does the student stay out of situations that might help him or her into trouble?

30. Keeping Out of Fights: Does the student figure out ways other than fighting to handle difficult situations?

31. Making a Complaint: Does the student tell others when they are responsible for creating a particular problem for the student, and then attempt to find a solution for the problem?

32. Answering a Complaint: Does the student try to arrive at a fair solution to someone's justified complaint?

33. Sportsmanship after the Game: Does the student express an honest compliment to others about how they played a game?

34. Dealing with Embarrassment: Does the student do things which help him or her to feel less embarrassed or self-conscious?

35. Dealing with Being Left Out: Does the student decide whether he or she has been left out of some activity, and then do things to feel better about the situation?

36. Standing Up for a Friend: Does the student let other people know when a friend has not been treated fairly?

37. Responding to Persuasion: Does the student carefully consider the position of another person, comparing it to his or her own, before deciding what to do?

38. Responding to Failure: Does the student figure out the reason for failing in a particular situation, and what he or she can do about it, in order to be more successful in the future?

39. Dealing with Confusing Messages: Does the student recognize and deal with the confusion which results when others tell him or her one thing, but say or do things which indicate that they mean something else?

40. Dealing with an Accusation: Does the student figure out what he or she has been accused of and why, and then decide on the best way to deal with the person who made the accusation?

41. Getting Ready for a Difficult Conversation: Does the student plan on the best way to present his or her point of view prior to a stressful conversation?

42. Dealing With Group Pressure: Does the student decide what he or she wants to do when others want the student to do something else?

43. Deciding on Something to Do: Does the student deal with feeling bored by starting an interesting activity?

44. Deciding What Caused a Problem: Does the student find out whether an event was caused by something that was within his or her control?

45. Setting a Goal: Does the student realistically decide on what he or she can accomplish prior to starting on a task?

46. Deciding on Your Abilities: Does the student realistically figure out how well he or she might do at a particular task?

47. Gathering Information: Does the student decide what he or she needs to know and how to get the information?
48. Arranging Problems by Importance: Does the student decide realistically which of a number of problems is most important and should be dealt with first?
49. Making a Decision: Does the student consider possibilities and make choices which he or she feels will be best?
50. Concentrating on a Task: Does the student make those preparations which will help him or her get a job done?

If available in audiotape or videotape format, modeling displays should begin with a narrator's setting the scene and stating the name of the skill and the behavioral steps which make up that skill. Sets of actors should then portray a series of vignettes in which each behavioral step is clearly enacted in sequence. Content in the vignettes should be varied and relevant to the lives of the students. The narrator should then return onto the tape and make a summary statement. In our view, this sequence of narrator's introduction, modeling scenes, and narrator's summary constitutes the minimum requirement for a satisfactory modeling tape. We have described in detail elsewhere (see Goldstein, Sprafkin, & Gershaw, 1976) those characteristics of modeling displays which usually enhance or diminish the degree of learning that occurs. We refer the reader interested in developing modeling displays to this source. We have also found that live modeling by trainers often provides those elements that promote satisfactory learning by youngsters (Goldstein et al., 1979). Trainers may decide to enact or play only a portion of the modeling display in any given session. We recommend that the first exposure to a new skill include at least the introduction and two or three vignettes to provide an overview and some variety of skill applications.

Role Playing

Following the playing of the modeling display the trainer should direct discussion toward helping trainees relate the modeled skill use to their own lives. The trainer should invite comments on the behavioral steps and on how these steps might be useful in the real-life situations which trainees encounter. The focus should be on dealing with specific current and future skill use by trainees rather than only general issues involving the skill.

It is important to remember that role playing in structured learning is viewed as behavioral rehearsal or practice for future use of the skill. Thus, trainers should be aware that role playing of past events which have little relevance for future situations is of limited value to trainees. However, discussion of past events involving skill use can be relevant in stimulating trainees to think of times when a similar situation might occur in the future. In such a case, the hypothetical future situation rather than the past event would be selected for role playing.

Once a trainee has described a situation in his or her own life in which skill usage might be helpful, that trainee is designated the main actor. He or she chooses a second trainee (the coactor) to play the role of the significant other person (e.g., mother, peer, etc.) in his or her life who is relevant to the skill problem. The trainee should be urged to pick as a coactor someone who resembles the real-life person in as many ways as possible. The trainer then elicits from the main actor any additional information needed to set the stage for role playing—for example, a description of the physical setting, a description of the events immediately preceding the role play, a description of the coactor's mood or manner, and so on.

It is crucial that the main actor seek to enact the behavioral steps which have been modeled. The trainer should go over each step as it applies to the role-play situation prior to any actual role playing's being started, thus aiding the main actor in making a successful role-play effort. The main actor is told to refer to the skill card on which the behavioral steps are printed. As noted previously, the behavioral steps should also be written on a chalkboard visible to the main actor during the role playing. Before the role playing begins, the trainer should remind all of the participants of their roles: The main actor should be told to follow the behavioral steps; the coactor, to stay in the role of the person; and the observers, to watch carefully for the enactment of the behavioral steps. For the first several role plays, it is helpful for the trainer to coach the observers as to what kinds of cues to observe—for example, posture, tone of voice, content of speech, and so on. This also provides an opportunity to set a positive example for feedback from the observers.

Next, the trainer should instruct the role players to begin. It is the trainer's main responsibility, at this point, to provide the main actor with whatever help or coaching he or she needs in order to keep the role playing going according to the behavioral steps. The trainer should urge trainees who "break role" and begin to explain or make comments to get back into role and explain later. If the role play is clearly going astray from the behavioral steps, the trainer should stop the scene, provide needed instruction, and begin again. One trainer should be positioned near the chalkboard to point to each behavioral step, in turn, as the role play unfolds, thus helping the main actor (as well as the other trainees) to follow each step in order.

The role playing should be continued until all trainees have had an opportunity to participate (in either role) and preferably until all have had a chance to be the main actor. Sometimes this will require two or three sessions for a given skill. We again suggest that each session begin with two or three modeling vignettes for a skill, even if the skill is not new to the group. It is important to note that even though the framework (behavioral steps) of each role play in the series remains the same, the actual content can and should change from role play to role play. It is the problem as it actually occurs, or could occur, in each youngster's real-life environment that should be the content of the given role play. When completed, each trainee will thus be better armed to act appropriately in a real situation requiring skill use in his or her own life.

There are a few further procedural matters relevant to role playing which can increase the effectiveness of the role playing. Role reversal is often a useful role-play procedure. A trainee role playing a skill may on occasion have a difficult time perceiving his or her coactor's viewpoint, and vice versa. Having the trainees exchange roles and resume the role playing can be most helpful in this regard. Also, the trainer can assume the coactor role, in an effort to expose youngsters to handling types of reactions that might not otherwise be role played during the session. For example, it may be crucial to have a difficult adult role realistically portrayed in the role play. It is here that trainer flexibility and creativity will certainly be called upon. This may be particularly helpful when dealing with less verbal or more hesitant trainees.

Feedback

A brief feedback period should follow each role play. This helps the main actor to find out how well he or she followed or departed from the behavioral steps, to explore the psychological impact of his or her enactment on the coactor, and to provide encouragement to try out the role-play behaviors in real-life. To implement this process, the trainer should ask the main actor to wait until he or she has heard everyone's comments before talking. The trainer should then ask the coactor about his or her reactions. Next the trainer should ask the observers to comment on the behavioral steps and other relevant aspects of the role play. The trainers should comment in particular on how well the behavioral steps were followed, and provide social reinforcement (praise, approval, encouragement) for close following. For reinforcement to be most effective, trainers should follow the guidelines described in Chapter 4 for positive reinforcement in behavior modification (see pages 50 to 54).

After the main actor hears all the feedback, the trainer should invite him or her to make comments regarding the role play and the comments of others. In this way he or she can learn to evaluate the effectiveness of his or her skill enactment in the light of evidence from others as to its success or lack of success.

In all aspects of feedback, it is crucial that the trainers maintain the behavioral focus of structured learning. Trainer comments must point to the presence or absence of specific, concrete behaviors, and not take the form of general evaluative comments or broad generalities. Negative comments should always be followed by a constructive comment as to how a particular fault might be improved. At a minimum, a "poor" performance (major departures from the behavioral steps) can be praised as "a good try" at the same time as it is being criticized. Trainees should be given the opportunity to rerole play these same behavioral steps after receiving corrective feedback. At times, as a further feedback procedure, we have audiotaped or videotaped entire role plays. Giving trainees later opportunities to observe themselves on tape can be an effective aid to learning, because it enables them to reflect on their own behavior.

Since a primary goal of structured learning is skill flexibility, role-play enactment which departs markedly from the behavioral steps may in fact "work" in some situations. Trainers should stress that they are trying to teach effective alternatives and that the trainees would do well to have the behavioral steps in their repertoire of skill behaviors available to use when appropriate. As the final optional feedback step, after all role playing and discussion are completed, the trainer can enact one additional modeling vignette or replay portions of the modeling tape. In a sense, this step summarizes the session and leaves students with a final review of the behavioral steps.

Transfer of Training

Homework. Several aspects of the training sessions we have just described have as their primary purpose augmenting the likelihood that learning in the training setting will transfer to the youngster's actual real-life environment. We would suggest, however, that even more forthright steps need to be taken to maximize transfer. When possible, we would urge a homework technique which we have found to be successful with most groups. Trainees should first be told how important (i.e., that it is the most important step of all) this transfer aspect is, and they should be instructed in how best to implement it. Trainees should be instructed to try in their own real-life settings the behaviors they have practiced during the session. The name of the person(s) with whom they will try it, the day, the place, and so on, should all be discussed. The trainee should be urged to take notes on his or her first transfer attempt on the Homework Report form provided by the trainers. This form requests detailed information about what happened when the student attempted the homework assignment, how well he or she followed the relevant behavioral steps, the student's evaluation of his or her performance, and his or her thoughts about what the next assignment might appropriately be.

As is true regarding the order in which structured-learning skills are taught, it has often proven useful to start with relatively simple homework behaviors and, as mastery is achieved, work up to more complex and demanding assignments. Often it is best to make a first homework assignment something that can be done close by—that is, in the school, community center, or wherever the class is taking place. It may then be possible to forewarn and prepare the person(s) with whom the youngster is planning to try out his or her new skill, in order to ensure a positive outcome. For example, a trainee's homework assignment might be to ask the gym teacher a particular question. The trainer might then tell the gym teacher to expect the trainee's question so that he or she is prepared to answer in a positive way.* These success experiences at beginning homework attempts are crucial in encouraging the trainee to make further attempts at real-life skill use. The first part of each session is devoted to presenting and discussing these homework reports. When trainees make an effort to complete their homework assignments, the trainers should provide social reinforcement (praise, approval, encouragement). Trainers should meet trainee's failure to do their homework with some chagrin and expressed disappointment. It cannot be stressed too strongly that without these, or

---

*Trainers should be cautioned, however, that breach of confidentiality can damage a teenager's trust in the trainer. If persons outside of the group are to be informed of specific training activities, youngsters should be told of this, and their permission should be asked, early in the group's life.

similar attempts to maximize transfer, the value of the entire training effort is in severe jeopardy.

External Support and Self-Reward. Of the several principles of transfer training for which research evidence exists, the principle of performance feedback is clearly most consequential. A youngster can learn very well in the training setting and do all of his or her transfer homework, and yet the training program can be a performance failure. "Learning" concerns the question: Can he or she do it? "Performance" is a matter of: Will he or she do it? Trainees will perform as trained if and only if there is some "payoff" for doing so. Stated simply, new behaviors persist if they are rewarded, diminish if they are ignored or actively challenged.

We have found it useful to implement several supplemental programs outside of the structured-learning training setting to help provide the rewards or reinforcements trainees need so that their new behaviors are maintained. These programs include providing for both external social reward (by people in the trainee's real-life environment) and self-reward (by the student himself or herself).

In several settings, we have actively sought to identify and develop environmental or external support by holding orientation meetings for school staff and for relatives and friends of the youngsters—that is, the real-life reward and punishment givers. These meetings acquaint significant others in the youngster's life with structured-learning, the skills being taught, and the steps which make up these skills. The most important segment of these sessions involves presenting the procedures whereby staff, relatives, and friends can encourage and reward trainees as they practice their new skills. We consider these orientation sessions to be of major value for transfer of training. In such sessions, the trainers should provide the significant others with an overview of structured learning, much like the overview previously described for use with a new group of trainees. An accurate picture of what goes on in a structured-learning class—what procedures are typically used, and why—should be provided. Most important, participants should be informed as to how they might help in the transfer effort, and why their contributions are so necessary to the success of the program. Typically, such potential reward givers should be given instructions in how to reinforce appropriate behaviors, or the approximations of such behaviors. One might tell them what specific responses on their parts would be appropriate for the skills being covered in the structured-learning class. It is often worthwhile to engage these significant others in role playing the kinds of responses they might make, so they can get practice and feedback in these behaviors.

Self-Reinforcement. Frequently, environmental support is insufficient to maintain newly learned skills. In fact, many real-life environments in which youngsters work and live actually actively resist a youngster's efforts at behavior change. For this reason, we have found it useful to include in our transfer efforts a method through which students can learn to be their own rewarders: the method of self-reinforcement or self-reward. Once a new skill has been practiced through role playing, and once the trainee has made his or her first homework effort and gotten group feedback, we recommend that trainees continue to practice their new skill as frequently as possible. It is at this time that a program of self-reinforcement can and should be initiated. Trainees can be instructed in the nature of self-reinforcement and encouraged to "say something and do something nice for yourself" if they practice their new skill well. Self-rewards may be both things that one says to oneself and things that one does for oneself. The trainee should be taught to evaluate his or her own performance, even if his or her efforts do not meet with the hoped-for response from others. For example, if the youngster follows all of the steps of a particular skill well, he or she might be taught to reward himself or herself by saying something (e.g., "I'll play basketball after school") as a special reward. It is important that these self-rewards are indeed special—that is, that they are not things that are said or done routinely, but things that are done to acknowledge and reinforce special efforts. Trainees' notes can be collected by the trainer in order to keep abreast of independent progress made by trainees, without consuming group time. A trainer should advance a student to this level of independent practice only when it is clear that he or she can successfully do what is being asked.

Peer Cotrainers.   As an additional aid to transfer, it is important to acknowledge the power of peer-group pressure on the behaviors of adolescents. The natural peer leader is often far more influential in a youngster's life than any adult trainer could hope to be. In this regard it is sometimes possible to capitalize on the natural leadership qualities of some adolescents. Hence, the trainer may want to select a peer (adolescent) cotrainer whom he or she can train and use instead of a second adult trainer. If a peer cotrainer is selected, it is important, of course, that he or she is proficient in the particular skill being taught.

RESEARCH EVALUATION

We have conducted a number of investigations designed to examine the skill-acquisition efficacy of structured learning with adolescents. In most of these studies, the youngsters involved were aggressive, disruptive, or in similar ways antisocial. Table 6.2 presents the substance of this research program. As can be seen from this information, consistently positive findings have emerged. Structured learning successfully trains adolescents in such prosocial skills as empathy, negotiation, assertiveness, following instructions, self-control, and perspective taking.

Beyond initial demonstrations that structured learning "works" with aggressive adolescents, these beginning studies have also highlighted other aspects of the teaching of prosocial behaviors. In an effort to capitalize upon adolescent responsiveness to peer influence, D. Fleming (1976) demonstrated that gains in negotiation skill are as great when the structured-learning group leader is a respected peer as when the leader is an adult. Litwack (1976), more concerned with the skill-enhancing effects of an adolescent's anticipating that he or she will later serve as a

TABLE 6.2. Structured-learning Research with Adolescent and Preadolescent Trainees

INVESTIGATOR	TARGET SKILL	TRAINEES	SETTING	RESULTS
Berlin, 1976	Empathy	Aggressive adolescents (JD and PINS)[a] ($N = 58$); $\bar{x}$ age $= 13.6$	Residential center	1. SL with conflict content $>$ SL with nonconflict content 2. SL with conflict content $>$ no treatment 3. I level 3 and 4 $>$ I level 2
D. Fleming, 1976	Negotiation	Aggressive preadolescents ($N = 80$); $\bar{x}$ age $= 10.5$	Regular classes in elementary urban school	1. No difference between high and low self-esteem trainees 2. No difference between adult-led and peer-led SL groups 3. All SL groups: significant acquisition but nonsignificant transfer
L. Fleming, 1976	Negotiation	Aggressve ($N = 48$) and passive ($N = 48$) educable mentally retarded preadolescents; $\bar{x}$ age $= 10.5$	Special-education classes in urban elementary school	1. SL $>$ attention control for aggressive and passive students
Golden, 1975	Resistance reduction with authority figure	Aggressive adolescents ($N = 60$); $\bar{x}$ age $=15.2$	Regular classes in urban senior high school	1. SL $=$ discrimination training 2. SL $>$ no treatment control on acquisition and transfer criteria
Greenleaf, 1977	Self-control	Aggressive preadolescents ($N = 60$); $\bar{x}$ age $= 14.6$	Regular classes in urban junior high school	1. SL $+$ transfer programming $>$ attention control on acquisition and transfer measures of self-control 2. SL $>$ attention control on acquisition and transfer measures of self-control 3. No significant effects for transfer programming alone
Hummel, 1977	Self-control	Aggressive adolescents ($N = 60$); $\bar{x}$ age $= 15.8$	Regular classes in rural senior high school	1. SL (stimulus variability) $>$ SL (constant) on acquisition and transfer measures for self-control and negotiation skills

Jennings, 1975	Interviewee behaviors (initiation, elaboration, etc.)	Emotionally disturbed adolescents ($N = 40$); $\bar{x}$ age = 13.7	Children's unit of state mental hospital	1. SL > minimal treatment control on subskills of initiation and termination of silence 2. SL > minimal treatment control on attractiveness to interviewer
Litwack, 1976	Following instructions	Passive-resistive adolescents ($N = 53$); $\bar{x}$ age = 14.10	Regular classes in urban junior high school	1. SL + anticipate serving as peer trainer > SL alone > no treatment on both acquisition and transfer criteria
Raleigh, 1976	Assertiveness	Aggressive ($N = 37$) and passive ($N = 37$) adolescents; $\bar{x}$ age = 13.5	Regular classes in urban junior high schools	1. SL (in groups) > SL (individual), discussion (groups), discussion (individual), no treatment on assertiveness or acquisition and transfer criteria
Swanstrom, 1977	Self-control	Aggressive preadolescents ($N = 42$); $\bar{x}$ age = 9.0	Regular classes in urban elementary school	1. SL = structured discussion 2. SL > no treatment control on acquisition criteria
Trief, 1976	Perspective-taking (PT.) cooperation[b]	Aggressive adolescents (JD and PINS)[a] ($N = 58$); $\bar{x}$ age = 15.5	Residential center	1. SL (affective + cognitive focus) > SL placebo control and brief instruction control on PT[b] 2. SL (affective focus) > SL placebo control and brief instruction control on PT[b] 3. SL (cognitive focus) > SL placebo control and brief instruction control on PT[b] 4. SL (combined focus) > SL placebo control and brief instruction on cooperation
Wood, 1977	Assertiveness	Aggressive and passive adolescents ($N = 70$); $\bar{x}$ age = 14	Regular classes in urban senior high school	1. SL > brief instructions control on acquisition and transfer measures of assertiveness across type of trainer 2. Greater assertiveness acquisition and trend toward greater transfer if teacher trained

[a] JD = juvenile delinquents; PINS = persons in need of supervision.

peer leader, showed that such helper-role expectation increases the degree of skill acquired. Apparently, when the adolescent expects to teach others a skill, his or her own level of skill acquisition benefits, a finding clearly relevant to Reissman's (1965) helper-therapy principle. Trief (1976) demonstrated that successful use of structured learning to increase the perspective-taking skill (i.e., seeing matters from other people's viewpoint) also leads to consequent increases in cooperative behavior. The significant transfer effects both in this study and in the Golden (1975), Litwack (1976), and Raleigh (1976) investigations have been important signposts for us in planning further research on transfer enhancement in structured learning.

We have also begun to examine the value of teaching certain skill combinations. Aggression-prone adolescents often get into difficulty when they respond with overt aggression to authority figures with whom they disagree. Responding to this type of event, Golden (1975) successfully used structure learning to teach such youngsters "resistance-reducing behavior," defined as a combination of reflection of feeling (the authority figure's) and assertiveness (forthright but nonaggressive statement of one's own position). Others have examined structured learning in yet other ways relevant to aggressive adolescents. Jennings (1975) was able to use structured learning successfully to train adolescents in several of the verbal skills necessary for satisfactory participation in more traditional, insight-oriented psychotherapy. Guzzetta (1974) was successful in providing means to help close the gap between adolescents and their parents by using structured learning to teach empathic skills to parents.

In similar studies in progress or being planned we are seeking to teach other prosocial skills listed in Table 6.2. In these investigations, we are attempting to further implement two experimental design strategies characteristic of our completed studies, both of which we feel are highly desirable components of treatment-evaluation research with delinquent and aggressive populations. The first concerns combinations of procedures designed to increase the transfer of the newly learned skills from the therapy setting to real-life settings. The second is use of factorial designs in order to derive change-enhancing prescriptive matches of treatments, trainers, and trainees.

CRITIQUE AND RECOMMENDATIONS

As a systematized, research-based, scientific movement, psychological skills training is still in its infancy. Many relevant theoretical and applied issues remain unresolved, a number of training methods and curricular concerns remain to be dealt with, and, in general, a great deal of needed research is yet to be conducted. It is to these matters we now turn.

Assessment

Though its history as a formal, systematic, psychoeducational intervention is quite brief, a wide variety of means have already been utilized in order to determine the nature and level of a given individual's social-skills deficiency. These include use of projective testing, case files or other biographical data, interviews of various structuredness, skill inventories or questionnaires completed by either the potential trainee or someone familiar with his or her daily behavior (peers, teacher, parent), and direct observation of trainee overt behavior in either naturally occurring or contrived situations. In all instances, the goal of such assessment has been to reliably estimate the individual's proficiency and deficiency levels across a variety of skills. In our view, most of these procedures—except direct behavioral observation—have largely failed in this effort.

Some have been too inferential, requiring too great a leap from assessment data to the skill behaviors one is seeking to predict. This is especially true of assessment via projective testing and global or comprehensive (nontargeted) interviews and, often, of case files or school records. Skill inventories or questionnaire's often do not suffer from this fault, but typically are weak in another regard shared by all but behavior observational assessment. Reliable estimation of skill levels has been thwarted by the failure to sufficiently reflect in the assessment process the fact that skill proficiency-deficiency is not only a characteristic of the person, but also of the situation or context (i.e., where and when) the use of the skill is appropriate. A youngster may respond with skilled self-control when admonished by a police officer, but with overt aggression when admonished for the same skill by a teacher. Clearly, an appraisal of the youngster's self-control skill level must reflect, at absolute minimum, *both* interpersonal contexts. Such situational assessment may be approximated in inventory or questionnaire assessment, as we have done in an assessment device we designed for one of our trainee populations. For example, our Skill Inventory items included:

10. *Expressing Anger:* Communicating your angry feelings to someone in a direct and honest manner.
    a. I express my angry feelings to my spouse for accepting a party invitation when he/she knew I wanted to stay home.
    b. I express my angry feelings to my friend for not telling me about his/her change in plans.
    c. I express my angry feelings to my coworker for leaving the hardest part of the job for me.
17. *Responding to a Complaint:* Trying to arrive at a fair solution to someone's justified complaint.
    a. I listen openly and respond to my spouse's complaint about my buying something that he/she thought was unnecessary.
    b. When my boss becomes angry about a detail I have overlooked, I respond calmly and rationally, without becoming sullen.
    c. When my neighbor nastily complains about a problem I am causing, I listen and take appropriate action about the problem.
22. *Self-Control:* Controlling your temper so that things do not get out of hand.
    a. I control my temper when my children disobey my requests.
    b. I control my temper when my spouse does something that I find annoying.
    c. I control my temper when a salesman treats me rudely in a store.
23. *Negotiation:* Arriving at a plan which satisfies both yourself and another person who has taken a different position.
    a. I negotiate with repairmen on a fair price for a job.

b. When my spouse and I encounter family problems, we compromise on a mutually agreeable solution.

c. I negotiate with my friend when each of us wants to do something different. (Goldstein et al., 1979)

We are, however, considerably more supportive of a behavior-observational assessment approach. In our view, such assessment is ideally conducted to be cross-situational, cross-temporal, and cross-observer. That is, the potential trainee should be observed in an array of naturalistic and/or contrived situations in which competent skill use is judged to be appropriate. This array of assessment situations should reflect diverse samples of times, places, and stimulus persons. Potential trainee behavior in given contexts is ideally observed on multiple occasions by two or more independent observers. When the exigencies of the real-life school, work, home, or any other observational context preclude implementation of such ideally structured behavioral observation, approximations thereto are typically still preferrable over the more inferential and less situational alternatives noted earlier.

Selecting Effective Trainers

In addition to the characteristics of successful skill trainers suggested earlier, there exists a substantial, if largely speculative, literature pointing to yet other, likely effectiveness-enhancing qualities of skill trainers. Considerable research sorting through these speculations, verifying or rejecting their impact on trainee learning, is an endeavor to be strongly recommended. In doing such research, we would urge the investigators to look for leads not only in the training, psychotherapy, and educational literature. There exist thousands of very competent social-skills trainers, persons who—often without premeditation—are regularly able to increase the prosocial skill level of diverse individuals, many of whom characteristically had behaved in consistently antisocial ways. Just as in formal social-skill training, the title, position, or credentials of such "natural trainers" seems largely irrelevant. They may be parents, high-school athletic coaches, teachers' aides, drugstore owners, prison guards, clergy, friends. What we are urging here is that those interested in maximizing social-skills trainer potency seek out and observe potent "natural trainers," and try to identify the means by which they successfully "train," so that we might seek to formally incorporate such wisdom into planned skill-training programs.

Transfer of Training

Prosocial skill acquisition that is essentially limited to the training setting, that fails to find consistent expression in the variety of real-life settings which constitute the trainee's world, is in our view a largely worthless accomplishment. We have reviewed evidence elsewhere indicating that a substantial majority of training-room, therapy-room, and classroom gains do *not* currently maintain in or transfer to real-life settings (Goldstein, Lopez, & Greenleaf, 1979, Goldstein & Stein, 1976). This is a dismal but accurate conclusion, testifying to the largely functionally autonomous manner in which so much training, therapy, and education exist. In our earlier presentation of the procedures which constitute structured learning we began to sound a more hopeful note, and presented a small number of experimentally substantiated procedures which have begun to show they can reliably improve the rate of positive transfer.

But this very important research domain, this quest for procedures which can be used as reliable transfer-enhancers, is still in its early infancy, at least as far as transfer-enhancement in the social-skills arena is concerned. Many *potential* transfer-enhancers exist. The trainer may provide general skill selection and implementation principles; conduct social-skills training in vivo, or otherwise reflect in the training transfer-enhancement via "identical elements"; provide a sufficient number of succesful skill-use trials to maximize "overlearning"; see to it—following the transfer principle of "stimulus variability"—that these successful skill practices are done in conjunction with *several different* types of co-role players; maximize, by the numerous means described earlier, the likelihood that the trainee will be rewarded by others and/or himself or herself when he or she seeks to use the newly learned skills outside of the training context. There exist additional *potential* means for enhancing transfer, means which draw upon research on social-support systems, social climates, biofeedback, drug treatment, and other diverse and often novel bodies of experimentation (Goldstein & Kanfer, 1979; Karoly & Steffen, 1980; Kazdin, 1975; Wildman & Wildman, 1975). Building upon the offerings of these researchers is a most crucial need in the social-skills training domain.

Ethical Considerations

In social-skills training, as in all psychotherapeutic, educational, or other endeavors which seek to alter human behavior, serious consideration of relevant ethical matters must be an integral part of intervention planning. Ethical issues may be even more of a concern when target trainees are persons who frequently engage in aggressive or other antisocial behaviors, and whose very participation in the skills-training program may be less than fully voluntary. The relevant ethical questions are many, and easy to find. Their answers are often harder to come by. Whose values will the training program try to reflect, especially when behaviors which "society" defines as antisocial are defined as prosocial by the person's smaller reference group? Shall we respond to the trainer's values here? The trainee's? The administrative agency involved (school, detention center, prison)? Who will select the skills to be taught? To be omitted? Will participation be voluntary, and based upon informed consent? What risks—obvious or subtle, immediate or long-term—may be associated with program participation? We do not offer our own answers to these ethical questions as necessarily optimal nor, certainly, final. They are, however, our best current attempt.

Skill Selection. Selection of concrete training goals—that is, the decisions about which skills should be taught to a particular trainee and which omitted—must, in our view, be a collaborative decision reached via mutual consultation between trainer and trainee. When made by the trainer alone such decisions run serious risk of imposing on the trainee trainer biases regarding what constitutes "good" or "proper" or "competent" skill functioning. Since trainer and trainee often differ in social class, educational background, life style, and aspiration level, the likelihood that serious skill-selection biases might actually (if subtly) operate are not negligible. Skill selection made solely by the trainee is, we feel, an equally serious threat to an heuristic set of training goals. By definition, the trainee is deficient in and inexperienced with an array of skills. To then place such skills before him or her, cafeteria-style, and propose that he or she choose those he or she wishes as the sole means of skill selection, is to risk serious miscalculation of appropriate and reachable training goals.

With the procedures that constitute academic counseling as our model, we have opted for a "negotiated-curriculum" solution to this ethical dilemma. A student seeking to register for an academic program will typically seek out an academic counselor or advisor. After a suitable exchange of background and aspirational information, the student will often indicate a desire to enroll in courses A, B, and C. The counselor, responding from his or her own perspective, may propose that courses D, E, and F are more suitable, or would be more useful for the student. The two negotiate, exchange reasons, consider alternatives, and ideally reach a negotiated curriculum superior in quality for that student than either of the one-person determined curricula which they brought to their meeting.

Analogously, in our skill selection in structured learning, both trainer and trainee complete parallel versions of the Structured Learning Skill Inventory. These Inventories are constructed to reflect a broad array of skills and situational contexts and, at least for the trainer version, can be derived from behavioral observation. After trainer and trainee independently complete their Inventories, they come together and engage in precisely the type of curricular negotiation just described as part of the academic counseling process. In a large majority of instances, we feel, a superior curricular outcome results.

Volition and Informed Consent. The trainee's decision to participate in social-skills training must be made on as fully a voluntary basis as his or her pretraining competencies and capacities permit. This view is appropriate, we feel, whether the trainee is a juvenile delinquent on probation, an adolescent incarcerated in a prison, a moderately retarded youngster, or an elementary-school pupil. We can identify no compelling examples of appropriate exceptions to this recommendation.

The potential trainee's right to free choice requires that the decision to participate or not be made in response to accurate and adequate information. Thus, potential participants in social-skills training should be provided clear and comprehensive information about the planned training experience and any evaluation associated with it. If it is consistent with the potential trainee's reading ability, this information should be written, nontechnically, and it should fully explain the content, procedures, and goals of the training program. Particular emphasis should be placed on the voluntary nature of participation; consistent with such an intent, use of subtle pressure on persons leaning toward or electing not to participate, should actively be avoided by trainers or others. When possible, invitees should be asked to respond to the invitation to participate in writing.

Risks. Risks associated with social-skills training do not seem to us to be appreciable. Those threats to the trainee that are relevant essentially parallel those characteristic of any educational endeavor. Some trainees will learn a given skill more slowly than other trainees in their groups, a discrepancy with some potential for feelings of embarrassment and discomfort. Those trainees who prove to be particularly slow may develop feelings of failure and lowered self-esteem. Good pedagogic practices—homogeneous grouping based upon shared skill deficiencies, appropriate pacing, ample use of reinforcement (even for "just trying")—can effectively serve to minimize such outcomes.

A perhaps more serious risk follows from the possibility that an apparently well-learned skill may fail to "work" in the real world and bring the trainee not reward, but either indifference or, worse, some form of punishment. To minimize the likelihood of such outcomes we would recommend the following:

1. Teach trainees "backup" skills—for example, responding to failure, responding to contradictory messages, and so on—early in their skill-training participation.
2. Teach trainees self-reward skills, to at least partially compensate for failures to receive rewards from others.
3. Be certain that real-life, skill-use homework assignments are
   a. made only when the trainee demonstrates high levels of proficiency in the skill in the training setting, and
   b. graduated such that real-life implementation attempts, while always somewhat challenging, start with relatively easy target persons and situations and *slowly* move toward more difficult ones.

Social-skills training is an energetic and growing movement in the United States today. We have examined its recent antecedents, its current programmatic representations, its problems, and its promise. As we have noted repeatedly, aggression control and the development of prosocial alternatives to aggression are complex, multifaceted challenges. Such challenges require complex solutions, consisting of a variety of diverse interventions. Social-skills training, while no panacea, is in our view one important such intervention. Its potential is considerable when implemented in a preplanned, systematic, and broad manner. It is our hope that the present section may serve as both a stimulus and a guideline for such implementation.

PROBLEM-SOLVING TRAINING

In 1939, Dollard, Miller, Doob, Mowrer, and Sears published *Frustration and Aggression,* a classic contribution to our subsequent understanding of aggressive behavior and its instigation. At the heart of their position lay the hypothesis that a universal causal relationship existed between frustration and aggression. In its initial formulation, frustration was posited to always cause aggression; aggression was predicted to always be a consequent of frustration. It was, early in its history, in several ways an attractively simple hypothesis. It turned the thinking of many individuals away from mythological and untestable notions of instinctual bases for aggression, it stimulated literally hundreds of investigations, and ultimately it led to considerable advance in our knowledge of the antecedents of aggression and the consequents of frustration.

Stated as a universal causality, however, the hypothesis has proven to have severe limitations. Frustration was shown to lead to aggression as predicted in only some instances. In young children, regression was often a more typical response (Barker, Dembo, & Lewin, 1941), and in others fixation or displacement (Johnson, 1972) have sometimes resulted. Wright (1942, 1943), Bateson (1941), Montague (1978), and other anthropologists have identified cultures in which aggression is an unusual consequent of frustration. Buss (1961) and others have shown that only some kinds of frustration lead to aggression, while other kinds do not. And Pastore (1952) demonstrated that how justifiable the frustration seems to the individual is a major determinant of whether he or she responds to it with aggression. Bandura & Walters (1959) present the multiplicity of potential consequents of frustration well with their observation:

> When distressed, some people seek help and support; others increase achievement strivings; others show withdrawal and resignation; some aggress; others experience heightened somatic activity; still others anesthetize themselves against a miserable existence with drugs and alcohol; and most intensify constructive efforts to overcome their adversities. (pp. 53–54)

Not only may frustration have consequents in addition to aggression, but aggression also has a number of potential antecedents in addition to frustration. These latter include one's reinforcement history for aggressive behavior, competing instigative and inhibitory tendencies, opportunity for the displacement of aggression, degree of exposure to aggressive models, previous history of punishment for behaving aggressively, the likelihood of counteraggression, and broader social sanctions for aggressive behavior. As Berkowitz (1969) comments, "In the long run, the frustration-aggression hypothesis contains considerable truth, but it is too simple and too sweeping . . . " (p. 19).

Even though notions of universal causality have clearly failed to sustain, there are many instances in which frustration *does* lead to aggression, and in which aggression *is* the individual's dominant response to frustration. Aggression is the individual's prepotent response to frustration when he or she has *learned* that the thwarting, goal-blocking, or other aversive component of the frustrating circumstance is most rapidly, thoroughly, or expeditiously resolved by aggression. Frustration is likely to lead to aggression when one is rewarded for such behavior. As many observers have noted, aggression very often pays. The more frequently it does, the more likely aggressive responses become in the individual's response hierarchy or repertoire. One means for decreasing the likelihood of prepotency of such a response is to increase the relative potency of other, more socially desirable responses. If some individuals can respond to frustration by, as Bandura (1969) notes, "increasing achievement striving" and "intensifying constructive efforts to overcome their adversities," perhaps we can actually teach such constructive behaviors to individuals more prone to respond with aggression. This was our goal in our consideration of psychological skills training, and it is toward this same goal that the present section is devoted.

In the previous section, we noted that for most individuals the learning of interpersonal and social skills was often a chance affair. The development of such skills, we observed, was rarely the object of concrete and systematic training. One "picked up" interpersonal and social-skill behaviors haphazardly, as part of the overall socialization process, or one typically learned them quasisystematically in spurts at home, at school, at church or synagogue, or elsewhere. Very much the same inadequate teaching picture exists with regard to the focus of the present section: problem-solving skills. Some people, some of the time, may be fortunate enough to receive systematic problem-solving instruction, but this is a relatively rare event. As with psychological skills training, the rather little problem-solving training which does occur tends to be irregular and unsystematic in occurrence and incomplete and inadequate in scope. We can do better. Individuals in general, and aggressive youngsters in particular, can be provided systematic training in problem-solving skills both for purposes of building general competence in meeting life's challenges, and as a specific means of supplying one more reliable, prosocial alternative to aggression.

Toward these broad goals, in this section we examine the leading approaches available to *interpersonal* problem solving. Our concern is how youngsters faced with frustrating, aggression-instigating, problematic events involving a peer, parent, teacher, or other person may be effectively trained to engage not in aggressive behavior vis-à-vis such important figures in their interpersonal world, but, instead, in competent problem solving. Although this body of literature is not yet very large, what does exist is both substantial and of proven efficacy. It is a body of literature well worth our serious attention.

The notion that problem-solving ability might be among the factors helping determine the quality of an individual's psychological adjustment, and might also be relevant to his or her level of aggressive and impulsive behavior, is both relatively recent and not frequently advanced. Jahoda (1953, 1958) was an early advocate of this view. More recently, a similar position is evident in Weinstein's (1969) focus on the development of interpersonal competence and in D'Zurilla and Goldfried's (1971) delineation of stages in the problem-solving process. The general stance advanced here is that inadequate problem-solving skills in the interpersonal and personal spheres of functioning result in too frequent reliance on socially unacceptable and nonenduring solutions, especially solutions of an acting-out nature. Note that this viewpoint parallels quite directly the position we took earlier regarding psychological skills training. There we proposed that skilled social behaviors could successfully be taught as viable substitutes for aggression, even in situations in which aggression—at least on a short-term basis—paid off. Similarly with problem-solving skills. In lieu of hitting, grabbing, insulting, pushing, threatening, or other aggressive behavioral solutions to interpersonal problems, individuals can successfully be taught the cognitive, reasoning, delaying skills necessary to reach satisfying, nonaggressive solutions to the same problem situation. In the remainder of this section we examine the specific attempts made thus far to train such problem-solving skills. In doing so, we look very briefly at a number of beginning, modest attempts at such training, and then make an in-depth examination of the one effort in this domain which has yielded a comprehensive, elaborate, and seemingly valid series of problem-solving training programs and materials.

Pilot Training Programs

Small, pilot efforts aimed at enhancing problem-solving skills were initiated by Holzworth (1964) and Giebink, Stover, and Fahl (1968). Using gamelike and other instructional materials, each sought to teach impulsive children adaptive means for handling frustrating situations. Each found suggestively (small N) positive results. Branca, D'Augelli, and Evans (1975) provide similarly encouraging early results from their training program in decision-making skills for preadolescents. Not unlike most of the programs we examine in this section, the focus of the Branca et al. program is upon teaching the *process* of decision making or problem solving, and not upon the rightness or wrongness of any particular decision or solution. Also as is true of several other programs, the decision-making process is segmented, and viewed as a phase or step-wise process involving problem definition, identification of alternative solutions, choice of one solution as probably optimal, test of this selection, and evaluation of this trial solution. In a program of this nature named *Thresholds,* Burglass and Duffy (1974) sought to teach a problem-solving process whose sequential steps were:

1. Defining the situation.
2. Expanding possibilities.
3. Evaluating possibilities.
4. Establishing decisional criteria.
5. Making a decision.
6. Acting on the decision.
7. Ratifying the decision.

Whereas Branca et al. (1975) and Burglass and Duffy (1974) implement their training efforts via an array of didactic, discussional, and simulational activities, Blechman (1974) has taught problem-solving skills utilizing a game format. Her *Family Contract Game* is designed to be employed by family units experiencing marked conflict and inability to successfully deal with interpersonal problems which involve them. The game is structured to circumvent or minimize the conflictual behaviors which usually characterize the behavior of the participating families: complaining, criticizing, interrupting, unresponsiveness, and so forth. Instead, again following a stage model, participation seeks to teach:

1. Definition of the problem.
2. Collection of relevant information.
3. Examination of alternatives.
4. Selection of course of action.
5. Evaluation of consequences.

In an important article, D'Zurilla and Goldfried (1971) explored the manner in which an array of behavior-modification approaches, especially those concerned with self-control, might constitute an effective clinical reflection of experimental psychology's efforts in the problem-solving arena. They describe separate behavior-therapy procedures for teaching what they view as the essential stages of effective problem solving: (1) general orientation; (2) problem definition; (3) generation of alternatives; (4) decision making; and (5) verification. Goldfried and Davison (1976) have described actual clinical applications of these suggested, problem-solving methods, and a few investigators have begun to conduct the necessary evaluation research in order to test the actual efficacy of these applications (Ross & Ross, 1973; Stone, Hinds, & Schmidt, 1975; Wagner, Breitmeyer, & Bottum, 1975).

Impulsive youngsters have been the target of the problem-solving training effort put forth by Bash and Camp's (1975) *Think Aloud Program*. By use of an extended series of didactic lessons, games, and other activities, trainees are taught a variety of self-instructional procedures aimed at increasing their reflectiveness, as well as such specific problem-solving skills as the ability to develop alternative solutions to interpersonal problems, to consider possible consequences, and to formulate plans of action based upon this formulation. It is skills such as these, in much more refined and elaborated form, which are the skill-development targets of the major, problem-solving training program which we now give in-depth consideration.

The Interpersonal Cognitive Problem-Solving Program

The pioneering work on problem-solving training we examine in this section was conducted over a fifteen-year period by George Spivack, Myrna B. Shure, Jerome J. Platt, and their coworkers. The fruits of their efforts appear in three volumes: *Social Adjustment of Young Children* (Spivack & Shure, 1974), *The Problem-Solving Approach to Adjustment* (Spivack, Platt, & Shure, 1976), and *Problem-Solving Techniques in Childrearing* (Shure & Spivack, 1978). While we seek herein to do justice to this seminal research and materials-development program in our discussion of it, the reader is strongly encouraged to examine directly the just-cited references.

In its earliest phase, Interpersonal Cognitive Problem Solving training (ICPS) was oriented primarily toward young children. The following comment by Spivack and Shure (1974) communicates a sense of why, in the context of aggressive behavior, they view problem-solving skills as worth teaching:

What might an adult say to a preschool child who hits another child or grabs a toy or cries? One possible response is, "Kevin, I know you feel angry at Paul, but I can't let you hit him." Another is, "Paul doesn't like to be hit." Sean snatches a truck from Robert and the adult asks him why he has taken the truck. "I want it!" is the answer. "Wait until Robert is finished and then you can play with it," says the adult. . . . In handling such behaviors as hitting and grabbing, many teachers and parents of young children demand that the behavior stop "Because I said so." They often explain why the behavior is unacceptable. ("You can't hit Paul because you might hurt him.") If the hitting persists in school, the child might be isolated from the other children until he calms down or is judged to be ready to play without hitting.

We believe that such techniques have serious limitations if one's goal is to help children develop effective ways of handling personal and interpersonal problems. First, the adult is too often doing the thinking for the child. The child is told he should wait his turn or stay away from another child or not hit. . . . The child neither solves his problem nor is helped to discover a solution of his own. Second, the adult in attempting to help a child often assumes that the child has a real understanding of the language of emotions ("I know you feel angry") or of negation ("but I *can't* let you hit him") or of causal relationships ("because you might hurt him"). Many young children do not have mastery of the language concepts necessary to solve interpersonal problems. . . . Finally, solving a problem for a child does little to help him feel good about himself. He is simply told what he can or cannot do, even though the reasons may be explained and the solution may work in that particular instance. He does not experience mastery that emerges when one has solved a problem. He may feel protected, but not competent. (pp. *IX–X*)

It is from this rationale that the ICPS Program emerged. Children (and later adolescents and adults) are to be taught *how* to think, not *what* to think. ICPS training teaches the problem-solving process, not problem solutions. In the case of young children trainees, prerequisite language and conceptual skills must also be taught. More generally, from the viewpoint articulated previously, there emerged a series of principles or guidelines from which the specific content and procedures of the ICPS Program would follow.

Principles Underlying ICPS. The first principle concerned prerequisite language and conceptual skills. For later ability to learn to construe alternative solutions, games and other activities are used first to teach the meaning of words such as *or, and,* and *not.* To aid in later understanding of individual preferences and interpersonal differences, words such as *some, same,* and *different* must be understood. And in the affective realm, of relevance to interpersonal sensitivity and empathy, notions of *happy, sad, mad,* and the like are provided.

The second principle underlying ICPS training for young children is that it is easier to teach new concepts with words already familiar to the child. Thus, a major effort is made to utilize previously learned content to teach new materials. The third principle is that program content and situations should center around interpersonal themes, not impersonal problems. The fourth principle emphasizes conceptual learning and understanding, rather than the use of specific words or sentences. For example, emphasis is on the *idea* of negation rather than on its necessarily accurate grammatical representation in any given sentence. The fifth principle, one lying at the heart of ICPS training, emphasizes teaching the child the habit of seeking alternative solutions and evaluating them on the basis of their potential consequences. With regard to this principle Spivack and Shure (1974) observe that no emphasis in training is placed upon the absolute merits of any given solution. If a child states "Hit him." as a solution to getting a toy from another child, the teacher-trainer says (just as he or she would say if a more socially acceptable solution were offered): "That's one idea. Can you think of a different idea?" (if he or she is teaching the seeking of alternatives). Or the trainer might comment: "That's one idea. What might happen next if you hit him?"* (if he or she is teaching the seeking of consequences). To further buttress the subsequent implementation of this principle, and thus aid trainee ability to evaluate alternative solutions, additional prerequisite skill words and concepts are taught—for example, *maybe, why-because, if-then.*

The sixth guiding principle underlying ICPS training stresses that the child think of and evaluate his or her own ideas, and be encouraged to offer them in the context of problem situations. This principle, Spivack and Shure note, rests on the belief that a child is more likely to act on a conclusion he or she views as his or her own, than he or she is upon problem solutions provided by others.

Finally, ICPS training grows from the principle that the prerequisite language skills and the cognitive problem-solving skills, which together constitute the training goals of this program, are not ends in themselves but, instead, should be conceptualized as antecedent, mediating skills necessary to enhance behavioral adjustment and reduce such maladaptive behaviors as impulsivity, aggressiveness, and overemotionality.

ICPS Skills. It is appropriate at this point in our presentation to more fully define and examine the specific problem-solving skills which constitute the focal training targets of the ICPS program. To do so most understandably we end our exclusive consideration of ICPS efforts with young children and move on in this and the following sections of this chapter to a more comprehensive consideration of the skills, aggression-relevant research results, and age-related training methods and materials of the ICPS Programs across age samples, including young children, but also preadolescents and adolescents.

ALTERNATIVE SOLUTION THINKING

A person's ability to generate different options or solutions that could potentially be utilized to solve a problem defines that person's capacity for alternative solution thinking. ICPS training for this skill has typically centered upon problems

---

*Spivack and Shure (1974) have demonstrated, in this context, that well-adjusted and poorly adjusted children do not differ in the frequency with which they verbally offer aggressive solutions such as "Hit him." to problems such as these. They do, however, differ significantly in the frequency with which they actually use such aggressive behaviors overtly in attempts to resolve problematic situations.

in trainee interpersonal relationships with a variety of types of persons, but especially with peers and authority figures. Spivack et al. (1976) observe, in partial explanation of their interest in promoting this skill, that if someone has but one or two solutions available to him or her in any given problematic situation, his or her chances of success are less than for individuals who can turn to alternative solutions when the first option attempted fails to succeed in problem resolutions.

> Among four- and five-year-olds, for instance, a girl may want her sister to let her play with her doll. She may ask her, and her sister may say no. Of interest is whether the child who wants the toy would conceive of an alternative way to get her sister to let her play with the doll. . . . If the girl's sister consistently says no every time she is asked for something, and no other options are available to the girl, she would soon become frustrated with her sister. She might react aggressively and exhibit impulsive behavior (for example, she might grab the toy) or she might avoid the problem entirely by withdrawing. (Spivack et al., 1976, p. 19)

CONSEQUENTIAL THINKING

This second ICPS skill is defined as an ability to consider how one's actions may affect both other people and oneself, as well as the subsequent reactions these behaviors may engender. The process of consequential thinking includes consideration of pros and cons to an interpersonal act that goes beyond the simple enumeration of alternative events that might ensue. As is seen in our later examination of ICPS training procedures and materials, consequential thinking is stimulated by having the trainer follow the offering of problem solutions with such questions as: "What might happen next?" "How will this make Mary feel?" "What will happen in the short run?" "What will happen in the long run?"

CAUSAL THINKING

Causal, or cause-and-effect, thinking associated with interpersonal problem situations is the ability to relate one event to another over time with regard to the "why" that might have precipitated any given act. At the simplest level, to continue the example just described, if the girl wishing to obtain a doll from her sister hit her sister, accurate cause-and-effect thinking would make her aware that she hit her sister because her sister would not let her play with the doll or because of her anger at not being given the doll. If her sister hit her back as a result of having been hit, accurate causal thinking should lead the child to be aware that her sister hit her because she hit first. The inclusion of causal thinking as a skill-training goal in the ICPS Program was initially based, in part, on the position of Muuss (1960). His concern was social causal thinking across developmental levels. At its optimal levels, Muuss viewed causal thinking as:

... an understanding and appreciation of the dynamic, complex and interacting nature of the forces that operate in human behavior. It involves an attitude of flexibility, of seeing things from the point of view of others as well as an awareness of the probabilistic nature of knowledge. A causally oriented person is capable of suspending judgment until sufficient factual information is available ... (p. 122)

Relevant to our present purposes, in Muuss' view, low levels of causal thinking and its companion, low insight into the dynamics of behavior, make it difficult to react logically and appropriately to the behavior of others and, hence, " ... behavior of others may be misunderstood and perceived as threatening, and such misunderstanding could lead to heightened conflict between the parties involved" (Spivack et al., 1976, p. 75).

INTERPERSONAL SENSITIVITY

This problem-solving skill concerns an individual's awareness that an interpersonal problem in fact exists. It is the ability to perceive such problems combined with skill in focusing upon its interpersonal problematic components. Spivack et al. (1976) comment:

To carry our example of the girl who wanted her sister's doll one step further, it seems reasonable to assume that if she were aware that a [interpersonal] problem or potential problem could develop once she decides to ask for a doll, her behavior and/or problem-solving strategies may differ from what might ensue in the absence of such sensitivity. (p. 177)

As we see shortly, however, empirical evidence examining the degree to which the various ICPS skills discriminate between well-adjusted and poorly adjusted individuals, or between aggressive and impulsive versus nonaggressive and more reflective persons, does not support interpersonal sensitivity as among the highly potent ICPS skills.

MEANS-END THINKING

Means-ends thinking is careful, step-by-step planning in order to reach a given goal. Such planning, Spivack et al. (1976) observe, includes insight and forethought to forestall or circumvent potential obstacles and, in addition, having available alternative means, when needed, to deal with realistic obstacles in the way of reaching one's goal. Means-ends thinking involves, in addition, awareness that goals are not always reached immediately and that the timing of one's behavior is also often relevant to goal attainment. Spivack et al. (1976) comment illustratively:

A child adept at means-ends thinking may consider, I can go visit the boy next door [means] but he won't know me and won't let me in [obstacle]. If I call first and tell him I just moved in and ask if I can come over [means], he'll say okay. But I better not go at dinnertime or his mother will be mad [time and obstacle] and he won't like me. (p. 202)

PERSPECTIVE TAKING

This interpersonal problem-solving skill is reflected by the extent to which an individual recognizes and can integrate the fact that different people may have different motives and viewpoints, and thus may respond differently in a given situation. Perspective taking closely resembles what others have termed role taking or empathy. A fuller sense of the meaning of this ICPS skill can be understood from its measurement. In ICPS research on perspective taking, Feffer and Jahelka's (1968) Thematic Apperception Test (TAT) procedure was used. The trainee, after creating stories to four TAT cards following standard TAT instructions, is presented the same cards again, and is asked to retell the initial story from the viewpoint of each of its characters. Among the qualities necessary for taking the perspective of others, scoring reflects the degree of coordination between the various versions.

Competence in the six problem-solving skills we have now presented is the overall training goal of the ICPS Program. The success of the Program in achieving these goals, and its impact on the overt aggressive and impulsive behavior of ICPS trainees, as well as their more general adjustment, are the concerns to which we now turn.

ICPS Research.   A substantial number of evaluative ICPS studies have been conducted. Many have been comparisons, on each ICPS skill, of trainees high versus low in adjustment, aggressiveness, impulsiveness, or inhibition. Others, seeking to provide complementary information, have examined the degree of correlation between the skills and these same criterion measures. Table 6.3 summarizes the major results of these experimental and correlational studies. For each of the major ICPS trainee age groups, Table 6.3 indicates the presence or absence of a significant impact of each skill upon the criteria studied.

Before turning to specific results—especially those relevant to aggression and its reduction—with particular trainee samples, an overall comment on Table 6.3 appears appropriate. Recall that the developers of ICPS set forth as their final guiding principle in undertaking this work the notion that the problem-solving skills are not taught as ends in themselves, but as antecedent, mediating skills necessary to enhance behavior adjustment and reduce aggressiveness, impulsivity, and over-inhibition. Table 6.3 tells us that, even though not all the skills thus impact in all the samples, Spivack, Shure, and Platt have essentially succeeded in their goal.

With regard to specific findings, let us examine alternative thinking first. Shure, Spivack, and Powell (1972) found that youngsters whose behavior ratings indicated a predominance of either acting-out behaviors or inhibition conceptu-

TABLE 6.3. ICPS Skills Relevant to Training Criteria: Adjustment, Aggression, Impulsivity, Inhibition

TRAINEE	SKILL					
	ALTERNATIVES	CONSEQUENCES	CAUSALITY	INTERPERSONAL SENSITIVITY	MEANS-END THINKING	PERSPECTIVE TAKING
Early childhood (age 4–5)	YES	YES	NO	NO	—	—
Middle childhood (age 9–12)	YES	NO	YES	—	YES	—
Adolescence	YES	YES	NO	NO	YES	YES

193

alized significantly fewer solutions to problem situations than did children rated as well adjusted. Elardo and Caldwell (see Spivack et al. 1976) found that as alternative thinking improved, disrespect, defiance, inattentiveness, withdrawal, and over-reliance on others all decreased. Two studies demonstrated that increased levels of alternative thinking on posttraining, test situations are also paralleled by analo-gously high levels in real-life contexts (Larcen, Chinsky, Allen, Lochman, & Selinger, 1974; McClure, 1975). As was true for children, poor levels of adjustment also correlates with deficient alternative thinking in adolescents (Shure & Spivack, 1978).

Consequential thinking was examined by Shure, Newman, and Silver (1973) and Spivack and Shure (1974). These studies indicate that 4 year olds rated as be-haviorally adjusted conceptualize a greater number of different, relevant conse-quences to such aggressive acts as grabbing toys and taking objects belonging to others without permission than do children rated as impulsive or inhibited. Shure and Spivack (1972) found that the number of consequences given by a youngster increases as a function of ICPS training. Comparisons of normal versus impulsive adolescents (Spivack & Levine, 1963) reveals that the normal sample provided significantly more consequences.

Larcen, Spivack, and Shure (1972) found a significant relationship between causal thinking and measures of both impulsivity and inhibition in 9 to 12 year olds, with well-adjusted youngsters identifying causal statements significantly more often than those displaying behavior deviance. No such result emerged in other exami-nations of this relationship involving 4 to 5 year olds or adolescents.

Level of interpersonal sensitivity, in the sense defined earlier—that is, degree of awareness that an interpersonal problem exists—did not differentiate between adjusted and more deviant child (Spivack & Shure, 1974) or adolescent (Platt, Spivack, Altman, Altman, & Peizer, 1974) samples. Perspective taking, a separate skill reflecting a different type of interpersonal sensitivity (role taking, empathy) has found greater success in ICPS evaluative research. Platt et al. (1974) found significantly greater ability on this skill in normal adolescents than in disturbed youngsters.

Finally, let us consider research on means-ends thinking. In a sample of 9 to 12 year old children, Larcen et al. (1972) found a significant inverse relationship between the level of means-ends thinking skill and such behavior as social aggres-sion, inability to delay, and emotionality. Working at the same age level, Shure and Spivack (1972) obtained evidence that normal, as compared to disturbed, young-sters conceptualized more means (steps) to reach a goal, more obstacles that might be met on the way to that goal, and more consideration of the importance of time. In addition to mentioning fewer means, obstacles, and time considerations in reach-ing a goal, less well-adjusted youngsters expressed stories more limited to impulsive and aggressive means.

This brief overview of ICPS outcome research confirms the conclusion we drew earlier in summary of Table 6.3. The skills examined, with only few excep-tions, appear to meaningfully and significantly relate to and differentiate among samples varying in levels of adjustment, aggression, impulsivity, and inhibition. Their importance seems well established.

We have focused in this section on one important approach to interpersonal problem solving: as a viable alternative to aggressive responses to frustrating situations. If problem-solving skills are, as we believe, important curricula for aggressive youngsters, we should not limit our vision only to Interpersonal Cognitive Problem Solving. Many other approaches to systematic problem solving exist. Most are impersonal rather than interpersonal in focus, and thus are one further step removed from the primary concerns of this book. Still, given our view championing a multifaceted intervention for multiply-determined school violence and vandalism, and given the scope of such behavior, we feel it to be premature at best and foolhardy at worst to rule out potential sources for effective interventions. We therefore urge the creative teacher, the creative researcher, the creative administrator to seriously consider the array of impersonal problem-solving programs as yet additional sources of valuable technology for teaching this important prosocial alternative to aggression. Specifically, these programs include Brainstorming (Osborn, 1953), Synectics (Gordon, 1961, 1971; Prince, 1970), Bionics (Papanek, 1969), Creative Problem Solving (Parnes, 1967), Attribute Listing (Crawford, 1950, 1954), Morphological Analysis (Zwicky, 1957, 1969), Checklists (Whiting, 1958), Vice-Versa Approach (Goldner, 1962), Fresh Eye (Whiting, 1958), the Total Creativity Program (Williams, 1972), Purdue Creativity Program (Covington, Crutchfield, & Davies, 1972), the Productive Thinking Program (Crutchfield & Covington, 1965), and Inquiry Training (Suchman, 1961). This suggestion completes our consideration of the problem-solving domain.

SUMMARY

In this chapter we have examined in depth two major contemporary approaches to the teaching of prosocial behavior. Psychological skills training and interpersonal cognitive problem solving each rest on a strong empirical foundation and have demonstrated their potency in enhancing overt prosocial behaviors in an array of real-world contexts. Their continued and expanded utilization in schools in general, and with aggressive youngsters in particular, is to be strongly recommended.

REFERENCES

ADKINS, W. R.   Life skills: Structured counseling for the disadvantaged. *Personnel and Guidance Journal*, 1970, *49*, 108–116.
ADKINS, W. R.   Life coping skills: A fifth curriculum. *Teachers College Record*, 1974, *75*, 507–526.
AUTHIER, J., GUSTAFSON, K., GUERNEY, B. G., JR., & KASDORF, J. A.   The psychological practitioner as teacher. *The Counseling Psychologist*, 1975, *5*, 1–21.

BANDURA, A. *Principles of behavior modification.* New York: Holt. Reinhart & Winston, 1969.
BANDURA, A., & WALTERS, R. H. *Adolescent aggression.* New York: Ronald Press, 1959.
BARKER, R. G., DEMBO, T., & LEWIN, K. Frustration and regression: An experiment with young children. *University of Iowa Studies in Child Welfare,* 1941, *18,* 1–314.
BASH, M. A., & CAMP, B. W. *Think Aloud Program Group Manual* (unpublished manuscript). Boulder, Colorado: University of Colorado Medical Center, 1975.
BASH, M. A., & CAMP, B. W. Teacher training in the Think Aloud Classroom Program. In G. Cartledge & J. F. Milburn (Eds.), *Teaching social skills to children.* New York: Pergamon Press, 1980.
BATESON, G. The frustration-aggression hypothesis and culture. *Psychological Review,* 1941, *48,* 350–355.
BERKOWITZ, L. *Roots of aggression.* New York: Atherton, 1969.
BERLIN, R. J. *Teaching acting-out adolescents prosocial conflict resolution through structured learning training of empathy.* Unpublished doctoral dissertation, Syracuse University, 1976.
BLECHMAN, E. A. The family contract game. *The Family Coordinator,* 1974, *23,* 269–281.
BRANCA, M. C., D'AUGELLI, J. F., & EVANS, K. L. *Development of a decision-making skills education program* (unpublished manuscript). University Park, Pa.: Pennsylvania State University, 1975.
BURGLASS, M. E., & DUFFY, M. G. *Thresholds: Teachers manual.* Cambridge, Mass.: Correctional Solutions Foundation, 1974.
BUSS, A. H. *The psychology of aggression.* New York: Wiley, 1961.
CARKHUFF, R. R. *Cry twice.* Amherst, Mass.: Human Resources Development Press, 1974.
CARSON, G. *The polite Americans.* New York: Morrow, 1966.
CARTLEDGE, G., & MILBURN, J. R. The case for teaching social skills in the classroom: A review. *Review of Educational Research,* 1980, *1,* 133–156.
COVINGTON, M. V., CRUTCHFIELD, R. S., & DAVIES, L. B. *The productive thinking program.* Berkeley, Calif.: Brazelton Printing, 1972.
COX, R. D., & GUNN, W. B. Interpersonal skills in the schools: Assessment and curriculum development. In D. P. Rathjen & J. P. Foreyt (Eds.), *Social competence: Interventions for children and adults.* New York: Pergamon Press, 1980.
CRAWFORD, R. P. *How to get ideas.* Lincoln, Neb.: University Associates, 1950.
CRAWFORD, R. P. *Techniques of creative thinking.* New York: Hawthorn, 1954.
CRUTCHFIELD, R. S., & COVINGTON, M. V. Programmed instruction and creativity. *Programmed Instruction,* 1965, *4,* 1–10.
DEACOVE, J. *Cooperative games manual.* Perth, Ontario: Family Pastimes, 1974.
DEACOVE, J. *Sports manual of cooperative recreation.* Perth, Ontario: Family Pastimes, 1978.
DOLLARD, J., MILLER, N. E., DOOB, L. W., MOWRER, O. H., & SEARS, R. R. *Frustration and aggression.* London: Kegan Paul, Trench, Trubnes, 1939.
D'ZURILLA, T. J., & GOLDFRIED, M. R. Problem solving and behavior modification. *Journal of Abnormal Psychology,* 1971, *78,* 107–126.
ELARDO, P., & COOPER, M. *AWARE: Activities for social development.* Reading, Mass.: Addison-Wesley, 1977.

FEFFER, M. H., & JAHELKA, M.   Implications of decentering concept for the structuring of projective content. *Journal of Consulting and Clinical Psychology,* 1968, *32,* 343–441.

FLEMING, D.   *Teaching negotiation skills to pre-adolescents.* Unpublished doctoral dissertation, Syracuse University, 1976.

FLEMING, L.   *Training passive and aggressive educable mentally retarded children for assertive behaviors using three types of structured learning training.* Unpublished doctoral dissertation, Syracuse University, 1976.

FLUEGELMAN, A.   *The new games book.* Garden City, N.Y.: Dolphin Books, 1974.

GIEBINK, J. W., STOVER, D. S., & FAHL, M. A.   Teaching adaptive responses to frustration to emotionally disturbed boys. *Journal of Consulting and Clinical Psychology,* 1968, *32,* 366–368.

GOLDEN, R.   *Teaching resistance-reducing behavior to high school students.* Unpublished doctoral dissertation, Syracuse University, 1975.

GOLDFRIED, M. R., & DAVISON, G. C.   *Clinical behavior therapy.* New York: Holt, Rinehart & Winston, 1976.

GOLDNER, B. B.   *The strategy of creative thinking.* Englewood Cliffs, N.J.: Prentice-Hall, 1962.

GOLDSTEIN, A. P.   *Structured learning therapy.* New York: Academic Press, 1973.

GOLDSTEIN, A. P.   *Psychological skill training.* New York: Pergamon Press, 1981.

GOLDSTEIN, A. P., & KANFER, F. H.   *Maximizing treatment gains.* New York: Academic Press, 1979.

GOLDSTEIN, A. P., LOPEZ, M., & GREENLEAF, D.   Introduction. In A. P. Goldstein and F. H. Kanfer (Eds.), *Maximizing treatment gains.* New York: Academic Press, 1979.

GOLDSTEIN, A. P., SPRAFKIN, R. P., & GERSHAW, N. J.   *Skill training for community living.* New York: Pergamon Press, 1976.

GOLDSTEIN, A. P., SPRAFKIN, R. P., GERSHAW, N. J., & KLEIN, P.   *Skill-streaming the adolescent: A structured learning approach to teaching prosocial behavior.* Champaign, Ill.: Research Press, 1979.

GOLDSTEIN, A. P., & STEIN, N.   *Prescriptive psychotherapies.* New York: Pergamon Press, 1976.

GORDON, W. J.   *Synectics.* New York: Collier Books, 1961.

GORDON, W. J.   *The metaphorical way.* Cambridge, Mass.: Porpoise Books, 1971.

GREENLEAF, D.   *Peer reinforcement as transfer enhancement in structured learning therapy.* Unpublished masters thesis, Syracuse University, 1977.

GUZZETTA, R. A.   *Acquisition and transfer of empathy by the parents of early adolescents through structured learning training.* Unpublished doctoral dissertation, Syracuse University, 1974.

HARE, M. A.   *Teaching conflict resolution simulations.* Paper presented at a meeting of the Eastern Community Association, Philadelphia, March 1976.

HARRISON, M.   *For the fun of it!* Philadelphia: Religious Society of Friends, 1975.

HAWLEY, R. C., & HAWLEY, I. L.   *Developing human potential: A handbook of activities for personal and social growth.* Amherst, Mass.: Education Research Association, 1975.

HEIMAN, H.   Teaching interpersonal communications. *North Dakota Speech and Theatre Association Bulletin,* 1973, *2,* 7–29.

HERSEN, M., & EISLER, R. M.   Social skills training. In W. E. Craighead, A. E. Kazdin, & M. J. Mahoney (Eds.), *Behavior modification: Principles, issues and applications.* Boston: Houghton Mifflin, 1976.

HOLZWORTH, W. A. *Effects of selective reinforcement therapy in a miniature situation in nursery school children.* Unpublished masters thesis, University of Illinois, 1964.

HUMMEL, J. W. *An examination of structured learning therapy, self-control, negotiation training and variation in stimulus conditions.* Unpublished doctoral dissertation, Syracuse University, 1977.

JAHODA, M. The meaning of psychological health. *Social Casework,* 1953, *34,* 349-354.

JAHODA, M. *Current concepts of positive mental health.* New York: Basic Books, 1958.

JENNINGS, R. L. *The use of structured learning techniques to teach attraction enhancing interviewee skills to residentially hospitalized, lower socioeconomic emotionally disturbed children and adolescents: A psychotherapy analogue investigation.* Unpublished doctoral dissertation, University of Iowa, 1975.

JOHNSON, R. N. *Aggression in man and animals.* Philadelphia: Saunders, 1972.

JUDSON, S. *A manual on nonviolence and children.* Philadelphia: Religious Society of Friends, 1977.

KAROLY, P., & STEFFEN, J. J. (Eds.). *Improving the long-term effects of psychotherapy.* New York: Gardner Press, 1980.

KAZDIN, A. *Behavior modification in applied settings.* Homewood, Ill.: Dorsey Press, 1975.

L'ABATE, L. Toward a theory and technology for social skills training. *Academic Psychology Bulletin,* 1980, *2,* 207-228.

LARCEN, S. W., CHINSKY, J. M., ALLEN, G., LOCHMAN, J., & SELINGER, H. V. *Training children in social problem solving strategies.* Paper presented at a meeting of the Midwestern Psychological Association, Chicago, 1974.

LARCEN, S. W., SPIVACK, G., & SHURE, M. *Problem-solving thinking and adjustment among dependent-neglected pre-adolescents.* Paper presented at a meeting of the Eastern Psychological Association, Boston, 1972.

LITWACK, S. E. *The helper therapy principle as a therapeutic tool: Structured learning therapy with adolescents.* Unpublished doctoral dissertation, Syracuse University, 1976.

McCLURE, L. F. *Social problem-solving training and assessment: An experimental investigation in an elementary school setting.* Unpublished doctoral dissertation, University of Connecticut, 1975.

McFALL, R. M. *Behavioral training: A skill acquisition approach to clinical problems.* Chicago: General Learning Press, 1976.

MONTAGUE, A. *Learning non-aggression.* New York: Oxford, 1978.

MUUSS, R. D. The relationship between "causal" orientation, anxiety, and insecurity in elementary school children. *Journal of Educational Psychology,* 1960, *51,* 122-129.

NIETZEL, M. T., WINETT, R. A., McDONALD, M. L., & DAVIDSON, W. S. *Behavioral approaches to community psychology.* New York: Pergamon Press, 1977.

ODEN, S. A child's social isolation: Origins, prevention, intervention. In G. Cartledge & J. Milburn (Eds.), *Teaching social skills to children.* New York: Pergamon Press, 1980.

ORLICK, T. *The cooperative sports and games book.* New York: Pantheon Books, 1978(a).

ORLICK, T. *Winning through cooperation.* Washington, D.C.: Acropolis Books, 1978(b).

ORLICK, T., & BOTTERILL, C. *Every kid can win.* Chicago: Nelson Hall, 1975.

OSBORN, A. F. *Applied imagination.* New York: Scribner, 1953.

PAPANEK, V. J. Tree of life: Bionics. *Journal of Creative Behavior,* 1969, *3,* 5-15.
PARNES, S. J. *Creative behavior guidebook.* New York: Scribner, 1967.
PASTORE, N. The role of arbitrariness in the frustration aggression hypothesis. *Journal of Abnormal and Social Psychology,* 1952, *47,* 728-731.
PLATT, J. J., SPIVACK, G., ALTMAN, N., ALTMAN, D., & PEIZER, S. B. Adolescent problem-solving thinking. *Journal of Consulting and Clinical Psychology,* 1974, *42,* 787-793.
PRINCE, G. M. *The practice of creativity.* New York: Collier Books, 1970.
RALEIGH, R. *Individual vs. group structured learning therapy for assertiveness training with senior and junior high school students.* Unpublished doctoral dissertation, Syracuse University, 1976.
RATHJEN, D. P., & FOREYT, J. P. *Social competence: Interventions for children and adults.* New York: Pergamon Press, 1980.
REISSMAN, F. The helper therapy principle. *Social Work,* 1965, *10,* 27-32.
RINN, R. C., & MARKLE, A. Modification of social skill deficits in children. In A. S. Bellack & M. Hersen (Eds.), *Research and practice in social skills training.* New York: Plenum, 1979.
ROBIN, A. Parent-adolescent conflict: A skill-training approach. In D. P. Rathjen & J. P. Foreyt (Eds.), *Social competence: Interventions for children and adults.* New York: Pergamon Press, 1980.
ROSS, D. M., & ROSS, S. A. Cognitive training for the EMR child: Situational problem solving and planning. *American Journal of Mental Deficiency,* 1973, *78,* 20-26.
ROTHERAM, M. J. Social skills training programs in elementary and high school classrooms. In D. P. Rathjen & J. P. Foreyt (Eds.), *Social competence: Interventions for children and adults.* New York: Pergamon Press, 1980.
SHURE, M. B., NEWMAN, S., & SILVER, S. *Problem-solving thinking among adjusted, impulsive and inhibited head start children.* Paper presented at a meeting of the Eastern Psychological Association, Washington, 1973.
SHURE, M. B., & SPIVACK, G. Means-ends thinking, adjustment and social class among elementary school-aged children. *Journal of Consulting and Clinical Psychology,* 1972, *38,* 348-353.
SHURE, M. B., & SPIVACK, G. *Problem-solving techniques in childrearing.* San Francisco: Jossey-Bass, 1978.
SHURE, M. B., SPIVACK, G., & POWELL, L. *A problem-solving intervention program for disadvantaged preschool children.* Paper presented at a meeting of the Eastern Psychological Association, Boston, 1972.
SPIVACK, G., & LEVINE, M. *Self-regulation in acting-out and normal adolescents* (report M-4531). Washington, D.C.: NIMH, 1963.
SPIVACK, G., PLATT, J. J., & SHURE, M. B. *The problem-solving approach to adjustment.* San Francisco: Jossey-Bass, 1976.
SPIVACK, G., & SHURE, M. B. *Social adjustment of young children.* San Francisco: Jossey-Bass, 1974.
STADSKLEV, R. *Handbook of Simulation Gaming in Social Education.* Birmingham, Ala.: University of Alabama, 1975.
STEPHENS, T. M. *Directive teaching of children with learning and behavioral handicaps.* Columbus, Ohio: Merrill, 1976.
STEPHENS, T. M. *Social skills in the classroom.* Columbus, Ohio: Cedars Press, 1978.
STONE, G. L., HINDS, W. C., & SCHMIDT, G. W. Teaching mental health behaviors to elementary school children. *Professional Psychology,* 1975, *6,* 36-40.

SUCHMAN, J. R. Inquiry training: Building skills for autonomous discovery. *Merrill-Palmer Quarterly*, 1961, *7*, 147–170.

SWANSTROM, C. *Training self-control in behavior problem children.* Unpublished doctoral dissertation, Syracuse University, 1977.

TERKELSON, C. Making contact: Parent-child communication skill program. *Elementary School Guidance and Counseling*, 1976, *11*, 89–99.

TRIEF, P. *The reduction of egocentrism in acting-out adolescents by structured learning therapy.* Unpublished doctoral dissertation, Syracuse University, 1976.

TWENTYMAN, C. T., & ZIMERING, R. J. Behavioral training of social skills: A critical review. In M. Hersen, R. M. Eisler, & P. M. Miller (Eds.), *Progress in behavior modification* (Vol. 7). New York: Academic Press, 1979.

WAGNER, B. R., BREITMEYER, R. G., & BOTTUM, G. Administrative problem solving and the mental health professional. *Professional Psychology*, 1975, *6*, 55–60.

WEHMAN, P., & SCHLEIEN, S. Social skills development through leisure skills programming. In G. Cartledge & J. F. Milburn (Eds.), *Teaching social skills to children.* New York: Pergamon Press, 1980.

WEINSTEIN, E. A. The development of interpersonal competence. In D. A. Goslin (Ed.), *Handbook of socialization theory and research.* Chicago: Rand McNally, 1969.

WHITING, C. S. *Creative thinking.* New York: Reinhold, 1958.

WILDMAN, R. W., II, & WILDMAN, R. W. The generalization of behavior modification procedures: A review. *Psychology in the Schools*, 1975, *12*, 432–448.

WILLIAMS, F. E. *A total creativity program for individualizing and humanizing the learning process.* Englewood Cliffs, N.J.: Educational Technology Publications, 1972.

WOOD, M. *Adolescent acquisition and transfer of assertiveness through use of structured learning therapy.* Unpublished doctoral dissertation, Syracuse University, 1977.

WRIGHT, M. E. Constructiveness of play as affected by group organization and frustration. *Character and Personality*, 1942, *11*, 40–49.

WRIGHT, M. E. The influence of frustration upon the social relations of young children. *Character and Personality*, 1943, *12*, 111–112.

ZWICKY, F. *Morphological astronomy.* Berlin: Springer-Verlag, 1957.

ZWICKY, F. *Discovery, invention, research: Through the morphological approach.* New York: Macmillan, 1969.

7
The School

Too often the problem of violence in schools becomes entangled in a vicious cycle of scape-goating, finger-pointing, and avoidance of responsibility by individuals and those segments of the society that must work together to solve the problem. The cycle goes something like this: Teachers blame the problem of student violence on parents and school administrators; administrators blame it on the teachers, parents, and the board of education; boards of education blame it on society; different segments of the society blame it on the schools and the homes and the breakdown of moral values; parents blame it on the bad company that the student runs around with; and the student blames it on the boring teachers and dull schools. (McPartland & McDill, 1977, p. 86–87)

The American school, which just a few decades ago was looked upon as a key instrument in solving many of society's problems, has, as the just-cited quotation reflects, become part of the violence problem. The perception of school has changed from the claim that "education prevents delinquency" to the belief held by many observers today that "schools create rather than prevent delinquency and discipline problems" (Duke, 1978a, p. 425).

Throughout this volume we have discussed different aspects of the school-violence problem and have presented some ways and ideas by which the youngsters involved in these problems can be helped. Why then do we have a separate chapter in which we focus on the school as a school? The answer to this question lies in the very nature of the school itself and the role it plays in our society. This role, as we just noted, is a dynamic one, and we need to understand it if we hope to come to grips with the disruptive actions that often take place within its confines.

The increase in violent and disruptive behavior has been attributed to the school by various individuals who have characterized the school as elitist (Stinchcombe, 1964), promoting of competitive individualistic values (Sexton, 1967), "mindless" (Silberman, 1970), restrictive of achievement opportunity (Cullen & Tinto, 1975), fostering of "immorality" (West, 1975), bureaucratic (Duke, 1976), and even more hostile terms. Probably all of these descriptions are valid in some form, and the contribution of the school itself to school violence and vandalism will continue to be a matter of controversy and conjecture.

The school uniquely is the institution where the forces bearing upon the behavior of youth all come together. On entering school youngsters reflect the influence of their family and the social, psychological, economic, and political environments in which their development has taken place. The school may help the youngsters solve or at least cope with the problems resulting from these environments, or it may even create new ones (Glasser, 1969). The school acting alone probably will have difficulty ameliorating the problem of violence, but the school is the crucial agent. Other agencies and institutions have neither the opportunity nor the focus and concentration of youth that the school has.

In Chapter 1, we presented an overview of the nature and extent of the problem, together with a list of 126 proposed solutions which have been attempted (Table 1.3). In the present chapter, we first consider the role of the school vis-à-vis violent and disruptive behavior. We then look at some specific school-focused programs that have attempted to reduce school violence and follow that by outlining some approaches for dealing with the multifaceted nature of the problem.

THE ROLE OF THE SCHOOL

Does the school provoke or ameliorate aggressive behavior? There is considerable controversy over the answer to this question. Gold (1978) maintains that the school controls "the major social psychological forces that generate delinquency" (p. 290) and consequently is a significant provoker of delinquent behavior. Gold's argument is consistent with the findings of Elliott and Voss (1974), who conducted a longitudinal study of school behavior and its relationship to delinquency and dropout. They claim that "the school is the critical generating milieu for delinquency" (p. 203), because it creates in one setting all of the necessary conditions for aggressive or disruptive behavior. Youngsters do not arrive at school categorized as failures or successes, but the school soon identifies them as such and makes their failure obvious to themselves and others. Delinquent or disruptive behavior in school is a face-saving way of defending themselves from such humiliations.

As a result of their longitudinal research, Polk and Schafer (1972) attributed delinquent and violent behavior to the way in which schools operate within their organizational structure. They argue that particularly with respect to students from low-income families the way most American schools are organized guarantees that some students will fail and that some will be discipline problems. In sum, Polk and Schafer believe that a youngster's commitment to violent behavior is largely a consequence of negative school experiences.

The finding (Elliott & Voss, 1974) that dropouts had a higher rate of police contacts while in school than did graduates, but that their police contacts declined to a lower rate than that of graduates after they dropped out of school, is one of the crucial pieces of evidence presented by those who regard the school as a contributor to the violence problem. The research of Frease (1973) and Kelly (1975) on tracking systems used in secondary schools also suggests that organizational structures, such as tracking, used by educational institutions may contribute to the incidence of disruptive and delinquent behavior. Frease (1973) reported that youngsters in low academic tracks become increasingly dissatisfied with and less committed to school and develop more associations with peers who are predelinquent or delinquent. Kelly (1975) found that tracking position was the best predictor of delinquent behavior when the effects of such variables as achievement in school, sex, and socioeconomic status were controlled. Simply stated, those individuals who maintain that the school is the main cause of disruptive behavior argue that very early on children entering school become labeled as "losers" by teachers, administrators, and other youngsters, and end up fulfilling that expectation.

But others who have examined the problem of school violence believe that the school, though it is an important factor, is not the principal source of disruption and delinquency. McPartland and McDill (1977) concluded that the school, even though it contributes to student aggression, is not the source of the problem. Feldhusen and his colleagues agree with this view (Feldhusen, Aversano, & Thurston, 1976; Feldhusen, Roeser, & Thurston, 1977; Feldhusen, Thurston, & Benning, 1973). They collected and analyzed longitudinal data on over 1,500 children who could be categorized as evincing persistent prosocial or disruptive behavior in grades three, six, or nine. The youngsters were followed for eleven years through extensive testing, parental interviews, and behavioral measures. Feldhusen and his associates found that school-related factors were not as important as family variables in differentiating the prosocial and aggressive children. They also report that variables such as the original teachers' assessments of behavior and I.Q. can predict delinquency over the long term with considerable accuracy.

Another view of the role of schools comes from the Bayh Subcommittee Report (Bayh, 1977). Gangs use schools as their base of operations and recruiting. Drug sales, extortion, robberies, and meetings all take place within the school, especially in big-city schools. Much of the vandalism and violence by these gangs is not necessarily for material gain (McPartland & McDill, 1977) and may reflect the extension of street-corner norms and behavior into the school (Foster, 1974). Neill (1978) believes that currently gangs are at the root of fear among teachers and students, and that Latin gangs, in particular, are the most serious problem confronting big-city schools.

In sum, the school's role in relation to gangs may be described as providing an accessible target of opportunity—opportunity to carry out all of the gangs' activities with relatively little risk. But this role obviously makes the school a victim rather than a provoker of violence as noted earlier. More importantly, violence and aggression are not the exclusive province of low-income, inner-city, or minority students.

As the data in Chapter 1 show, the increase in school-related aggressive behavior has occurred in urban, suburban, and rural schools, schools in which gangs are difficult to find.

Wenk (1975) provides yet another perspective on the school's contribution to school violence. He attributes the increase in disruptive behavior across all schools as a reflection of the disparity between society's greater complexity and instability and the school's maintenance of programs intended for and geared to a simpler, more predictable world. In sections that follow we consider some of the options posited by Wenk and others to counter school violence. At this juncture, we stress that irrespective of how the school's role is viewed with regard to causation, all perspectives are in agreement about the centrality of the role of the school regarding violent and disruptive behavior by youth.

SCHOOL-MODIFICATION PROGRAMS FOR PREVENTION AND REMEDIATION

Every school desires to prevent and remediate violent and disruptive student behavior. In a sense, there are at least as many programs to counter violence in the schools as there are schools. Indeed there are probably more programs than school systems, because some schools have several different efforts under way. Marvin, McCann, Connolly, Temkin and Henning (1977) report that Los Angeles, for example, has more than forty programs to combat violence in the schools. And, as enumerated in Table 1.3, we were able to identify 126 programs designed to combat school violence in America today.

Programs to curb aggressive and disruptive behavior in schools vary considerably in terms of their financial support, location, conceptual base, duration, level of implementation, district size, and other factors. In the present chapter, as noted previously, our concern focuses on those programs designed to modify aspects of the school itself.

Many of these programs, if not the majority, are based on intuitive insights rather than on research evidence and have undergone no systematic evaluation (Feldhusen, 1979). As a rule, they all report some degree of success and may be extremely different from one another. For example, Van Avery (1975) outlined "the humanitarian approach" he implemented at the high-school level in Sarasota, Florida. The essence of Van Avery's program centered around the collaboration among students, teachers and staff, administration, parents, school board, and community in the enforcement of school rules. According to Van Avery, there were few complaints about student behavior and no violence.

But school-modification programs approaching the problem of violence from a completely different perspective also report successful results. For example, Wint (1975) described a "law and order" approach in Wyandach, New York, which emphasized strict discipline, rules, quiet classrooms, and the learning of basic skills.

Rules were made clear and explicit on the first day of school; the principal was in charge and supported teachers; and misbehaving students were punished quickly and consistently. After three years, the school, once full of violence and disorder, was reported as "peaceful and well-organized" (p. 176).

As we noted earlier, schools are not wanting because of a paucity of programs designed to combat violence. In their survey of such school programs, Marvin and his colleagues (Marvin et al., 1977) found that (1) each of these programs is tailored to the individual needs of the particular school; (2) many different approaches have been attempted; (3) many of these programs seem to reduce violence and disruption in the schools; and (4) one of the major factors in the successful reduction of school violence appears to be close cooperation among school personnel, outside community agencies, parents, students, and the community at large. This last finding is essentially the approach advocated in this volume, and we say more about it later.

A factor not identified by Marvin et al. (1977), and one that might be a crucial antecedent to any successful program to counter school violence, may be the explicit admission that there is a violent-behavior problem in the school. In other words, schools which initiate a specific program to reduce disruptive and aggressive behavior by taking this step have acknowledged and defined a problem that needs attention. It may well be that the reason why most programs designed to reduce school violence are reported as successes is less a matter of what they do than a result of the fact that they do something.

Duke's (1978b) survey of 100 randomly selected high schools in New York and 100 in California adds support to this thesis. In both states, urban and non-urban high-school administrators identified their three most severe discipline problems as skipping class, truancy, and lateness to class. Duke presents some data that teachers, on the other hand, identify classroom disruption, fighting, and disrespect for teacher authority as the most pressing problem. What is interesting in this study is that administrators ranked fighting, disruption, drug use, and profanity among the least important discipline problems in school. Duke speculates that students would rate theft and fighting as their most serious problems and notes the following:

> If my speculations concerning teacher and student perceptions of the most pressing discipline problems are accurate, it becomes somewhat more understandable why a "crisis" in school discipline seems to exist. *Each of the three major role groups involved in high schools is concerned primarily about a different set of discipline problems.* Self-interest dictates priorities. (Duke, 1978b, p. 326)

Thus, the perception of the problem of school violence may not necessarily be shared by its various constituencies. Resolving the differences and clearly defining the problem may be the first most important step in reducing school disruptions.

Marvin et al. (1977) were able to classify and summarize the findings of their survey of 137 school-modification programs into four major categories: security systems, counseling services, curricular/instructional programs, or organizational changes. A brief description of each of these four types of program modifications along with some exemplars follows.

Security Systems

Programs under this label concentrate on protecting staff and students from outsiders and from violence, vandalism, and other aggressive and criminal acts within the school. Examples of security-system programs include such activities as (1) having teams of student leaders patrol the halls during free time; (2) providing access to the school on at least one protected street for all students; (3) monitoring, after school hours, signals from crime-detection devices placed in a security center in the school; (4) giving police assigned to schools office space in which to counsel students; (5) using K-9 units to control burglaries and vandalism; (6) implementing a security plan involving I.D. cards, bright lighting, police, electronic monitoring for weapons, teachers on hall duty; and (7) providing a personal alarm system for staff and students.

Counseling Services

In Chapter 4 we examined counseling programs which focus specifically on the aggressive student. Here we list some of the ways schools can proceed to implement programs which might provide services for students in trouble or which might coordinate these services among these youth, their families, the school, and other agencies. Examples of programs are: (1) weekly group counseling of students with individual follow-up; (2) having disruptive students removed from class to work with a counselor to cool off and to clarify their problems; (3) having a counseling center coordinate help from various agencies in an attempt to keep children in school instead of having them go to court for minor offenses; (4) having street workers look for students with problems and counsel them on the spot; and (5) having youngsters discuss with a counselor all aspects of their lives—drugs, peers, parents, and so on—for a ten-week period.

Curricular/Instructional Programs

This group of programs focuses on helping disruptive students attain or develop skills through various specific curricula or instructional programs such as reading, mathematics, personal management, conflict resolution, and so on. The following are examples of this group: (1) training teachers to help students accept responsibility for their personal actions; (2) training students in security careers and providing them with on-the-job experience in the schools; (3) providing students with a wide variety of minicourses from which they can choose instead of going to study halls; (4) teaching students topics in criminal law and taking field trips to put workers in the criminal justice system; (5) providing internships for teachers who learn techniques in teaching special basic skills and crisis-intervention techniques.

Organizational Modifications

The intent of this last set of programs is to change the structure of the schools by making them more responsive to the problems and situations brought on by disruptive youngsters. Examples of programs that schools have implemented include: (1) dividing the school into five independent communities; (2) setting up a nongraded alternative school which emphasizes basic skills, career education, and parental involvement; (3) allowing students in trouble to sign contracts by which they can have their privileges restored; and (4) providing a review board to which students can appeal disciplinary actions.

The problem of violence and delinquency is much greater than the schools can manage alone in their current state. All of the activities listed in the preceding categories underscore the likelihood that schools can at best begin to come to grips with disruptive behavior in a variety of ways. Deciding which approach is most appropriate for a particular school depends not only on the nature of the violence problem in that school, but also on how and by whom the problem is defined. What may be viewed as a problem of violence in one setting may in another setting be considered as "normal" or "acceptable" behavior. Parents' perspectives of misbehavior and disruption may vary considerably from the teachers' and, in turn, from the students' perspectives. Moreover, community characteristics will to a considerable degree reflect how disruptive behavior is labeled and consequently handled. Aggressive behavior in one setting may be viewed as a learning problem to be overcome, whereas in another it may lead to expulsion from school and more severe consequences.

We need to consider the question of learning disabilities and learning problems explicitly. The issue is posed succinctly by Zimmerman, Rich, Keilitz, and Broder (1978) who in their study of delinquency and disability ask the question, "Is it possible that children are sentenced in court not because of what they did on the streets, but because of what they could not do in the classroom?" (Zimmerman, Rich, Keilitz, & Broder, 1978, p. 20). Estimates of the extent of learning disabilities among delinquent youth range as high as 73 percent (Zimmerman et al. 1978). The school's response to such youth has often involved a chain of events described by Rector, Barth, and Ingram (1980) as follows:

> An acting-out child can be seen as disruptive by a teacher who then treats the child accordingly. While this may be an indication of learning disability or of a learning problem, the child may be labeled as disruptive. This affects the child's self-esteem, which can already be affected by his inability to understand or control his behavior. Not only does he feel incompetent, but he is perceived as incompetent by others. The result can be rejection, alienation, and hostility. The end product can be delinquency. (p. 129)

Regardless of the many sources and explanations of disruptive behavior, in the end it is still the school that must cope with aggression and must help cope with violent youth by providing alternatives to detention and institutionalization. There is reason for some optimism in even the most difficult situations. The New York City public schools have recently reported reading and mathematics scores above national norms for the first time in years. School crime such as assaults, narcotics, and arson also declined between 1977 and 1982, but weapon possession, robbery, larceny, and sex offenses increased over the same time period (Maeroff, 1982). In the other chapters of this book we have provided a range of pupil-oriented, teacher-oriented, or community-oriented approaches together with their rationale for dealing with violent individuals in school. In the rest of this chapter, we want to look specifically at some school-oriented strategies or changes which the school might employ to reduce overt aggression. Because most of these suggestions are based on intuitive or theoretical positions rather than on accumulation of evidence, they should be thought of as guides for decision making by schools and should not necessarily be construed as hard and fast rules with wide-ranging generalizability. Their applicability will depend on the particular type and level of problem confronting the school, the human and material resources available to the school, and, perhaps most crucially, on the willingness of the school to be open to alternatives which all involve change to some degree.

TOWARD THE REDUCTION OF VIOLENCE

Although the evidence as to which approach works best to counter aggression in schools is moot, there is general agreement that what is currently occurring is insufficient. Consequently, if a school intends to alleviate some of the problems of violence confronting it, change of some sort is necessary.

If we view the school as an ecological system or part of a system, any change in one aspect of the system implies changes or adjustments in other aspects. Schools, like most institutions, resist change for any number of reasons. Change may threaten the insecure, may involve risk taking by teachers and administrators, may require leadership that is not available, may run counter to union priorities, or may involve a complex set of other reactions. There are many other reasons why schools will not do something about the problem of school crime, but increasingly both the public and school personnel themselves find inertia on the school's part an unacceptable response to school violence and vandalism. What we hope to do is to identify various strategies and approaches that have been suggested and tried as ways of reducing crimes in school. These suggestions cut across a number of dimensions, such as cost, complexity, duration, and so on, which have a bearing on the feasibility of their implementation.

An example illustrates succinctly what may be involved. Both evidence and experience strongly suggest that if schools and classes had smaller enrollments, lower incidences of disruptive behavior would result. A recommendation to have smaller-sized classes would make sense from other perspectives as well in that evidence indicates that class size is negatively related to school achievement (Glass &

Smith, 1979). The consequences of implementing a change toward smaller-sized groupings for instruction would embroil the schools in far-reaching political and economic decisions, to say the least, and would involve a host of additional societal issues including increased employment opportunities for teachers, architectural and structural consideration of school buildings, the training of teachers, and so on. Nonetheless, during a period when decreasing school enrollments are resulting in school closings and the aggregating of students in fewer and sometimes larger units, the implications of such decisions on the incidence of disruptive behavior needs to be examined.

Let us look now at some other school-relevant factors which educators have perceived as contributing to school violence (Marvin et al., 1977). In addition to disruptions being affected by building and class size, educators also believe that disruptions in school would be fewer if buildings were less dreary; if the staff had higher and more realistic expectations of their students—that is, if they focused on what students were capable of accomplishing rather than on what they could not do; if teachers and other personnel were aware of legal due process; if there were more agreement and unity about what school was all about among parents, teachers, administrators, and students; if school personnel were more friendly and less hostile to students and to one another; and if both the staff and curriculum could respond more adequately to the problems reflected by disruptive behavior—that is, if teachers were more skilled and had more knowledge to handle such situations, and if the curriculum provided more alternatives for aggressive youngsters (Marvin et al., 1977). It would be difficult to disagree with any of these perceptions, but how they become implemented in a school is another matter.

How something becomes part of a school's way of doing things is largely a reflection of its principal. There is a considerable amount of evidence both in the United States and Great Britain which supports the position that what a principal or head of school does affects the social-psychological climate in that school. The climate, in turn, influences not only the academic accomplishments of the students but the incidence of delinquent behavior as well (Rutter, Maughan, Mortimore, & Ouston, 1979; Wynne, 1980). To put it simply and directly, for the fortunate school the problems of violence and vandalism are often on their way to being solved by the appointment of the right person as principal.

On the basis of forty case studies of all types of schools (elementary, secondary, public, private, church or synagogue related, inner city, suburban), Wynne (1980), in particular, has concluded that a return to more conservative principles in which the authority of the teacher and the school are restored is required. Wynne would establish discipline by writing, publishing, and circulating a clear set of rules for student behavior, and he would enforce the rules firmly and fairly by providing swift and appropriate punishment.

In contrast, to reduce violence Wenk (1975) would completely restructure the public-school system. He believes that schools, as currently structured, fail to provide students sufficient opportunity to develop into responsible citizens. To make the schools more responsive to all of their students, Wenk has proposed a continuum of five levels of strategies for school programs, as follows:

Primary Action. An a priori education and human-services model to improve the lives of students.

Primary Prevention. A strategy that is aimed at children in need who are not necessarily "delinquency prone." The focus is on providing help to the youngster who requires it and not on delinquency prevention per se.

Prevention. A program that focuses on individual children who are likely to become deviant. These children are "targeted" as delinquency prone.

Treatment or Sanctions. This strategy is aimed at youngsters manifesting inappropriate or maladaptive behaviors that have become unacceptable and have elicited responses from school or community authorities and in all likelihood will involve the criminal justice system.

Rehabilitation and Correction. This strategy addresses delinquents who have returned to the school on probation or parole.

Wenk's approach is important to note, because it provides schools with a comprehensive and integrated set of programs. Unfortunately, it has not been implemented in its totality, but it does provide schools with a long-range blueprint of what is possible.

Another broad-scale approach to school modification has been developed by Duke (1980) through his Systematic Management Plan for School Discipline. Duke maintains that schools can deal with behavior problems by acknowledging that a school is made up of interdependent units and by making sure that each of these organizational units is functioning properly and is related to the others. Of particular importance in Duke's model are school rules and sanctions, school records and information processing, conflict-resolution methods, trouble-shooting mechanisms, community involvement, environmental design, and staff development. To implement Duke's model, a three-phase process is presented: (1) preliminary assessment; (2) planning and enactment of the plan; and (3) review and revision. The strategy involves much deliberation and participation in order to effect changes that would reduce disruptive behavior.

SPECIFIC RECOMMENDATIONS
FOR SCHOOLS

Although we have not exhausted all of the school-modification strategies and models for controlling school violence in the preceding models, we have sampled the spectrum of extant approaches that have been proposed. As Feldhusen (1979) points out:

From this review of the problems, the causes, and the cures for violence, crime, delinquency, vandalism, and truancy in the high schools, it is apparent that we know the problem very well, the causes only moderately well, and the solutions least well of all. There is very little evidence from research to guide practitioners in developing programs to deal with disciplinary problems. Only in the field of behavior modification is there a sizable body of research. (p. 242)

But as we noted earlier, schools which have undertaken steps to counter violence and vandalism report at least anecdotal evidence of positive payoffs. On the basis of the current state of available knowledge, the following recommendations seem warranted as ways of reducing school crime:

1. Positive behavior of students should be rewarded and recognized much more than currently occurs.
2. The principal should have available discretionary resources and must take the initiative in creating a positive humanistic climate in the school.
3. All constituencies of the school—teachers, students, administrators, and parents—should cooperate in the development and enforcement of school rules.
4. Special courses and other explicit efforts must be made in helping students develop self-control, self-direction, conflict resolution, and personal management.
5. Multiple measures of success in school should be utilized. Grades should not be the sole measure of success.
6. Illegal behavior in the school should not be condoned. Crime and delinquency should be prosecuted.
7. Schools should offer alternative programs that meet the individual needs of noncollege-bound youngsters.
8. Inservice programs such as techniques of behavior management should be developed for teachers and administrators.
9. Task forces and other linkages should be established between and among parents, administrators, teachers, and students to assess and to develop plans for combatting school crime.
10. To resolve conflicts among parents, students, and school personnel, counseling services for the family and for family and school staff together should be available.
11. School should have a coordinated guidance system to diagnose, plan, and assess programs for disruptive students.
12. Teachers should have clear and explicit objectives and standards, particularly when teaching skills that are prerequisite to further learning.
13. Work-study and career education should be available or developed for students.
14. School buildings should be used during the evenings and weekends to serve the community.
15. Teachers and administrators should live in the community.
16. Security guards and devices should be employed to protect students and staff from perpetrators of violence from both within and outside schools which have severe disruptive problems.
17. For students with serious behavior problems, special settings should be created for short-term treatment.

Which, if any, of these recommendations will be appropriate in a specific school will depend, of course, on the particular circumstances of that situation. We offer the preceding recommendations not as simple prescriptions but as some apparently viable steps that can be taken to curb school crime. Public schools in America have taken on or have had imposed on them a tremendous array of tasks which some have said has brought "purposive disorder" into the school (Sennett, 1980). But when the "purposive disorder" has been accompanied by increases in violence, vandalism, theft, arson, and so on, it is time for the school to consider some of the alternatives we have just presented. Curbing school crime will require more than the everyday response, as indicated by the following quotation:

> It seems to be characteristic of the creation of settings (although by no means peculiar to it) that there is no systematic effort to understand the universe of alternatives of thought and action relevant to any decision that has to be made. For any step in the growth of the setting, there is always a universe of alternatives which could be considered, but in practice there seems to be awareness only of a very constricted universe, and this is largely due to the weight of tradition, a pessimistic assessment of what others will allow, and the lack of an organizational vehicle devoted to a description of the universe of alternatives. The results are that virtues are made of presumed necessities, courage is not seen as a relevant characteristic, and imagination is viewed as a luxury relevant to some future world and not the present one. When the concept of the universe and alternatives is taken seriously, the personal consequences can be as profound as the intellectual ones. (Sarason, Zitnay, & Grossman, 1971, pp. 91–92)

What this chapter has tried to say is that although there is no simple panacea to school violence, it has been and can be confronted successfully by schools and school personnel who have been creative risk takers. Throughout, the underlying theme has been that the reduction of school violence will require a renewed spirit of cooperation and effort on the part of all of the constituencies encompassing the school. Not one of the just-cited recommendations can be implemented without consideration of some of the others. If, for example, formal mechanisms are established for student participation in the governance of the school, the students may relegate this responsibility to teachers and administrators, not because they are indifferent to the school, but because they have never adequately mastered the necessary basic social and political skills that will enable them to participate. Providing instruction in these basic skills may, in turn, require teachers to participate in inservice education to acquire the requisite knowledge and skills. Thus, a chain of events is precipitated which can be understood through the ecological perspective of the school, a perspective which promises payoff in combatting school violence.

REFERENCES

BAYH, B. (Chairman). *Challenge for the third century: Education in a safe environment—final report on the nature and prevention of school violence and vandalism.* Washington, D.C.: U.S. Government Printing Office, 1977.

CULLEN, F. T., & TINTO, V. A. *A Mertonian analysis of school deviance.* Paper presented at the annual meeting of the American Educational Research Association, Washington, D.C., 1975.

DUKE, D. L. Challenge to bureaucracy: The contemporary alternative school. *Journal of Educational Thought,* 1976, *10,* 34–38.

DUKE, D. L. The etiology of student misbehavior and the depersonalization of blame. *Review of Educational Research,* 1978, *48,* 415–437(a).

DUKE, D. L. How administrators view the crisis in school discipline. *Phi Delta Kappan,* 1978, *59,* 325–330(b).

DUKE, D. L. *Managing student behavior problems.* New York: Teachers College, Columbia University, 1980.

ELLIOTT, D. S., & VOSS, H. L. *Delinquency and dropout.* Lexington, Mass.: Lexington Books, 1974.

FELDHUSEN, J. Problems of student behavior in secondary schools. In D. L. Duke (Ed.), *Classroom management* (seventy-eighth yearbook of the National Society for the Study of Education, Part II). Chicago: The Society, 1979.

FELDHUSEN, J. F., AVERSANO, F. M., & THURSTON, J. R. Prediction of youth contacts with law enforcement agencies. *Criminal Justice and Behavior,* 1976, *3,* 235–253.

FELDHUSEN, J. R., ROESER, T. D., & THURSTON, J. R. Prediction of social adjustment over a period of six or nine years. *Journal of Special Education,* 1977, *11,* 29–36.

FELDHUSEN, J. F., THURSTON, J. R., & BENNING, J. J. A longitudinal study of delinquency and other aspects of children's behavior. *International Journal of Criminology and Penology,* 1973, *1,* 341–351.

FOSTER, H. L. *Ribbin', jivin', and playin' the dozens.* Cambridge, Mass.: Ballinger, 1974.

FREASE, D. E. Schools and delinquency: Some intervening processes. *Pacific Sociological Review,* 1973, *16,* 426–448.

GLASS, G. V., & SMITH, M. L. Meta-analysis of research on class size and achievement. *Educational Evaluation and Policy Analysis,* 1979, *1,* 2–16.

GLASSER, W. *Schools without failure.* New York: Harper & Row, 1969.

GOLD, M. Scholastic experiences, self-esteem, and delinquent behavior: A theory for alternative schools. *Crime and Delinquency,* 1978, *24,* 290–294.

KELLY, D. H. Status origins, track positions, and delinquent involvement. *Sociological Quarterly,* 1975, *12,* 65–85.

MAEROFF, G. I. The state of the city's schools. *The New York Times,* September 12, 1982, 6E.

MARVIN, M., McCANN, R., CONNOLLY, J., TEMKIN, S., & HENNING, P. Current activities in schools. In J. M. McPartland & E. L. McDill (Eds.), *Violence in schools.* Lexington, Mass.: Lexington Books, 1977.

McPARTLAND, J. M., & McDILL, E. L. *Violence in schools: Perspectives, programs and positions.* Lexington, Mass.: Lexington Books, 1977.

NEILL, S. B. Violence and vandalism: Dimensions and correctives. *Phi Delta Kappan,* 1978, *59,* 302–307.

POLK, K., & SCHAEFER, W. E. *Schools and delinquency.* Englewood Cliffs, N.J.: Prentice-Hall, 1972.

RECTOR, M. G., BARTH, S. M., & INGRAM, G. The juvenile justice system. In M. Johnson (Ed.), *Toward adolescence: The middle school years* (seventy-ninth yearbook of the National Society for the Study of Education, Part I). Chicago: The Society, 1980.

RUTTER, M., MAUGHAN, B., MORTIMORE, P., & OUSTON, J. *Fifteen thousand hours: Secondary schools and their effects on children.* Cambridge, Mass.: Harvard University Press, 1979.

SARASON, S. B., ZITNAY, G., & GROSSMAN, F. K. *The creation of a community setting.* Syracuse, N.Y.: Syracuse University, 1971.
SENNETT, R. *Authority.* New York: Knopf, 1980.
SEXTON, P. C. *The American school: A sociological perspective.* Englewood Cliffs, N.J.: Prentice-Hall, 1967.
SILBERMAN, C. E. *Crisis in the classroom.* New York: Vintage Books, 1970.
STINCHCOMBE, A. L. *Rebellion in a high school.* Chicago: Quadrangle Books, 1964.
VAN AVERY, D. The humanitarian approach. *Phi Delta Kappan,* 1975, *57,* 177–178.
WENK, E. A. Juvenile justice and the public schools; mutual benefit through educational reform. *Juvenile Justice,* 1975 (August), 7–14.
WEST, W. G. Adolescent deviance and the school. *Interchange,* 1975, *6,* 49–55.
WINT, J. The crackdown. *Phi Delta Kappan,* 1975, *57,* 175–176.
WYNNE, E. A. *Looking at schools: Good, bad, and indifferent.* Lexington, Mass.: Lexington Books, 1980.
ZIMMERMAN, J., RICH, W., D., KEILITZ, I., & BRODER, P. K. *Some observations on the link between learning disabilities and juvenile delinquency.* Williamsburg, Va.: U.S. Government Printing Office, 1978.

8
Beyond The School:
Community Intervention

Aside from these (previously) stated efforts of the school to gain support from parents, the present day movement toward the wider use of the school building, making the school a social center of the community, contributes to a development of community spirit, with its consequent favorable reaction toward the school in the minds of the parents. The more favorably the parents react in this way, the more likely are they to support the principal and the teachers in their efforts to discipline pupils intelligently and effectively. Moreover, the closer the community relates itself to the school, the closer the pupils feel themselves to be to the throbbing life of the community, and the more real the school exercises become to them. The more nearly adjusted the pupil feels to real life, the less likely is he to rebel in misconduct. (Perry, 1915, pp. 226–227)

The problem of school violence may be "bigger" than the school context in which it occurs. In fact, the preceding quotation, reprinted from Perry's book, demonstrates the long-standing belief that outside-of-school interventions may have a substantial impact upon in-school problems. Perry also points to the critical need for schools to tie their programs to community needs and concerns if they are to effectively serve their students.

In previous chapters, we have examined a variety of in-school methods for dealing with the problem of violence in schools. Though we believe that the interventions we have described, and the research we have summarized, have great utility in efforts to prevent or decrease violent episodes in schools, our discussion in this chapter suggests that the picture is not yet complete.

Here, we take a broader view by looking beyond the walls of the school for examples of strategies and techniques with a base in community life and an impact on school violence. We examine, for instance, the community-education movement, which may represent the most comprehensive attempt to forge formal and long-lasting school-community linkages. We also describe a variety of less formal community programs that touch on the school-violence issue, and we provide examples of the most relevant programs. Finally, we discuss some of the rationale for developing home-school linkages, offer some guidelines for the development and implementation of such programs, and focus on the actual operations of some model programs in this area.

Before we begin, however, it seems appropriate to build a basis for the consideration of the need for community involvement in the problem of school violence. Consequently, this chapter opens with a brief summary of the ecological or systems viewpoint.

ECOLOGICAL PERSPECTIVE

Instead of focusing only on individuals, ecologists are more interested in examining ecosystems: interaction systems comprised of living things and the nonliving habitat. In order to do this, ecologists engage in naturalistic research in an attempt to understand human behavior in its natural setting. Ecologists typically do not consider emotional disturbance to be a physical disease located solely within a child, but prefer to look at it as a disturbed ecosystem, in which disturbance can more profitably be described as a "failure to match."

The ecological orientation to emotional disturbance is based on the assumption that each child must be viewed as a complete entity surrounded by a unique mini social system of ecosystems. When the various aspects of a child's system are working together harmoniously, ecologists say that the ecosystem is congruent or balanced, and the child appears to be "normal."

On the other hand, when such congruence does not exist, the child is likely to be considered deviant (out of harmony with social norms) or incompetent (unable to perform purposefully in the unchanged setting). When this is the case, ecologists say that the system is not balanced, that particular elements are in conflict with one another. Such conflicts are termed *points of discordance*: specific places at which there is a "failure to match" between the child and his or her ecosystem. According to ecologists, the search for solutions to the problem of inappropriate behavior must focus on these points of discordance and the resulting failure to match. When systems function harmoniously, a state of balance exists, and the stage is set for positive behavior, competent functioning, and increasing psychological growth and development.

The words *ecological orientation* carry a number of meanings, depending upon the perspective and viewpoint of the persons involved. In its most general sense, ecology can be defined as the biologist saw it, "the study of living things in their natural habitat." While this may not appear to be a particularly useful definition for those of us interested in the development of psychological and educational programs for children with special emotional and behavioral needs, consider the

contrast between this definition and the following quotation: "Mu~~
developmental psychology is the science of the strange behavior o~~
strange situations with strange adults" (Bronfenbrenner, 1972).

Bronfenbrenner refers, of course, to the predominant tendency of m~~
psychology to attempt to improve understanding of children's development and ~~
havior by studying very small bits of information produced under usually artificia~~
laboratory surroundings. What is missing from the picture thus gained is any understanding of what *really* happens to children within the context of the systems in
which they live. Can we understand the experience of being a child in a family, a
neighborhood, a school, a community?

The ecological viewpoint stresses the need to go beyond narrow visions of behavior and development and to find ways to focus on the *interactions* of children
with critical aspects of their environments. We must increase our knowledge of the
actual conditions in which children live, according to the ecologists, before we can
use what we learn from such experiences as the basis for our intervention programs.
Without such comprehensive knowledge, it could not be reasonable to expect our
efforts to impact on children within the context of their systems. What we learn in
the laboratory, at this point, may simply be too far removed from reality to be of
much use in the construction of programs for children with special emotional and
behavioral needs.

OVERVIEW OF ECOLOGICAL
INTERVENTIONS AND PROGRAMS

It may be helpful to review some of the major assumptions made by persons who
develop intervention programs based upon ecological principles:

1. Each child is an inseparable part of a small social system. Just as every child is
    considered to be unique, so is every ecosystem. When there is too much dis-
    cordance for the ecosystem to function harmoniously, the system is con-
    sidered to be troubled (though the youngster will probably be identified as
    the disturbed party). Efforts to help "troubled children," then, should be ad-
    dressed to the problems of "troubled systems," with the goal of making the
    system work in the interests of the child.
2. Disturbance is not viewed as a disease located within the body of the child,
    but rather as discordance (a lack of balance) in the system.
3. Discordance may be defined as a disparity between an individual's abilities
    and the demands or expectations of the environment—"failure to match"
    between child and system.

According to Bricker (1966), deviancy "reflects a discrepancy between what
the individual is capable of doing (his repertoire) and the demands made upon that
repertoire by the various environmental situations in which the individual is located" (p. 6). Bricker points out that deviance is a relative, not an absolute, concept

le interaction between behavior and the demands of

h a number of seriously troubled youngsters, Bricker

behavior could be traced to either skill deficits or an
nt. By reducing the discrepancy between environ-
havior, the deviancies of those children were reduced
r focusing directly on them. (p. 4)

As Bricker (1966) has described, behavior is the result of the interaction between skills and competencies that an individual already has and the demands or
expectations of others in a given situation. The bigger the discrepancy between abilities and expectations, the more likely "deviant" behavior will result.

4. The goal of any intervention is to make the system work, and to make it
   work, ultimately, without the intervention.
5. Improvement in any part of the system can benefit the entire system.
6. This broader view of disturbance gives rise to three major areas for intervention:
   a. Changing the child.
   b. Changing the environment.
   c. Changing attitudes and expectations.

At those times when the ecological system is disrupted (points of discordance), intervention is called for. The ecological viewpoint allows a variety of interventions (including those that may follow from behavioral or psychodynamic
beliefs) but demands that all intervention be examined with regard to potential
effect on the entire ecosystem. Intervention can focus on any element or combination of elements within a particular ecosystem, and all interventions must strive
to be as comprehensive, coordinated, and functional as possible.

Such a perspective raises a number of important implications, some of which
are listed here:

1. Emotional disturbance must be viewed, at least in part, as culturally relative.
   Behavior that is "normal" in one environment may be viewed as deviant in a
   different behavior setting.
2. Interventions must focus on all elements of a given ecosystem—not only on
   the identified child.
3. Interventions must focus on the realities existent in a given ecosystem. While
   it is obviously difficult to change the environmental conditions which surround many of the youngsters involved in school violence, ignoring those conditions is not likely to reduce the level of aggression in schools.
4. Especially in schools, whose focus for so long has been to change the child to
   fit the system, this perspective advocates considerable change in program planning. For example, the following is a list of interventions that might be developed in response to a troubled system. Clearly, targeting intervention on
   the identified child is just one of many strategies:

WORK WITH THE CHILD

Build new competencies.
Change priorities.
Obtain necessary resources.
Find more appropriate environments.

WORK WITH THE ADULTS

Alter perceptions.
Raise or lower expectations.
Increase understanding or knowledge.
Restructure activities.

WORK WITH THE COMMUNITY

Bring more resources into school.
Allow more entry into community.
Develop coordinating ties.

DEVELOP NEW ROLES

Resource teacher.
Diagnostic-prescriptive teacher.
"Linking" person.

DEVELOP NEW PROGRAM MODELS

Community education/schools.
Outdoor education.
Alternative public schools.
Focus on prevention.
    Teach "mental health."
    Preventive mainstreaming.

5. Finally, one major implication of an ecological orientation is that we must give up our search for a magical answer to the problems presented by troubled children. Instead we must learn to think in terms of troubled systems and increase our understanding of the reciprocal person-environment interaction patterns. The rationale for thinking ecologically about the problem of violence in schools may be seen in the following points:

   a. On the whole, we must realize that traditional children's mental-health and educational programs have not been successful in reducing the problem of school violence. The ecological orientation proposes that this failure may be due to the narrowness of previous efforts.

   b. A systems viewpoint seems to be essential in examining the problem of aggression in schools. Even in the case of severely troubled youngsters, it seems clear from a reading of the current literature that the targeted child is seldom, if ever, *the whole problem*.

   c. In order to be effective, diagnosis and treatment of troubled children must be much more comprehensive and functional than it has been in the past. It seems clear that we can benefit by gathering data from as many sources as possible—that is, we need to be inclusive instead of exclusive in what information we utilize in our thinking about the youngsters we attempt to serve. New strategies like ecological mapping, profile systems, comprehensive case reports, and so on, are important additions to ecological understanding.

d. Everyone has needs and we must pay attention to them. The ecological orientation stresses the importance of looking at the entire system surrounding each child. Our own experiences and the documentation of efforts by many others indicates the importance of understanding and responding to the needs and concerns of significant others (parents, teachers, friends, etc.) in each child's environment. Hobbs (1975) has clearly documented the inadequacy of our current categorization system and the limited diagnosis-intervention child-only focus on which it is based. Focusing all our attention on the child while ignoring the family, school, and community that surround him or her can make the identification and remediation of difficulties almost completely impossible.

e. Building strong ecosystems should be the ultimate goal of intervention with troubled children. Linkages between various aspects of each child's world are critical elements (not "fringe extras" to be considered if time allows) in the development of successful programs.

f. Ecological interventions can use numerous resources ignored by other approaches. Children live and learn within the context of their own environments. Parents, siblings, neighborhood peer groups, church or synagogue, school, playground are all potential elements of a particular child's world. Each element has an impact on the child and, through the child, on each other element; a youngster's difficulty in one part of his or her system (i.e., home) can have serious repercussions in another part (i.e., school). Concern is with the whole child.

g. Ecological interventions can have a broad positive impact benefiting others as well as the "target" child. The implications of an ecological perspective for the *prevention* of emotional disturbances are enormous.

ECOLOGICAL PERSPECTIVE
AND SCHOOL VIOLENCE

As we have seen, it is not always possible to understand school violence by focusing on individual youngsters. The ecological view emphasizes the importance of *interactions*: Which individuals at what particular points in time in which physical and psychological environments are prone to violence? Consequently, the ecological perspective can also emphasize a variety of setting-focused as well as individual-focused targets for intervention.

There is some evidence for this interactionist point of view. For example, Chess, Thomas, Rutter, and Birch (1963) have studied the interaction of youngsters' temperament and environment in the production of behavioral disturbances. They concluded that temperament alone could not account for behavioral disturbances.

> Rather, it appears that behavioral disturbance as well as behavioral normality is the result of the interaction between the child with a given patterning of temperament and significant features of his developmental environment. Among these environmental features, intrafamilial as well as extrafamilial circumstances such as school and peer-group, are influential. (p. 147)

In a discussion of emerging themes in the study of social-emotional development, Parke (1979) agrees with the interactionist view expressed earlier and with the conclusions reached by Chess et al. Parke (1979) points out that social-emotional development must be seen as having multiple causes and multiple sources of influences:

> The child is embedded in a variety of social systems and settings in which various agents shape the child's social-emotional development. These range from smaller immediate settings and systems such as the family or peer group, in which the child has considerable influence, to larger or more remote systems such as the school, the community, or the wider culture, over which the child has less control. (pp. 930–931)

The interaction (or lack thereof) between home and school may be an especially significant factor in school violence. For example, Walberg (1972) has noted that "a general propensity to be a delinquent and to be apprehended" (p. 295) is negatively associated with frequency of school talks with parents, frequency of family outings, and the amount of scheduled study time. Similarly, Goldstein, Cary, Chorost, and Dalack (1970) studied the relationship between family patterns and school performance of youngsters labeled emotionally disturbed and concluded "that any comprehensive attempt to predict school success should include family background variables ... " (p. 17). We continue our discussion of school-family interactions in the next section.

Finally, we could not conclude this introduction without some discussion of the relationship between school violence and broader societal conditions. McPartland and McDill (1977) have noted that there "appears to be a significant negative association between the health of the economy or the availability of jobs and the level of youth crime ... " (pp. 7–8).

Hyman (1979) reminds us that we "often forget that schools can only be a reflection of a society, not the light that leads it" (p. 1027). Hyman also points out that it is unrealistic for us to believe that youngsters who perceive little hope for justice in society at large will expect to be treated fairly by schools. Instead, schools' emphasis on competition and grades and labeling may only serve to increase the alienation of already alienated youth.

In Hyman's view, programs such as Head Start, which attempt to enrich the family and community systems that surround youngsters, are very useful interventions but are plagued by a lack of resources and the impossible task of coordinating seemingly paradoxical regulations and philosophies. Nevertheless, such programs can hopefully lead the way to an increased emphasis on the development of healthy and appropriate learning environments and to the prevention of violent behavior in schools.

WORKING WITH FAMILIES

Earlier, we touched on the importance of home-school interactions. Families are important, it should be noted, not only for their ability to supplement the school's educational program or behavioral regulations, but also because they represent the context in which children learn how to satisfy their needs and, ultimately, how to get along in the outside world of school and community. Better perhaps than any other aspect of a youngster's ecosystem, families can provide the appropriate atmosphere for positive growth and development. As a result, efforts to intervene in the behavior of violence-prone youngsters that neglect the potential of family contact may often represent self-defeating activities.

Recently, more attention has been paid to the place of parents in educational programs for behaviorally disordered children. Fortunately, and contrary to earlier efforts when parents were likely to be "blamed" for the behavior of their children, current strategies focus much more clearly on the development of parent-professional partnerships.

For example, Lightfoot (1981) has argued that schools must view families as educative environments of their own not simply as supplements to the school program. Thus, a goal for school-family interaction might be a single educational program that expands upon appropriate experience in both the home and school settings. The fact that this does not happen very often is attributable, according to Lightfoot (1981), to parents' and teachers' misperceptions:

> Parents' and teachers' perceptions of each other as uncaring about children and as not valuing the educational process lead to distance and distrust and the need to blame one another. Rather than search for the origins of conflict and finding effective strategies for real (rather) than contrived participation of parents and teachers in a collaborative task, schools develop sophisticated methods of exclusion; parents draw farther and farther away from parental responsibilities in the schooling process; and children fail—often experiencing the failure as their own individual inadequacy, incompetence, and lack of motivation. (p. 7)

Perhaps the best example of the new parent-professional partnership approach may be found in the writings of Nick Hobbs (1975) and colleagues. Hobbs noted that even though parents hold the continuing responsibility for their children's welfare, they seldom receive the support they need to fulfill their role as parents. Instead, in many instances, professionals seem to enter, assume some responsibility, and disappear from the scene in a sequence that can give the appearance of random and purposeless activity. The ways in which professionals relate to parents are critical skills, according to Hobbs, and he offers the following suggestions for professionals involved with youngsters with special needs to consider:

1. Involve the parents every step of the way in your process. Establish a dialogue.
2. The end result of assessment should be a realistic management plan with potential for improving the day-to-day situation.
3. Be aware of community resources and be prepared to help parents gain access to appropriate programs.
4. When possible, include the parent as a team member in your process.
5. Be sure that your reports are written in clear and understandable language. Avoid jargon!

6. Provide copies of your reports for parents. It takes time to digest findings and recommendations.
7. Help parents understand the labeling process: the use of terms (when necessary) for communication, the changing nature of diagnosis, etc.
8. Help the parent develop a view of life with a special needs youngster as an ongoing process of problem-solving: a role for which parents are especially well-suited and a process for which you can provide assistance.
9. Emphasize the youngster's abilities, not just his or her weaknesses. Help parents see the importance of what their child *can* do.
10. Help the parent learn how to find a way through the system of helping services. Be sure parents understand their rights and warn them about service insufficiencies.
11. Finally, try to equip parents with the armor they may need to combat the negative orientations of many professionals and "friends." (Hobbs, 1975)

Hobbs and his colleagues also developed a series of recommendations for parents to follow in their interactions with professionals. They are summarized here:

1. You are the primary advocate (helper, coordinator, record-keeper, decision-maker, etc.) for your chid. You have the right to be involved in any decisions about your child's current or future educational programs.
2. It is important for you to keep very well informed. You may need to develop your abilities to persuade others, to assert your rights, to overcome resistance.
3. Try to find one person, from the many with whom you have contact, who can help you understand and integrate the information that you gather.
4. Learn to keep records! Develop a system that can provide documentation of your efforts (and the efforts of others) on behalf of your child.
5. Make sure you understand what is said to you. Question professional jargon. Ask for examples. Don't leave a meeting until you're clear about what is being said.
6. Ask for copies of your child's records and any deliberations about your child's program.
7. Read. Educate yourself about your child's problem.
8. Talk to people: professionals, parents, others. Join a parent group and benefit from the experience of others who've been in similar situations.
9. Try to establish a sense of teamwork with your child's teacher. Stay in contact.
10. Listen to your child's perspective on his/her situation.
11. Help your child accept the existence of problems and model a calm and positive problem-solving approach.

SCHOOL VIOLENCE
AND PARENTS

The Parents' Network of the National Committee for Citizens in Education (NCCE) has produced a handbook (*Violence in our Schools: What to Know about It—What to Do about It*) for parents and others concerned with the problem of school violence. This fifty-two-page pamphlet is full of useful information including: recent survey results of school-violence rates; guidelines to help recognize warning signs of increasing violence in your local school; ideas for involving teachers, students, community residents, and others in plans to decrease school violence; names and addresses of organizations that might provide even more information or assistance; a summary of recent relevant state legislation. One of the most useful sections is Appendix B, *Some Do's and Don'ts for your Child's Safety,* which is reproduced here:

Some Do's and Don'ts for Your Child's Safety

DON'T
- Send your child to school early without being sure another adult on the school end knows about it and approves.
- Ignore your children if they complain or say they are worried about being in certain places in the school or on the school grounds.
- Allow your children to remain in or around school buildings after school is over. If you pick them up and can't get there at the regular time, advise your children and make arrangements with someone you trust to pick them up for you.
- Assume that the present security system for the school is the best possible. Ask about how visitors are handled—how access to doors is controlled. Ask for written information on these matters, review it, think about it and ask questions. Make suggestions.
- Try to correct the problems in your school on your own. The odds are very high against success if you go it alone. Get others to join you.

DO
- Caution your children about talking with adults they don't recognize while in school in the halls, bathrooms or other places.
- Talk with school personnel about using children to run errands. This usually means they would be alone and increases danger to their safety.
- Encourage your child to report trouble—lunch money taken, physically roughed up, threatened. There seems to be plenty of convincing evidence that part of the reason why things have reached the crisis stage is that more and more people (adults and other students) began to realize that there was only a slim chance anyone would report the problem. If you do this, please remember the children deserve protection if someone tries to get back at them; assure them something will be done to follow-up on their report.
- Encourage your junior and senior high age child to think about talking with their friends if they are worried about violence in their schools and seeing if they want to form their own committee or become a part of a larger committee which includes adults.
- Make sure the rules, regulations and expectations you have for your child are clearly understood and followed. Remember your attitude is bound to set a tone for school behavior and response to school rules. (NCCE, 1975, pp. 21-22)

The Parents' Network suggested that pamphlet readers might want to duplicate the preceding list and distribute it to interested persons. Clearly, the publication of materials such as these must be viewed as one very important kind of community intervention into the problem of school violence.

COMMUNITY EDUCATION

QUESTION: Does enrolling of community support through establishment of Community Education programs reduce violence, vandalism, and delinquency in community schools?

ANSWER: There is limited evidence to suggest that there may be less violence, vandalism, and delinquency in some schools with programs of Community Education, but there is not enough information upon which to draw conclusions. If community support represents students and residents in the development of and participation in relevant programs, it is likely that school violence and vandalism may be reduced. (Steele, 1978, p. 84)

As Steele notes, it is difficult to draw firm conclusions about the impact of community-education programs on school violence. There is, however, a considerable body of evidence that supports the potential of community education for the reduction of violent school episodes.

Community education may be defined as having the following program components:

1. A school building base, which also represents a community center. While "school" may be the major program offered in the building from 9:00 A.M. to 3:00 P.M., other educational programs for children and adults are available there before and after regular school hours.
2. The staff includes at least one person (Community School Director) who is responsible for the development and implementation of appropriate program offerings.
3. The community school is governed by a community advisory council whose membership represents the school's community.
4. Community schools support cooperative efforts with other community agencies and resources and frequently conduct neighborhood needs assessments to determine local educational needs.

Finally, to summarize this brief definition of community education, Steele (1978) said:

The critical element identifying Community Education is the involvement in decision-making of citizens at the neighborhood level in determining needs, priorities, programs, and evaluation of factors affecting the quality of life in their own communities including the schools. (p. 85)

At the current time, approximately 40 percent of the nation's schools may be involved at some level in community-education programs. Often, participating schools are found in small rural districts. Most community-education programs in urban areas are concentrated in central city areas where drop-out rates are high, attendance is low, and violence is frequent.

Both urban and rural community-education programs may be aimed at least in part at reducing student alienation and isolation, a probable major cause of school violence. One strong belief held by community-education advocates is that the provision of meaningful opportunities for the involvement of neighborhood citizens in school program development can lead to increased citizen participation in the educational process and ultimately to increased community support for the schools. Similarly, increased opportunities for student involvement should lead, from this perspective, to increases in youth support for school programs, to decreased student alienation, and ultimately to a reduction in school violence. In order for this to occur, however, there must be available youth programs as well as opportunities for involvement. Further, programs must be viewed as relevant and meaningful by the youngsters for whom they are intended. As Steele (1978) notes:

> Youth recreation limited to an available gymnasium, basketball, and hoop under the rubric of Community Education for youth cannot be expected to produce results which are significantly better than noncommunity schools. (p. 87)

What can we say about the impact of community education on school violence? A number of studies bear on the issue. For example, Ellison (1974) analyzed the impact of community schools in a problem-filled district near San Francisco. Ellison's community schools were preselected, not randomly chosen, and there were clear differences between the community schools and the "control" schools on a number of dimensions (community schools had a higher percentage of student turnover and students from broken homes, and a lower percentage of students achieving at or above grade level). Not surprisingly, Ellison found that conversion to community schools had little or no impact on rates of school vandalisms. Unexpectedly, however, Ellison did find a community-wide decrease in vandalism during the time of the study.

Palmer (1975) found a positive correlation between citizen participation in community-education programs and decreased levels of school vandalism. Palmer also noted a significant decrease in four (of the sixteen) crime categories used for the study, but because increases were noted in other categories and no differences found in a third group, results pertaining to community crime were obviously inconclusive.

Perhaps the most complete documentation of the impact on school violence and vandalism by programs of community education may be found in school districts with the strongest commitment to the principles of the community-education movement. Flint, Michigan, can serve as the primary example, since community education was born in Flint nearly fifty years ago when Charles Stewart Mott contributed funds to provide school-based recreational programs for neighborhood children. It was not long before every school in Flint became a true community school, governed by a local advisory council, administered by a community-school director, and so on.

At least by comparison to national statistics, Flint schools appear to be in large measure escaping the frequently reported increases in school violence and vandalism. Steele (1978) reports that for the 1973 to 1976 period, the frequency of "homicides, robberies, assaults on students and teachers, burglaries of school buildings, and drug and alcohol offenses on school property were lower than national statistics" (p. 90).

Although these figures appear quite promising, it is difficult to know to what extent they are attributable to the program of community education or if they are tied more directly to other features of the Flint system. For example, the Flint schools have a written statement of "student rights and responsibilities" which holds students (and their parents) responsible for their actions (and for restitution of any damage they may cause). Also, Flint employs neighborhood adults as security aides in secondary schools. Flint schools also utilize sensitive electronic security devices, though having school buildings in active use until 10:00 P.M. every night may be a more effective vandalism deterrent than the security system.

Despite these mitigating factors, however, the potential of community-education programs to reduce incidents of school violence and vandalism seems clear. At a vocational-skills center operated by the Flint school district, usage is constant, security guards and devices are not utilized, and vandalism is almost nonexistent. In "community schools" in Washington, D.C., few serious crimes have been reported. Vandalism is minimal at the John F. Kennedy School and Community Center in Atlanta, Georgia, home of an Atlanta middle school and twelve community agencies. The same can be said for the Dana P. Whitmer Human Resources Center, a combination elementary school and community facility in the heart of the downtown business district in Pontiac, Michigan.

Howard (1978) has hypothesized that community-education programs may be effective in reducing school violence to the extent that they meet the perceived needs of the area residents. That is, residents must have opportunities to offer input *and* their views must be incorporated into the developing community-education programs.

Similarly, Rubel (1976) has noted that school violence may actually be elicited when school decisions are made in a seemingly arbitrary manner without soliciting or incorporating student involvement. Finally, Steele (1978) has concluded:

Community schools in name only, irrelevant to community youth, are likely to reflect the increasing violence, vandalism, and crime common to large urban school districts. The underlying premise of Community Education is that the outcome of community involvement is school programs that reflect community wants and needs. Students who feel powerless to control the outcome of their own education, who feel a sense of incomprehensibility of school affairs whose outcome they cannot predict, who anticipate that school disapproval is required to achieve their goals, who are completely disillusioned by school will resort to rulelessness, anarchy, and deviant behavior.

Schools that make a difference in the lives of young people are relevant because they "involve" the students at critical decision points in the educational process: in equitable and continuing planning, development, and evaluation of school-related programs. That is the substance of Community Education. (p. 93)

PUNITIVENESS
AS SCHOOL POLICY

Hyman (1979) has noted that the public response to children's misbehavior in America seems to be growing increasingly more punitive. Whether this attitude is a cause or an effect of the often-noted finding that *discipline* seems to be the most frequent public response to the question "What is the major problem in schools today?" is unclear. What is clear is that youngsters run a great risk of being hurt in school and the hurt is not always administered by other children.

One unfortunate result of the American public's punitiveness may be the institutional acceptability of the hitting of children. The Supreme Court's refusal to provide children with constitutional protection from paddling is, in Hyman's view and in ours, another contributing factor to increased levels of school violence. Thus, even though considerable evidence refuting the use of corporal punishment exists in the psychological literature, we have now legitimized such actions by school personnel. The end result of such a policy may very well turn out to be *increased* levels of school violence by youngsters.

The literature on child abuse is expanding rapidly and this is not the appropriate place for an extended discussion of that topic; interested readers are referred to a book by Garbarino, Stocking, and Associates (1980), and to a particularly comprehensive article by Belsky (1980). Our interest in school violence does, however, demand closer inspection of the relationship between the physical mistreatment of children and their eventual involvement in aggression against persons or property.

For example, it is increasingly concluded that aggressive, acting-out delinquents have been the victims of aggression themselves. Welsh (1976) used such findings to develop his "belt theory" of delinquency, which noted the near impossibility of finding a recidivist male delinquent who had not been whipped with a belt or other object during his early years.

The abuse of children by parents in the home is, then, likely to have an impact in other areas of a child's world—that is, in the school and in the community. Aggressive parents tend to have aggressive children, though the youngster's aggression may occur only when they are seemingly safe from parental "discipline."

But what about the use of such "discipline" not by family members but by school authorities? What are the effects of the use of "corporal punishment" on misbehaving youngsters in schools? *The Last Resort* is a newsletter devoted to discussion of just such questions. In one recent issue (May/June, 1981), articles reprinted from U.S. newspapers described the following incidents:

- A Florida teacher was accused of pulling children's teeth and of taking crutches away from an injured youngster.
- Two Virginia junior-high students required emergency-room treatment after being beaten on the heads with a stick by an angry teacher.
- A Colorado teacher was finally dismissed after twenty-nine incidents of violence against students that occurred over a ten-year period.
- An Alaska father filed a criminal complaint against a teacher who paddled and severely bruised his son.

- The (unsuccessful) fight against corporal punishment led by parents of young-sters in a Delaware school district.
- An Ohio first-grader spent parts of four consecutive days isolated in a 5-foot by 5-foot closet as punishment for misbehavior. The boy's father consented to the punishment, which the principal described as an effort to avoid further corporal punishment (the child had already been paddled several times).
- Reviews of corporal punishment policies were conducted in a number of school districts.
- Parents decided to leave an Arkansas community after a school paddling left a 4-inch by 6-inch welt on their son's backside.
- Successful attempts to replace corporal punishment by discipline were based on the work ethic in a Florida junior-high school and by a written policy of assertive discipline in an Ohio middle school.

If corporal punishment by a parent in the home can result in aggressive acts by youngsters in school and in the community, can we believe that the same punishment inflicted by school authorities will not have similar results? Do schools not have some responsibility for providing appropriate and effective models of intervention for their communities? How many parents "go along" with school policies of corporal punishment even when they approach physical and psychological child abuse, because teachers and administrators are professionals and "must know what's right for children"?

Further, do we not often use physical punishment on those children who are least likely to benefit and most likely to learn the wrong lesson: that if you are bigger, force is an appropriate intervention to get what you want? Is the public perception of the need for "old-fashioned discipline" not the major factor in the continual acceptance of a situation that frequently leads to the abuse of children and an increase in school violence? The line between corporal punishment and physical abuse is very easily transgressed. Should children not have the same protections against transgressions as do incarcerated criminals in prisons?

What, then, can communities do to nullify the negative effects of corporal punishment? They can abolish it, as Sweden has done in the "antispanking law" that has been in effect since 1979. The law, which is aimed primarily at educational settings, makes it clear that beating children is injurious to their physical and emotional health, that it is liable to increase the children's use of violence in the future, and that it is therefore simply not to be permitted in Sweden.

Carlson (1981) has noted some of the factors for the establishment of "anti-spanking legislation."

—A child who is spanked learns that someone who is bigger has the right to correct someone who is smaller with violence. This they of course use themselves towards their peers.

—A child who is spanked feels fear for the adult. In time this fear very easily turns into disrespect and hate which is bad ground for cooperation, understanding and love later in life.

—A child who is spanked is more likely to hit his own children.

—A child who is spanked for educational reasons runs a higher risk to be abused when the parent is at stress, than the child who is normally fostered without violence.

—A child who is spanked for educational reasons does not learn what the parent wants him to learn. A small child cannot, as grown-ups, see and understand the background for the punishment. The child often only sees the actual situation.

—A child who is spanked feels he has not the same right as the adult, namely, not to be physically attacked. If men and women walk around hitting each other they are prosecuted, but if they hit their own child they are only doing their job. (p. 5)

While the right for parents to spank their own children may be felt more strongly in the United States than it is in Sweden, legislation would be one step in the protection of youngsters from abuse in schools. In an editorial titled "Regents buckle on spanking," *The New York Times* (March 15, 1980) decried the New York State Board of Regents' decision (by a 7 to 6 vote) to favor corporal punishment in schools. The decision was a reversal of an earlier vote that would have urged repeal of corporal-punishment legislation, came after increased evidence of the dangers of school-paddling policies, and would have no impact on teachers' rights to self-defense, according to *The Times*.

Further, the editorial noted that:

The victims, as studies show, are almost never muscular, undisciplined adolescents; they are young children. Are children, then, not now safeguarded against abuse? Some insist they are protected. But as Regent Kenneth Clark, the distinguished psychologist, says, "There is no lobby for the children. They are subject to the degree of stability or instability of the particular individual responsible for them at that moment." (p. 28)

COMMUNITY-PROGRAM EXAMPLES

"Helping Hand" Programs

In most communities, the problem of school violence spills out of the school building into the surrounding neighborhood. While mild teasing and harassment of youngsters by other (often bigger and older) children on the way to and from school has seemingly always occurred, assaults, sometimes with weapons, are now increasingly reported. Such "on-the-way-to-school" violence creates a climate of fear for students and probably causes school attendance to decrease. Police cannot be expected to provide security along every route that youngsters take from home to school and back.

Helping Hand programs were initiated in Indianapolis, Indiana, in the mid-1960s as a citizen-participation effort to increase the safety of youngsters traveling to and from school. Since then, such programs have been adopted by a number of schools across the country.

According to the National School Resource Network (1980):

> The key to the Helping-Hand Program is the identification of places where children can go for assistance. This identification is generally a placard in the window with a symbol that all children are taught to recognize—most often a large, red handprint. Children being teased, attacked, or intimidated are taught that they can go to any place with a red hand in the window and that someone will be there who will "let them in" and assist them in obtaining whatever help may be necessary. (p. 2–2)

Helping hands may be placed in shops and restaurants in addition to private homes. Sometimes citizens volunteer to "watch the block" during peak hours and some schools designate a staff member as coordinator for the program. The coordinator can stay in touch with volunteers, be available at the school telephone in case a serious problem arises at a helping hand location, and maintain a steady flow of information about the program to parents, children, press, and so on.

Although formal evaluations of the impact of helping-hand programs on school violence are not available, the National School Resource Network notes that a number of schools and parent groups perceive the programs to be effective. For example, Washington, D.C., schools are expanding their helping hand programs to all the elementary schools because they believe that the model program resulted in a decrease in the number of to-and-from-school incidents and they are convinced that the existence of helping hand locations lowers the anxiety levels of many students.

Restitution Programs

Restitution programs are based on the premise that the punishment must fit the crime. When the reaction to criminal behavior is unrelated to the effect of the behavior, perpetrators will not understand the impact of their own actions and might be more likely to repeat the crime.

For example, institutionalization is a frequent but usually not very effective societal reaction to juvenile delinquency. "Victims are not compensated, and offenders are not rehabilitated. Juveniles may be left with the impression that their crimes have no consequences, thus reinforcing antisocial behavior" (National School Resource Network, 1980, p. 23-1).

Restitution programs have developed as an attempt to provide a more meaningful response to youth crime. In such programs, offenders may be required to make restitution (in the form of cash and/or services) to the victims of their crimes. Authorities may connect youngsters with jobs that will provide them with the funds they need to repay victims. For example, a youngster might be placed in a community job such as park improvement and have a sizable portion of his or her pay deducted for the restitution payment.

Youngsters may also pay their debts in services. When four young juveniles were caught breaking windows in their Quincy, Massachusetts, school, the "Earn-It" program required that they repair the windows (after school) under a custodian's supervision. A youngster convicted of making false fire alarms was assigned to the job of painting the inside of the local firehouse, where it was hoped he would learn something about the consequences of his actions.

Schools can be very involved in restitution programs. In Toldeo, Ohio, four "restitution counselors" supervise youngsters involved in the restitution program at school and at their work sites. Counselors also coordinate each youngster's case and provide follow-up information to the court.

As for effectiveness, the Toledo school-security specialist believes that the program has reduced vandalism and property crimes in the schools. The coordinator of the programs believes that restitution has maximal impact on younger children and first offenders.

In Quincy, the restitution program provides an average total "pay-back" to victims of 138 thousand dollars per year. In addition, approximately 30 percent of program participants manage to keep their jobs *after* restitution has been completed, a result that may certainly help prevent further problems in the future. Ninety percent of participants complete their assignments, and the program has attracted widespread community support.

Adopt-a-School Programs

Schools are faced with a very difficult challenge; even as budgets for programs decrease by ever-larger increments, the diversity of the student population demands a wider range of activities if schools are to maintain challenging and relevant learning environments. When schools fail to provide such programs, for whatever reasons, they can lose community support, be seen as unrelated to student needs, and open the doors for increased levels of violence.

Adopt-a-School programs are one response to this dilemma and they are working successfully in a number of communities across the country. Such programs may be described as follows:

> Adopt-A-School programs are models of school-community involvement and cooperation in which businesses, organizations, and industries adopt schools and contribute funds, personnel, or expertise to those schools for programs, projects, and services. Through such support and input, schools gain programs and services they would not otherwise have and are enabled to continue to grow, change, and provide students with the kinds of curriculum and growth-producing learning experiences they need. Faculty and students experience fresh viewpoints, ideas, and concepts and develop links with the world outside the classroom. (National School Resource Network, 1980, p. 25–1)

In Oakland, California, an Adopt-a-School program has been in existence since 1975 and has expanded to the point where more than twenty private companies are now involved. Kaiser Aluminum and Chemical Corporation, for example, has adopted Oakland High School and provided the school with a reading and math skill center filled with the latest electronic equipment. A number of students work on individualized programs at the center. Some students are now serving as tutors for new program participants. Students who make outstanding progress may earn part time jobs at the Kaiser plant.

Results indicate that the program is having an impact. Many youngsters have shown an increase in skills and some students have demonstrated dramatic turn-arounds in interest and enthusiasm for school programs. Morale of both students and teachers has received a substantial boost, and vandalism seems to have decreased.

Vandalism-Prevention Education

Finally, we turn to a program designed to meet the problem of school vandalism head-on, through an educational and preventive format. As we have discussed elsewhere in this book, school vandalism is a major social problem (with an estimated annual cost of somewhere between 200 and 500 million dollars) and many school districts are hoping that a vandalism-prevention campaign now will lead to reduced levels of school vandalism in the future. There is some basis for this assumption: Students who learn about the effects of vandalism, especially students who *teach* others about the costs of vandalism, tend not to become vandals themselves.

Vandalism-prevention programs may consist of both the direct transmission of information through lectures and demonstrations and/or the involvement of students in active projects. Programs have been funded and developed through schools, community agencies, state and federal programs, private foundations, and so on. Programs with broad community input and support seem to be most successful.

Examples include: an antivandalism curriculum developed in Colorado and partially funded by the local Board of Realtors; an Ohio program that developed specific topic worksheets for students and brought outside visitors (a deputy sheriff, a juvenile-court staff member, a locksmith) into schools to talk with students; poster contests on antivandalism themes; "vandalism-awareness" walks in which teachers can discuss vandalized and refurbished property with students, and so on.

Although pre- and postvandalism education data are seldom available, many schools have reported that such programs have made a difference. In Colorado Springs, some schools report as much as a 50 percent decrease in incidents of vandalism that they apparently felt could be attributed to an educational program.

A FINAL WORD

Schools reflect society and as we are frequently reminded, American society is characterized by violence. We have seen in this chapter, however, that in addition to serving as a model of violence for schools, communities also represent sources of energy and ideas and materials and support that can combine with school authorities and with students to combat increasing levels of school violence.

In order for this integrated attempt at intervention to succeed, better relationships between schools and communities will have to be developed. When schools are viewed as centers of community efforts to improve the quality of life, local residents are more inclined to offer assistance to school efforts. When corporations understand that they can make important contributions to the educational programs of schools in their community, they have often responded with good ideas and have backed them with professional expertise, time, and funds.

The fact that some programs such as community education and Adopt-a-School have demonstrated apparent success in reducing levels of school violence is impressive, but also makes it even harder to understand the overwhelming dimensions of the school-violence problem. Why do some schools seem able to develop effective programs while others do not? What is it about certain communities that causes citizens to pitch in and try to help while neighboring towns seem unable to even know where to begin? In the next chapter, we discuss the complexities behind these questions and offer some suggestions for finding answers to these dilemmas and to the problem of school violence in the future.

REFERENCES

BELSKY, J.   Child maltreatment: An ecological integration. *American Psychologist,* 1980, *35* (4), 320-325.
BRICKER, W.   Competence as a key factor in the study of children's deviant behavior. Paper presented to Tenn. Assoc. of Mental Health Centers, Nashville, TN, Oct. 1966.
BRONFENBRENNER, U.   Toward an experimental ecology of human development. *American Psychologist,* 1977, *32,* 513-531.
CARLSON, B.   Eight reasons not to spank a child. *The Last Resort,* 1981, *9* (5), 5.
CHESS, S., THOMAS, A., RUTTER, M., & BIRCH, H.   Interaction of temperament and environment in the production of behavioral disturbances in children. *American Journal of Psychiatry,* 1963, *127,* 142-147.
ELLISON, W.   *An analysis of the impact of community schools on the reduction of school vandalism in a selected district.* Doctoral dissertation, University of Michigan, 1974.
GARBARINO, J., STOCKING, S., & ASSOCIATES. *Protecting children from abuse and neglect.* San Francisco: Jossey-Bass, 1980.
GOLDSTEIN, K., CARY, G., CHOROST, S., & DALACK, J.   Family patterns and the school performance of emotionally disturbed boys. *Journal of Learning Disabilities,* 1970, *3* (1), 10-17.
HOBBS, N.   *The futures of children.* San Francisco: Jossey-Bass, 1975.
HOWARD, J.   Factors in school vandalism. *Journal of Research and Development in Education,* 1978, *11* (2), 53-63.
HYMAN, I.   Psychology, education and schooling: Social policy implications in the lives of children and youth. *American Psychologist,* 1979, *34,* 1024-1029.
LIGHTFOOT, S.   Family-school relationships. *Citizen Action in Education,* 1981 *8* (1), 6-7.
McPARTLAND, J., & McDILL, E.   *Violence in schools: Perspectives, programs, and positions.* Lexington, Mass.: Lexington Books, 1977.

NATIONAL COMMITTEE FOR CITIZENS IN EDUCATION. *Violence in our schools: What to know about it—What to do about it.* Columbia, MD: 1975.

NATIONAL SCHOOL RESOURCE NETWORK. *School Violence Prevention Manual.* Cambridge, MA: Oelgeschlayer, Gunn & Hain, Inc., 1980.

NEW YORK TIMES. The Regents Buckle on Spanking. March 15, 1980, p. 15.

PALMER, J. A study of community education programs as a deterrent of violence and vandalism in a small rural Michigan community. Doctoral dissertation, University of Michigan, 1975.

PARKE, R. Emerging themes for social-emotional development. *American Psychologist,* 1979, *34* (10, 930-931.

PERRY, A., JR. *Discipline as a school problem.* Boston: Houghton-Mifflin, 1915.

RUBEL, R. *Unruly school: Disorders, disruptions, and crimes.* Lexington, Mass.: D.C. Heath, 1977.

STEELE, M. Enrolling community support. *Journal of Research and Development in Education,* 1978, *11* (2), 84-93.

WALBERG, H. Urban schooling and delinquency: Toward an integrative theory. *Journal of the AERA,* 1972, *9* (2), 285-300.

WELSH, R. Severe parental punishment and delinquency: A developmental theory. *Journal of Clinical Child Psychology,* Spring, 1976, 17-21.

9
Conclusion

We began this book by presenting, and supporting with a litany of awesome statistics, a broad conclusion already very well known by most American teachers: There exists today a near-epidemic of violence in America's schools. Violence toward both persons and property, prominent in American society in general, finds chronic expression in all its diverse forms at almost all levels and settings of American public education. The broad formal and informal educational establishment—administrators, teachers, support-services personnel, academics, parents, community leaders—has responded creatively and energetically. In Chapter 1 we enumerated 126 different programmatic attempted solutions aimed at reducing school violence and vandalism. Consistent with our systems, multilevel viewpoint, these several attempted solutions are diversely oriented toward students, teachers, curriculum, school administration, physical alteration of the school, parents, security personnel, community intervention, and the state and federal levels.

How is the teacher or school administrator to choose from among this large number of potentially effective programs? What strategies might optimally be followed in selecting from among these many alternatives that small, implementable number of programs which best fit a given student, a given teacher, a given school? Chapter 2, *The Teacher as Decision Maker,* is our beginning answer to these questions. We sought there to describe concretely the decision-making process, its dynamics and components, its utilization in classroom contexts, and, in particular, its optimal nature and flow vis-à-vis student aggression.

The remainder of this book sought to further advance this decision-making effort. Chapters 3 through 8 describe in considerable detail those violence- and vandalism-control procedures and programs which *our* decision making suggests are especially worth recommending. We do so on both empirical grounds, as many of these procedures rest on a base of not inconsiderable research support, and on anecdotal grounds, based on the positive classroom experiences observed by us and reported to us by a broad array of classroom teachers. Behavior-modification procedures were thus described for the presentation or removal of either positive reinforcement or aversive consequences. The contingent presentation of rewards; the removal of such rewards by the use of extinction, time out, or response cost; and punishment by the use of verbal reprimands appear to be particularly worth considering for aggression-control purposes. Aggression in educational and related contexts has also long been a target for both psychodynamic and humanistic interventions. The former include restructuring central aspects of the youngster's milieu, Life-Space interviewing, and, perhaps particularly noteworthy, an extensive series of psychodynamic interventions developed by Redl and Wineman (1957). It is interesting to note that a number of these interventions—for example, planned ignoring, proximity and touch control, hypodermic affection, promises, and rewards—replicate (and anticipate) in their actual procedures several of the earlier-mentioned behavior-modification techniques. The humanistic interventions we focused upon as potentially of special value vis-à-vis school violence and vandalism were Gold's (1978) Alternative Education, Beatty's (1977) New Model Me Program, Dreikers, Grunwald, and Pepper's (1971) approach to classroom discipline, and Glasser's (1969) Reality Therapy. Each of these approaches, especially when viewed in a multilevel intervention context, appears to us to be well worth further utilization and evaluation.

In addition to behavioral, psychodynamic, and humanistic interventions at the student level, we also considered in depth and strongly recommended two other classes of approach to the aggressive youngster himself or herself. As what might appropriately be called psychoeducational interventions, we examined means for explicitly teaching youngsters prosocial values and prosocial behaviors. Values clarification (Raths, Harmin, & Simons, 1966) and moral education (Kohlberg, 1973) were the chief psychoeducational means recommended for prosocial-values enhancement. Psychological skills training (Goldstein, Sprafkin, Gershaw, & Klein, 1979) and interpersonal cognitive problem-solving training (Spivack, Platt, & Shure, 1976) were described as optimal means for enhancing certain important types of prosocial behaviors.

While the behavior-modification, psychodynamic, and humanistic interventions recommended by us can indeed function as powerful means for reducing antisocial behavior, they share a common assumption worth considering here. Each believes that the positive, effective, prosocial qualities which are among the chief targets of the three types of interventions reside *within* the individual. That is, all three positions assume that among the aggressive youngster's repertoire of potential behaviors there exist the prosocial values and skills which would result in constructive attitudes and behaviors were they only "set free." As we noted earlier in this book, the behavior modifier seeks to do so by judicious use of contingency management, the psychodynamicist seeks to elicit the prosocial assumed to already exist by use of an array of uncovering techniques, and the humanist-nondirectivist endeavors to create a positive, growth-enhancing therapeutic climate toward these same ends. The psychoeducational interventions rest on a contrasting assumption. The aggressive youngster is believed to be lacking, deficient, or, at best, weak in the prosocial values and behaviors which contrast so sharply with the antisocial underpinnings of overt violence. Such constructive qualities are essentially assumed to be absent from the individual's repertoire, and must be taught to him or her. Thus, as became clear in our presentation of the various psychoeducational methods designed to enhance prosocial values and behavior, the specific techniques involved are explicit didactic procedures employed to literally teach specific prosocial behaviors or encourage growth toward higher stages of prosocial values. It is our basic belief that a truly comprehensive and maximally effective set of interventions at the student level will include *both* procedures explicitly designed to decrease the antisocial—for example, reduce overt aggressive behavior—and other procedures, such as those just discussed, to explicitly enhance the likelihood of prosocial values and behavior. Youngsters must be taught not only what not to do, but what else to do instead!

Our theme throughout this book has been largely an ecological one. School violence has been viewed as multiply-determined—certainly by characteristics of youngsters, but also importantly by characteristics of the school, the home, and the larger community. Violence and vandalism, we held, may be diminished considerably or even inhibited altogether by policies and behaviors initiated by a school's principal, a school's use of various support services, the nature and consistency of its disciplinary procedures, administration-teacher and teacher-teacher coordination of both educational strategies and pedagogic tactics, and, as perhaps a summary reflection of these in-school factors, the school's prevailing psychological climate.

The ecology of school violence, we held in the immediately preceding chapter, also has significant community roots. School, home, and the larger community may not only be viewed as an interactive system but must, we feel, be worked with as such. Such an effort vis-à-vis school violence will at times find direct expression. Helping Hands, restitution programs, Adopt-a-School, and vandalism-prevention education are four community programs singled out by us as potentially valuable direct-intervention attempts by the community to reduce school violence. Other community resources, less explicitly targeted on school violence, exist and may be utilized with substantial benefit toward violence-reducing ends. Work with youngsters' families, concern with youngsters' peer groups, teacher-parent interaction programs, broader community education efforts are but a few examples.

We have, throughout this book and this chapter, identified, described, and encouraged the continued use of a series of apparently effective student-oriented, teacher-oriented, school-oriented, and community-oriented interventions designed to reduce violence and vandalism in school settings, and to increase prosocial alternatives thereto. To be of greatest assistance to the teacher-reader, we would have wished at this point to have been able to select and narrow down existing alternatives even further and to present to the reader *the* set of maximally effective interventions at all levels. But we cannot do so. The art of aggression control and prosocial enhancement cannot, must not, too greatly outdistance the science of aggression control and prosocial enhancement. The formal and informal evaluative research which does exist well supports the body of our earlier recommendations. But which combinations of interventions will prove optimal, for which youngsters, administered by which teachers, in which school settings, is a complex matter largely uninvestigated—in fact, largely even unasked—at the present time.

The seminal work of Hunt (1972), Cronbach (1967), and Stern (1970) on differential, tailored, or prescriptive education is most relevant to our theme and future perspective. Each of these investigators held that educational attainment would be most effectively promoted if the nature of the educational intervention employed (e.g., teaching methods, curricular content, teacher style) was differentially responsive to specific learning characteristics of the youngsters involved, most broadly describable as their individual channels of accessibility. We would energetically champion precisely the same prescriptive perspective vis-à-vis aggression-control interventions. Which combination of multilevel interventions will prove optimal for which youngster-teacher-school-community combinations will vary considerably, we believe, from combination to combination, and is thus a domain especially deserving of creative, energetic, and sustained research attention.

REFERENCES

BEATTY, F.   The new model me. *American Education,* 1977, *13* (1), 23–36.
CRONBACH, L. J.   How can instruction be adapted to individual differences? In R. M. Gagné (Ed.), *Learning and individual differences.* Columbus, Ohio: Charles C Merrill, 1967.
DREIKURS, R., GRUNWALD, B. B., & PEPPER, F. C.   *Maintaining sanity in the classroom: Illustrated teaching techniques.* New York: Harper & Row, 1971.
GLASSER, W.   *Schools without failure.* New York: Harper & Row, 1969.
GOLD, M.   Scholastic experiences, self-esteem, and delinquent behavior: A theory for alternative schools. *Crime and Delinquency,* 1978, 290–309.
GOLDSTEIN, A. P., SPRAFKIN, R., P., GERSHAW, N. J., & KLEIN, P.   *Skillstreaming the adolescent: A structured learning approach to teaching prosocial behavior.* Champaign, Ill.: Research Press, 1979.

HUNT, D. E.   Matching models for teacher training. In B. R. Joyce, & M. Weil (Eds.), *Perspectives for reform in teacher education.* Englewood Cliffs, N.J.: Prentice-Hall, 1972.

KOHLBERG, L.   *Collected papers on moral development and moral education.* Cambridge, Mass.: The Center for Moral Education, Harvard University, 1973.

RATHS, L. E., HARMIN, M., & SIMONS, S. B.   *Values and teaching: Working with values in the classroom.* Columbus, Ohio: Charles C Merrill, 1966.

REDL, F., & WINEMAN, D.   *The aggressive child.* New York: The Free Press, 1957.

SPIVACK, G., PLATT, J. J., & SHURE, M. B.   *The problem-solving approach to adjustment.* San Francisco: Jossey-Bass, 1976.

STERN, G. G.   *People in context.* New York: Wiley, 1970.

Author Index

243

Subject Index

244